EKΩN AND AKΩN IN EARLY GREEK THOUGHT

American Philological Association
American Classical Studies

The Harmonics of Nicomachus and the Pythagorean Tradition	Flora R. Levin
The Etymology and the Usage of ΠΕΙΡΑΡ *in Early Greek Poetry*	Ann L. T. Bergren
Two Studies in Roman Nomenclature	D.R. Shackleton Bailey
The Latin Particle Quidem	J. Solodow
On the Hymn to Zeus in Aeschylus' Agamemnon	Peter M. Smith
The Andromache of Euripides	Paul David Kovacs
A Commentary on the Vita Hadriani in the Historia Augusta	Herbert W. Benario
Creation and Salvation in Ancient Orphism	Larry J. Alderink
Eros Sophistes: Ancient Novelists at Play	Graham Anderson
Ancient Philosophy and Grammar: The Syntax of Apollonius Dyscolus	David Blank
Autonomia: Its Genesis and Early History	Martin Ostwald
Language and Metre: Resolution, Porson's Bridge, and Their Prosodic Basis	A. M. Devine
Descent from Heaven: Images of Dew in Greek Poetry and Religion	Deborah Boedeker
Iamblichus and the Theory of the Vehicle of the Soul	John F. Finamore
Epicurus on the Swerve and Voluntary Action	Walter G. Englert
Seneca's Anapaests	John G. Fitch
Xoana and the Origins of Greek Sculpture	A. A. Donohue
ANAΓKH in Thucydides	Martin Ostwald
Old Comedy and the Iambographic Tadition	Ralph M. Rosen
EKΩN and AKΩN in Early Greek Thought	GailAnn Rickert

GailAnn Rickert

EKΩN AND AKΩN
IN EARLY GREEK THOUGHT

Scholars Press
Atlanta, Georgia

EKΩN AND AKΩN
IN EARLY GREEK THOUGHT

GailAnn Rickert

© 1989
The American Philological Association

Library of Congress Cataloging in Publication Data

Rickert, GailAnn.
  Hekon and akon in early Greek thought.

  (American classical studies : 20)
  Based upon the author's 1985 Harvard doctoral
dissertation.
  Includes bibliographical references.
  1. Hekon (The Greek word) 2. Akon (The Greek word)
3. Greek language--Semantics. 4. Intentionality
(Philosophy) 5. Philosophy, Greek. I. Title.
II. Series: American classical studies : no. 20.
PA430.H37R5 1989   488.1   89-10633

ISBN 978-1-55540-372-0

To my parents
Joseph B. and Rita M. Rickert

Table of Contents

Preface IX

Introduction 1

Chapter 1: Βία and Ἀνάγκη 7
    Βία: general description 7
    Ἀνάγκη: general description 15
    Ἀνάγκη (i): βία 17
    Ἀνάγκη (ii): compelling social practices 23
    Ἀνάγκη (iii): unavoidable prevailing circumstances 29
    Summary 33

Chapter 2: The Functional Opposite View 35
    The FOV and ἀνάγκη (i): Part One 37
        Ἄκων or οὐχ ἑκών conjoined with ἀνάγκη (i) and (ia):
            description 38
        Discussion 41
        Ἑκών or οὐκ ἄκων opposed to ἀνάγκη (i): description
            and discussion 44
    The FOV and ἀνάγκη (i): Part Two 48
    The FOV and ἀνάγκη (ii) 52
        Part One 52
        Part Two 55
        Summary 60
    The FOV and ἀνάγκη (iii) 60
        Part One 60
        Part Two 63
            Constraing circumstances with supernatural influence 63
            Other prevailing circumstances 66
        Summary 71
    The Functional Opposite View: an assessment 71
    The Functional Opposite View: Appendix 75

Chapter 3: Other Occasions 79
    Agents who err 79
    Agents who do harm or wrong 86
    Third-party passages 88
    General statements 89

Preliminary conclusions 91

Chapter 4: Aristotle on τὸ ἑκούσιον and τὸ ἀκούσιον 93
    The Aristotelian Negative View (ANV) 96
        Actions which come about by force 96
        Μικταὶ πράξεις (mixed acts) and the Aristotelian
          Negative View 99
        Mixed acts in the Eudemian Ethics 103
        Μηδὲν συμβάλλεται (contributes nothing) in
          the Aristotelian Negative View 106
        Some examples and exceptions 108
        Actions which come about through ignorance 111
    The Aristotelian Positive View (APV) 118
        Description 118
        On the extensional equivalence of Aristotle's
          positive and negative accounts 120
        Summary 125

Chapter 5: The Occasions for Describing Attitude View 127
    Description 127
    Test passages for the Occasions for Describing Attitude View .. 128
        1. The ἑκών victim of force 129
        2. More on mixed actions 131
          More on the Aristotelian Positive View and
            intentional description 137
        3. Third-party passages 139
        4. Views of strong and weak desire 143
    Challenges for the Occasions for Describing Attitude View 149
        1. Animal agents 149
        2. Acting ἑκών opposed to acting under necessity 156
        3. Philoctetes and the aggressor's use of ἑκών 160
    Concluding Remarks 165
        1. A final comparison of the ODA View with the APV 165
        2. Is the ODA View too strong? 166
        3. A word on translation 168
        4. Making room for an ethical view 168

Index Locorum 171

General Index 185

Preface

This book is based upon my 1985 Harvard doctoral dissertation. I especially want to thank my dissertation committee, the director, Martha Nussbaum, always the challenging and engaging interlocutor, Ruth Scodel, and Zeph Stewart for guiding and encouraging me during the development and completion of the dissertation.

Since then, the chapters have been reorganized, and throughout the text, further supporting and methodological arguments have been added, while original arguments have been reformulated. What was formerly an appendix of the ancient sources studied has been integrated into the discussion.

I am most grateful to Ruth Scodel for additional help during the process of revision. Special thanks are due Martin Ostwald and Ludwig Koenen for their careful readings of the manuscript and much sound advice.

For proofreading, editorial and computer assistance, and cheerful patience, I am much indebted to Roger Macfarlane. I am grateful to both The University of Michigan's College of Literature Science and the Arts and the Horace H. Rackham School of Graduate Studies for their financial support of the final production of the manuscript, and to the editorial board of the Monograph Series of the American Philological Association for accepting the manuscript for publication.

Finally, I would like to thank Sherri Oden for many conversations which allowed me to try out and articulate my ideas.

Introduction

The prominence of ἑκών group words in contexts which are themselves of special interest (e.g., Athenian homicide law, Socratic, Platonic, and Aristotelian ethics, and Aristotelian action theory) makes them a topic of particular interest. More generally, the study of these words falls under the study of ancient Greek views of desire and intentionality. However, discussions and investigations of ἑκών group words, whether generated from a narrow or broad perspective, have failed to yield a satisfactory account of them. Studies of Plato and Aristotle have not done so because they show little if any interest in the prior usage of these words or the development of prior usage into the idiosyncratic employment of these words by the philosophers. Discussions of Greek homicide law have been rather complacent about the need to analyze the concepts borrowed from contemporary usage and have not regarded supposed modern equivalents as especially problematic. Studies of broader scope, e.g., studies of the development of the conceptualization of "will," although they may be attentive to ἑκών group words within their schemes, are prevented from giving sufficient due to ἑκών group words by the enormity and complexity of their aims.[1]

It is the task of this study, therefore, to begin the exposition of ἑκών group words by focusing on their use before they are consciously relied on by Plato and Aristotle in the pursuit of their own agenda. Although I do not mean to suggest that ἑκών group words can be fully understood apart from the larger issues of intentionality and desire, this investigation will be smaller in scope. It is my hope, however, that the approach applied here will prove useful to future attempts to integrate ἑκών group words into the broader sphere and to reconcile the philosophical and the popular perspectives.

---

[1]For a more recent discussion of the will, see e.g., A. Dihle, *The Theory of Will in Classical Antiquity*, Sather Classical Lectures, 48 (Berkeley, 1982), 20ff. R. Maschke, *Die Willenslehre im griechischen Recht* (Darmstadt, 1926; 2nd ed. 1968) bears the marks of its era but must still be consulted for its views of the importance of intention in Greek legal history. For a brief review of scholarly views of "will," see J.-P. Vernant, "Intimations of the Will in Greek Tragedy," ch. 3, J.-P. Vernant and P. Vidal-Naquet, *Tragedy and Myth in Ancient Greece*, trans. J. Lloyd (Sussex, 1981), 28ff. Cf. M. O'Brien's remarks on the will in Plato in *The Socratic Paradoxes and the Greek Mind* (Chapel Hill, 1967) esp. 216ff. See too the comparative study of C.A. Neuhausen, *De Voluntarii Notione Platonica et Aristolelea*, Klassisch-Philologische Studien, 34 (Wiesbaden, 1967).

Even a glance at some of the translations commonly used to render ἑκών group words (ἑκών or ἑκούσιος and ἄκων or ἀκούσιος) reveals these are difficult words: willingly and unwillingly, voluntarily and involuntarily, intentionally and unintentionally, deliberately and accidentally.[2] These words are themselves ambiguous and involve a wide range of psychological features, both cognitive and affective. They are clearly not synonymous and extensive analysis

---

[2]Most of these translations are familiar. "Deliberately" and "accidentally" are found especially in legal contexts; see for e.g., K. Maidment's translation of Antiphon's Second Tetralogy (*Minor Attic Orators*, vol.1, Loeb Classical Library [Cambridge, Mass., 1941]). But they are found elsewhere too; e.g., R. Warner (*Thucydides: History of the Peloponnesian War*, rev. ed., Penguin Books [New York, 1972]) used "deliberately" for ἑκούσιοι at Thuc. 1.32.4 and "involuntarily" for ἄκοντες as well as "not deliberate" for ἀκούσιοι at 3.40.1–2. Translations that focus on lack of knowledge or error are found especially for forms of ἄκων; e.g., in his translation of *Oedipus at Colonus* (*The Complete Greek Tragedies, Sophocles I*, ed. D. Grene and R. Lattimore [Chicago, 1954]), R.F. Fitzgerald renders ἑκών group words in a variety of ways, including "He never knew what he did" for ἔργων ἀκόντων, line 239–40, and "unmeditated" for ἄκον πρᾶγμα, line 977; R. Jebb (*Sophocles, The Plays and Fragments*, pt., 2, *The Oedipus Coloneus*, 2d ed. [Cambridge, 1899]) translates ἄκον πρᾶγμα, line 977, "the unknowing deed" (see too Jebb's comment on *OT* 1229–30 [*Sophocles, The Plays and Fragments*, pt.1, *The Oedipus Tyrranus*, 3rd ed. (Cambridge, 1893)]; and B.B. Rogers (*Aristophanes*, Loeb Classical Library [Cambridge, Mass., 1938]) translates οὐχ ἑκών at *Wasps* 992, "by mistake." See also the Appendix to ch. 2. Hesychius' lexicon (e 31) gives θέλων and βουλόμενος for ἑκών (K. Latte, ed., *Hesychii Alexanrini Lexicon*, vol. 2 [Copenhagen, 1966]). Modern etymological dictionaries employ several of these translations. For example, H. Frisk gives for ἑκών, "freiwillig, absichtlich"; for ἄκων, "unfreiwillig, wider Willen, unabsichtlich" (H. Frisk, *Griechisches etymologisches Wörterbuch*, vol. 1 [Heidelberg, 1960], 479). P. Chantraine gives for ἑκών, "qui agit volontairement, de son plein gré"; for ἄκων, "qui agit contre sa volonté, contre son gré" (P. Chantraine, *Dictionnaire étymologique de la langue grecque*, vol. 2 [Paris, 1970], 331). Both Frisk (p. 479) and Chantraine (p. 331) give βούλομαι and ἐθέλω as the Greek verbs corresponding to Hittite and Sanscrit parallels. See the first chapter of Maschke, *Willenslehre*, for a view of the relationship between ἑκών group words and ἐθέλειν and βούλεσθαι. Platonic and Aristotelian studies, of course, show no more agreement about renderings of these words. Even O'Brien, *Paradoxes*, who is sensitive to the problems imposed by the very words with which we are confronted in our study of Greek ethics uses "on purpose," "willingly," and "without restraint" for ἑκών in the Socratic paradox, and when speaking more broadly about evil-doing, he uses the pairs "voluntarily" and "involuntarily" and "intentionally" and "unintentionally," respectively, for ἑκών and ἄκων. Also, see Gauthier's complaints about the translation of ἑκών group words by the pair voluntary and involuntary and his comments about their richness even in Aristotle (R.A. Gauthier and J.Y. Jolif, eds., *L' Éthique à Nicomaque*, 2nd ed., vol. 2, pt. 1 [Paris, 1970], 170). Recent articles in *Phronesis* (30 [1985] 314–22: R. Weiss, "Ignorance, Involuntariness and Innocence: A Reply to McTighe" [29 (1984) 193–236]) make it all too clear that rendering these words in Aristotle's ethics is still a matter of controversy.

would be required in order to distinguish them and determine how they are related to one another even in our own language.³ The diversity of this list clearly indicates that whatever understanding we have of ἑκών group words does not derive from any straightforward comprehension of them apart from the contexts in which they appear, including the presence of other particular words which are understood to shade the ἑκών group words in a distinct way or even give them their various presumed meanings.

The procedure of this book will be to test the efficacy of four interpretative views to accommodate (or not) the occurrences of ἑκών group words collected, and out of the successes and failures of these views, to develop an interpretative view which will accommodate as many occurrences as possible. Because so many ἑκών group words appear in passages in which they are related to some kind of force or necessity, the first view from which progressive refinements are generated in order to accommodate more passages, the Functional Opposite View, is developed from a descriptive analysis of these passages. Since Aristotle was the first to launch a substantive investigation of τὸ ἑκούσιον and τὸ ἀκούσιον and produced related but different accounts of τὸ ἑκούσιον, a negative view and a positive view, his views are also tested for their satisfactoriness in accommodating the occurrences of ἑκών group words in the passages collected.⁴ The fourth view, the Occasions for Describing Attitude View, is generated from the insights and failures of these views.

To appreciate this way of proceeding, it will be helpful to consider the alternative it sets aside as well as address some of its implications and limitations.

The interpretative views to be tested are more complex descriptions of the function of ἑκών group words than can be captured or at least clearly conveyed by the substitution of some individual word used as an equivalent or translation. In this study I am, in effect, challenging the ordinary procedure or at least the readiness with which we adopt a wide range of *meanings* for a single word.

Rather than suppose that ἑκών group words are a resevoir for a series of different meanings or senses which emanate just from the ἑκών group word itself, my aim is to develop an interpretative view that accommodates as many occurrences as possible. After all, another way to evaluate the failure of an

---

[3]One is reminded of J.L. Austin's "Three Ways of Spilling Ink," *Philosophical Papers*, ed. J.O. Urmson and G.J. Warnock, 3rd ed. (Oxford, 1979), 272–287, in which he distinguishes and discusses the relationships among "intentionally," "deliberately," and "on purpose." But whereas Austin's explananda are primarily cognitive terms, translations of ἑκών and ἄκων involve concepts that have both cognitive and affective features.

[4] See ch. 4 p. 94 for further discussion of the use of Aristotle, a 4th century B.C.E. thinker, to investigate the use of ἑκών group words before Plato.

expression presumed to be an equivalent to accommodate a particular occurrence is to suppose it is simply incorrect, even if it does appear to accommodate occurrences elsewhere. I do not want to imply that a word cannot itself have or come to have a set of distinct stable meanings. But I do think we ought to wonder whether we have adequately understood a word to which several distinct meanings are ascribed.

If an interpretative view accommodates the usage of an ἑκών group word in a passage or passages, the ἑκών group word could be understood to function as the interpretative view claims. The passage makes sense when the ἑκών group word is understood through the interpretative view. I repeat, the ἑκών group word *could* be so understood. This possibility does not rule out there being some other interpretative view which could also be applied so that the passage still makes sense. Furthermore, it need not be the case that the interpretative view is acceptable simply because it does allow the passage to make sense. The accommodation of an interpretative view is weaker than ascribing a meaning. Typically, the failure of a particular meaning to fit a particular occurrence of a word tends to result in the multiplication of meanings for the word, including so-called rhetorical and technical usages. This issue is taken up with a specific example at the end of the Chapter 2. But in this study, the failure of an interpretative view to accommodate occurrences of ἑκών group words will result either in the refinement of the view in question or ultimately in its rejection.

Whatever sympathy one may have with my criticism of the meaning list approach, I expect it will be objected that an approach which aims to develop an interpretative view which can accommodate as many occurrences as possible has its own limitations. In particular, it assumes the words can be treated in the same way synchronically and across genres and authors.

I confess to being unworried if the procedure seems akin to the Socratic search for definitions. I see nothing inherently wrong with this. At the very least, I see no reason to suppose that providing a list of meanings themselves having important differences is intrinsically better.[5] My stance should not be understood as a denial or ignorance of the limitations of such a comprehensive approach. Rather, it is a response to the apparent indeterminacy of the meaning of ἑκών group words prompting this investigation. My interest is to understand these important words, and if my views can at least disrupt the complacency with which we make use of what seems to me something of a hodgepodge of translations and interpretations, I will be more than satisfied for the present.

---

[5]See ch. 2 pp. 73–76 for further discussion of the sense list approach.

Introduction 5

The interpretation of ἑκών group words I will offer in this study, the Occasions for Describing Attitude View (ODAV), is that a distinct and definable group of circumstances constitute the environment in which ἑκών group words appear and trigger their use, but are not themselves the meaning of ἑκών group words; the significance of ἑκών group words cannot be reduced to these circumstances. In sum, ἑκών group words describe the overall attitude of an agent or victim, positive or negative, as one of deep commitment to or divorcement from the action performed or suffered under these particular circumstances.

The virtue of this view, as I see it, is that it incorporates and does not reject outright the insights of the other interpretative views with which it is contrasted, and while maintaining a stable meaning, recognizes a relationship between ἑκών group words and other factors, even internal ones, that so frequently accompany their use. In addition to not reducing the meaning of ἑκών group words to the circumstances which occasion their use, this view does not identify the meaning of these words with some internal factor which in a particular case seems to be an important element in the explanation of why the agent or victim is called ἑκών or ἄκων. It is my view that inadvertently allowing substitution of that sort has produced the large variety of meanings and translations of ἑκών group words which obscures the essential role of these words, to tell whether or not the agent or victim has a strong positive or negative attitude toward what can be seen overtly, the action performed or suffered.

*   *

*

Relying on the citations in standard indexes, lexica, concordances, and editions with indexes, I have collected for study all occurences of ἑκών group words (primarily forms of ἑκών and ἄκων, ἑκούσιος and ἀκούσιος) from the following: Homer, the *Homeric Hymns*, Hesiod, Pindar, Lyric, the Presocratics, Aeschylus, Sophocles, Euripides, unassigned tragic fragments, Aristophanes, Epicharmus, unassigned comic fragments, Herodotus, and Thucydides.[6]

---

[6]The forms ἀεκαζόμενος, ἕκητι, and ἀέκητι are included only from Homer, the *Homeric Hymns*, and Hesiod. Consult Frisk, *Wörterbuch*, and Chantraine, *Dictionnaire*, for difficulties with these forms. The following is a list of indexes etc. used to locate the passages discussed in this study: G.L. Prendergast, *A Complete Concordance to the Iliad of Homer*, rev. and enl. ed., ed. B. Marzullo (Hildesheim, 1971); H. Dunbar, *A Complete Concordance to the Odyssey of Homer*, rev. and enl. ed., ed. B. Marzullo (Hildesheim, 1971), (this volume includes the Homeric Hymns); M. Hofinger, *Lexicon Hesiodeum* (Leiden, 1975–1978); W. W. Minton, *Concordance to the Hesiodic Corpus* (Leiden, 1976); G. Fatouros, *Index Verborum zur frühgriechischen Lyrik* (Heidelberg, 1966); E. Lobel and D. Page, eds., *Poetarum Lesbiorum Fragmenta* (Oxford, 1955); D.L. Page, ed.,

Although all these occurrences are accounted for in the study, their large number precludes individual discussion of each. In the body of the text I discuss representative and difficult passages and provide a substantial number of examples. But the Index Locorum includes all the passages, and lists circumstantial categories for each.

Poetae Melici Graeci (Oxford, 1962); M.L. West, ed., *Iambi et Elegi Graeci ante Alexandrum Cantati*, vol. 2 (Oxford, 1972); W.T. Slater, ed., *Lexicon to Pindar* (Berlin, 1969); H. Diels, *Die Fragmente der Vorsokratiker*, vol. 3, 6th ed., rev. with additions and index by W. Kranz (Berlin, 1952); G. Italie, *Index Aeschyleus*, 2nd ed., rev. and enl., ed. S.L. Radt (Leiden, 1965); F. Ellendt, *Lexicon Sophocleum*, 2nd ed., rev., ed. H. Genthe (Hildesheim, 1965); J.T. Allen and G. Italie, *A Concordance to Euripides* (Berkeley, 1954); C. Collard, *Supplement to the Allen and Italie Concordance to Euripides* (Groningen, 1971); R. Kannicht and B. Snell, *Tragicorum Graecorum Fragmenta*, vol. 2 (Göttingen, 1981); H. Dunbar, *A Complete Concordance to the Comedies and Fragments of Aristophanes*, rev. and enl. ed., ed. B. Marzullo (Hildesheim, 1973); H. Jacobi, *Comicae Dictionis Index*, pt. 1 (Berlin, 1857); *Comicorum Graecorum Fragmenta*, ed. G. Kaibel, vol. 1 (Berlin, 1958); J.E. Powell, *A Lexicon to Herodotus*, 2nd ed. (Hildesheim, 1977); M.H.N. von Essen, *Index Thucydideus* (Berlin, 1887).

1. Βία and Ἀνάγκη

The passages collected for this study give the general impression that ἑκών group words appear most frequently in contexts in which force and necessity are highly prominent. In fact, in over fifty passages ἑκών group words appear in contexts where they are directly related to circumstances of *force* or *necessity* expressed by forms of βία or ἀνάγκη (or both).[1] This chapter determines what these circumstances are by analyzing and cataloguing what counts as βία and ἀνάγκη in these passages. In Chapter 2 this information will be used as the basis for identifying similar circumstances in other passages where βία and ἀνάγκη words do not actually appear. It is important to collect and sort these circumstances because some relationship between ἑκών group words and force and necessity is fundamental to each of the interpretative views to be examined in this study, and the views do not all concur about what counts as force and necessity. Thus, in order to determine the adequacy of interpretative views to accommodate the uses of ἑκών group words and to develop my own view, it will be necessary first to describe what kinds of force and necessity are especially relevant to ἑκών group words.

Βία: general description

In the majority of passages where βία appears related to the use of an ἑκών group word, physical force exerted by a personal agent, *hands-on force*, is involved. A few passages offer some detail about the force involved. For example, at *Iliad* 15.178–88,[2] Zeus' message to Poseidon threatens hand to hand combat;

---

[1]Although the βία and ἀνάγκη words sometimes occur in the form of verbs, nouns, or adjectives, mostly they appear as instrumental, comitative, or circumstantial datives, or in equivalent expressions. (The equivalent expressions include an adverb, prepositional phrases governed by ἐκ, πρός, ὑπό, κατά, διά, and ἐν, and circumstantial participles. For the circumstantial use of these prepositions see R. Kühner, *Ausführliche Grammatik der griechischen Sprache*, 3rd ed., rev. B. Gerth, pt. 2 [Hannover, 1898]: ἐκ: 430.2.3.f; πρός: 441.III.3.b; ὑπό: 442.II.b.d; κατά: 433.II.3.d; διά: 434.I.3.e; ἐν: 431.3.b.) Circumstantial forms appear about twice as frequently as non-circumstantial forms, but I detect no essential difference in meaning based on this distinction. Passages containing non-circumstantial forms of βία: *Od.* 3.205–17/#1–2, 21.344–53; Ar. *Lys.* 223–28/#2; Theog. 1341–44; Bacchyl. 17.39–46 with lines 23 and 28; Pind. *Pyth.* 8.8–15; and Simon. Fr. 541.7–11 *PMG*. (See n. 2 for my use of #.)

[2]For the precise line in which the ἑκών group word appears, consult the Index Locorum. If there is more than one occurrence of a ἑκών group word in the pas-

and in *Prometheus Bound*, Hephaestus, accompanied by the personified pair Kratos and Bia, nails Prometheus to a rock (12–20/#1), and it is Zeus' fiery lightning bolt (663–72/#2) which threatens the progeny of Inachus.[3]

But usually, the type of situation itself, e.g., the abduction, restraint, or killing of persons, signals that some bodily force is being applied. Sometimes a verb like λεληισμένης (seize as booty or prey), ἁρπάσας (seize, snatch up) (Eur. *Tro.* 370–73 and 959–60 respectively), or ἀπηύρων (wrest from) (*Il.* 1.428–30) may conjure a more vivid picture, but the picture still lacks details of specific physical means. In some passages the physical nature of βία can be inferred because βία is paired and contrasted with what are clearly non-physical means. For example, βία is contrasted with a purchase and sale agreement (Eur. *Cyc.* 253–60/#1–2), persuasion (Aesch. *Supp.* 938–49), guile (δόλῳ) (*Od.* 9.403–12), and skill (ἰδρείη) (*Il.* 7.191–98/#2).

Even though detail is limited, the features just discussed make it clear that βία generally signals the hands-on force of one or more agents. It must be observed, however, that βία represents not only actual or in-progress physical force but also the force exerted by the threat of such force, and threatened βία compels as potently as βία in progress.

A good example is the case of Inachus in *Prometheus Bound*:

τέλος δ' ἐναργὴς βάξις ἦλθεν Ἰνάχωι
σαφῶς ἐπισκήπτουσα καὶ μυθουμένη
ἔξω δόμων τε καὶ πάτρας ὠθεῖν ἐμὲ
ἄφετον ἀλᾶσθαι γῆς ἐπ' ἐσχάτοις ὅροις·
κεἰ μὴ θέλοι, πυρωπὸν ἐκ Διὸς μολεῖν
κεραυνὸν ὃς πᾶν ἐξαϊστώσοι γένος.
τοιοῖσδε πεισθεὶς Λοξίου μαντεύμασιν
ἐξήλασέν με κἀπέκλῃσε δωμάτων
ἄκουσαν ἄκων· ἀλλ' ἐπηνάγκαζέ νιν
Διὸς χαλινὸς πρὸς βίαν πράσσειν τάδε.
(Aesch. *PrB* 663–72/#2)

Zeus compelled (ἐπηνάγκαζε) Inachus by force (πρὸς βίαν) to expel Io. What we know from the passage is that Zeus threatens the destruction of Inachus's progeny. If this threat is not counted as the reference of πρὸς βίαν, the substance of the compulsion, then some further untold violence against Inachus must be postulated. But to posit some further force here is to read much too

---

sage cited, the occurrence under discussion is noted by the sign / followed by # and a number. E.g., Aesch. *PrB* 12–20/#1 refers to the first occurrence of an ἑκών group word within lines 12–20.

[3] Zeus' lightning bolt may be less an actual weapon and more a metaphor for destruction. Cf. Aesch. *Ag.* 180. The "goad" of *Theog.* 371–72, however, is clearly not an actual instrument but part of a metaphorical love image.

much into the text. The more natural way to understand compulsion πρὸς βίαν simply is to identify it with Zeus' threat of violence.[4]

In some cases βία may be actual initially or applied to some members of a larger group which is affected, but the continued persistence of actual βία is doubtful. Rather, it is the threat of βία, a threat that is clearly realizable, which provides its own force and supports the description of the situation as occurring "by force." For example, in Euripides' *Trojan Women* (959–60 and 1010–22), Helen, even if initially taken by actual force, surely remains as the wife of Deiphobus under the threat of force. Herodotus (1.89.3) tells a story about some advice given by the conquered Croesus to Cyrus. Croesus advised Cyrus to recover some of the booty taken by the soldiers by claiming it as a tithe to Zeus. In this way, explains Croesus, Cyrus will not be hated by the soldiers for taking it "by force" (βίῃ). This implies that Cyrus could have taken the booty "by force." If we try to picture the soldiers being forced to give up booty, we can conclude that βία imposed on the soldiers might actually have been applied in some cases, but it is probably unrealistic to suppose each of the soldiers would have been subjected to actual force or even needed to be subjected to actual force. The force exerted by the threat of βία from the king would have been just as compelling. Similarly, in Euripides' *Helen* (391–96) and *Iphigenia in Aulis* (356–69) the use of βία is denied. But if we imagine how βία might have been used, it is likely that βία constitutes the threat of force and not actual force. In the *Helen*, we are told Agamemnon did not gather an army πρὸς βίαν. But what would it mean for a king to gather an army πρὸς βίαν? Surely it would be going too far to imagine reluctant men being dragged off to war by the minions of Agamemnon. However, a show of arms that would mirror the king's power and threaten such compliance or the removal of the king's protection that would result in bodily harm seems plausible. In the *Iphigenia in Aulis*, Menelaus insists Agamemnon was not forced to send for Iphigenia (καὶ πέμπεις ἑκών, / οὐ βίᾳ). But had he been forced to send for her, we can imagine the force involved would have been some threat to his life and/or leadership backed up by the sword of one or more soldiers anxious to leave for Troy.[5]

Exceptions to some kind of external and personal hands-on force, actual or threatened, are rare. In a few passages, the individuals described by the ἑκών group words are not affected by βία that is clearly of a hands-on sort. But the

---

[4]πρὸς βίαν in this passage has been understood by commentators in the sense "in defiance of his (Inachus') will." M. Griffith, ed., *Aeschylus: Prometheus Bound* (Cambridege, 1983), contrasts this sense with *PrB* 207–8 where he translates πρὸς βίαν straightforwardly as "through crude violence." See below, pp. 11–13 and n. 8, for my objections to the reading "in defiance of" here and in other passages. See below for the relationship between ἀνάγκη and βία.

[5]Cf. the tense condition of the troops at Aulis recalled by the Chorus of the *Agamemnon*, 188ff.

βία involved is a direct enough extension of such force that there is insufficient reason to seek some other explanation or to assume a separate sense of βία. Consider the following passage from Book 1 of the *Iliad*:

Ὥς ἄρα φωνήσασ' ἀπεβήσετο, τὸν δὲ λίπ' αὐτοῦ
χωόμενον κατὰ θυμὸν ἐϋζώνοιο γυναικός,
τὴν ῥα βίῃ ἀέκοντος ἀπηύρων·
(*Il.* 1.428–30)

Here Thetis leaves Achilles who is angered about Briseis (τήν) whom the heralds led away. Βίῃ could be taken with the verb and its object or closely with ἀέκοντος. On the first reading, Achilles is a third party described by a ἑκών group word but not under circumstances of βία marked by the presence of the word βία which applies to him directly.[6] The type of situation and verb do support actual or at least potential hands-on treatment of Briseis if βίῃ is taken to apply to her removal, but this passage contains no ἑκών group word describing Briseis. However, this passage can be taken together with earlier lines of Book 1 which refer to the same event and do directly describe Briseis as going ἀέκουσα:

Ὥς φάτο, Πάτροκλος δὲ φίλῳ ἐπεπείθεθ' ἑταίρῳ,
ἐκ δ' ἄγαγε κλισίης Βρισηΐδα καλλιπάρῃον,
δῶκε δ' ἄγειν· τὼ δ' αὖτις ἴτην παρὰ νῆας Ἀχαιῶν·
ἡ δ' ἀέκουσ' ἅμα τοῖσι γυνὴ κίεν·
(*Il.* 1.345–48)

This reading, involving only Briseis and not Achilles, provides a link between βία and the ἑκών group word and does not present any difficulty for understanding βία as actual or threatened hands-on force.

On the other hand, if we consider what seems the more natural reading, taking βίῃ closely with ἀέκοντος, we must discover whether βία could refer to actual or threatened hands-on force applied to Achilles. Achilles tells Agamemnon he will not fight for the girl (1.298–9) and hands her over to the two heralds without any show of force (1.324ff.). There is no direct hands-on force in the actual transaction or even a threat of force from the heralds. However, Agamemnon's orders to the heralds do contain a threat of physical force. He says he will come in person with many men if Achilles does not give up Briseis to the heralds (1.324–5). Thus, even if we think the threat of βία has no real influence on Achilles, the context contains a threat of force closely associated with the heralds and could account for βίῃ in lines 428–30.[7]

---

[6] Passages where the ἑκών group word attaches to an interested third party will be discussed in ch. 3.

[7] Cf. *Il.* 19.270–75, where Achilles refers to the time when Agamemnon led Briseis away, he says of himself ἐμεῦ ἀέκοντος ἀμήχανος. Since Achilles refers to the events of Book 1, βία can be operative here too. However, ἀμήχανος is

Another way to read βίη closely with ἀέκοντος is to assimilate it to the expression βίᾳ (or πρὸς βίαν) τινος (genitive of person). This expression is commonly understood and translated "against the will of" or "in defiance of."[8] My objection is not to the assimilation *per se* but to the general interpretation of the expression. It weakens βία unnecessarily and treats as completely interchangeable essentially distinct perspectives: the view from outside the person, what is happening to the person, and the view from within the person, the person's psychological attitude. Furthermore, in a passage like this which contains both the grammatical expression βίᾳ τινος and a form of ἄκων describing the same individual, I think we ought not assume these expressions are merely pleonastic rather than importing a significant nuance.

There are many familiar passages in which the expression βίᾳ τινος appears without any ἑκών group word, where it is the habit of translators and commentators to substitute the internal attitude of the person affected by the βία for the act of βία itself and to treat these different perspectives as interchangeable. I am not suggesting that there is no connection between the two perspectives; but I do think we should recognize the difference between the perspectives and the accompanying nuance of each. Take for example the well-known βίᾳ πολιτῶν of the *Antigone* (lines 79 [Ismene] and 907 [Antigone]). At line 79 Jebb translates "to defy the state" and at line 907, "in the city's despite." Neither of these translations captures what βία vividly conjures, an act of violence against the state. Kamerbeek aptly says of βίᾳ πολιτῶν at line 79

---

better taken within its own context as referring to the interference of Zeus or to Agamemnon's being difficult, rather than as evidence of βία and Agamemnon's threat to overpower Achilles. Another possible explanation for lines 428–30 is that, in consideration of the evidence for βία in Agamemnon's orders to the heralds concerning Achilles and in the treatment of Briseis and of the position of βίη between τήν (Briseis) and ἀέκοντος (Achilles), it might be best to see βίη as applying to both Briseis and Achilles.

[8]Cf. Liddell and Scott, *Greek-English Lexicon*, βία II.2: βία τινός. In his commentary, W. Leaf, ed., *The Iliad*, 2d ed., [London, 1900–02], reads βίη with ἀέκοντος and consider the expression pleonastic. Eustathius (M. Van der Valk, ed., *Eustathii Commentarii Ad Homeri Iliadem Pertinentes*, vol. 1 [Leiden, 1971]), 129.40–43 on verses 429 and 430) explains that by βίη ἀέκοντος the poet means Achilles was treated unjustly: πάντως δὲ τὸ βίᾳ οὐ δίκαιον. (Compare for example, Sophocles' *Antigone*, 907: βίᾳ πολιτῶν.) He understands ἀέκοντος to explain this βία which is only homonymous with βία as κατὰ ῥώμην δύναμις. Likewise, Eustathius says that according to the poet, Briseis too went ἀέκουσα: Ἀέκουσα δὲ καὶ ἐκείνη κατὰ τὸν ποιητὴν ἐπορεύθη. Even if Eustathius is right to infer that βίη ἀέκοντος amounts to unjust treatment, there is no need to go so far as to treat βία as ὕβρις and βία as physical force as mere homonyms or to think that the poet of the *Iliad* would have thought them homonyms. This sort of interpretation amounts to confusing the overall meaning of the passage with the meaning of particular words and expressions. (However, if we take the idiom βίᾳ with the genitive as "by doing injustice to X," this passage is akin to the passages of doing harm or wrong discussed in ch. 3.)

that "it combines as it were ἀπόρρητον πόλει 44 and νόμου βίᾳ 59." Jebb substitutes what is more an internal perspective even for νόμου βίᾳ: "in defiance of the law."[9] But what this phrase more accurately and succinctly depicts is transgression of the law as an act of violence against it. This is what Creon, not surprisingly, describes with great clarity at line 663: ὅστις δ' ὑπερβὰς ἢ νόμους βιάζεται (whoever transgresses or uses force on the laws).

Returning to *Iliad* 1.428–30, even if βία is not associated with Agamemnon's threat but is regarded as a variation of the expression βίᾳ τινος, it is still important to recognize that this phrase, here and elsewhere can and, I would argue, should be seen as extending from the core of βία, violent hands-on physical force. To be sure, there is a difference between the act of violence perpetrated against Achilles or the act of violence against the state in the *Antigone* (the burial of Polyneices) and the violent hands-on force of a murder or rape. But in contexts where force is especially relevant, there is no need to neglect the residue of hands-on force carried in βίᾳ τινος or to go so far so as to treat what is really a different perspective as a different sense of βία.[10] It is especially important to appreciate the nuance of βίᾳ in the *Iliad* passage since the objective genitive here is represented by ἀέκοντος. This phrase is not necessarily a mere pleonasm. Understanding it as merely pleonastic requires accepting a particular view about the relationship between βία and ἄκων. Since determining that relationship is the subject matter of this book, it would be premature to draw any conclusions now. However, on the view of ἑκών group words I will develop in the course of this book, the phrase is not pleonastic: βίᾳ describes the situation from the perspective outside of Achilles and ἀέκοντος the perspective from within Achilles.[11]

The same reasoning applies to a passage from Euripides' *Ion*, if βίαι is read closely with the genitive ἀκόντων θεῶν in line 378:[12]

οὐκ ἔστιν ὅστις σοι προφητεύσει τάδε.
ἐν τοῖς γὰρ αὐτοῦ δώμασιν κακὸς φανεὶς

---

[9]J.C. Kamerbeek, *The Plays of Sophocles: Commentaries*, pt. 3, *The Antigone* [Leiden, 1978]) and Σ understand ἀπόρρητον πόλει to mean "forbidden by the city" against R. Jebb (*Sophocles, The Plays and Fragments*, pt. 3, *The Antigone*, 3rd ed., [Cambridge, 1900]) and others who understand "forbidden to the city."

[10]It will do no good to object that this nuance has passed out of conscious usage. Since violence is especially relevant to these contexts, they may be special cases even if more generally the nuance of βία in the expression has lost its starkness.

[11]In the next chapter I will introduce such an interpretive view of ἑκών group words (the Functional Opposite View). See especially the Appendix to ch. 2 for evidence of this view among a variety of scholars.

[12]374–7 del. Badham; 375 ἄκοντας Brodaeus: ἑκό- L; 379 ἀνόνητα Stephanus; ἄκοντα L.

Φοῖβος δικαίως τὸν θεμιστεύοντά σοι
δράσειεν ἄν τι πῆμ'. ἀπαλλάσσου, γύναι·
τῶι γὰρ θεῶι τἀναντί' οὐ μαντευτέον.
[ἐς γὰρ τοσοῦτον ἀμαθίας ἔλθοιμεν ἄν
εἰ τοὺς θεοὺς ἄκοντας ἐκπονήσομεν
φράζειν ἃ μὴ θέλουσιν, ἢ προβωμίοις
σφαγαῖσι μήλων ἢ δι' οἰωνῶν πτεροῖς.]
ἂν γὰρ βίαι σπεύδωμεν ἀκόντων θεῶν,
ἀνόνητα κεκτήμεσθα τἀγαθ', ὦ γύναι·
ἃ δ' ἂν διδῶσ' ἑκόντες, ὠφελούμεθα.
(Eur. *Ion* 369–80)

In this passage Ion advises Creusa not to press Apollo to speak about self-incriminating matters. In the disputed lines, 374–77, Ion suggests that the gods can be prevailed upon to speak by means of sacrificial victims or birds. If the lines are retained, these means can be seen as summarized by or at least included under βίαι in line 378. Although it is impossible for humans to use actual hands-on force against the gods, the means gathered under βία here can be seen as weapons humans have in their arsenal as they deal with the gods.[13] But whether or not the disputed lines are retained, compared to the majority of passages discussed in this chapter, hands-on force seems too strong a reading of βία in this passage, especially since the gods are the object of the βία. However, here too the relevance of force to the context allows βία to make its point at least as an extension of hands-on force. Βία has enough residue from this core meaning that there is insufficient reason to recommend some new sense for this passage. Again, the nuance of βία can be (and I think should be) preserved; the phrase does not have to be reduced to a pleonastic expression.

There are a few passages, however, which do represent a more significant departure from hands-on force. In the following three passages, the force involved is an internal force. I will label this group (i/a).

Μή μ' ἀέκοντα βίηι κεντῶν ὑπ' ἄμαξαν ἔλαυνε
εἰς φιλότητα λίην, Κύρνε, προσελκόμενος.
(Theog. 371–72)

This couplet clearly contains a metaphor. The poet speaks of being driven to excessive love through the image of being goaded with βία and yoked to a cart. The image of "goading" might be taken to sustain by itself the use of βία and thereby confine βία to the metaphor. However, βία could directly represent the passions of the poet outside of the metaphor, i.e., passion is an actual form of βία, not just metaphorically represented by βία. Passion is not merely like

---

[13]Compare, for example the ἐπαγωγαί and συνδέσμοι Adimantus speaks about in Plato's *Republic* (364c4–5). The gods seem more bound by the magic of these door-to-door salesmen than "persuaded."

being shoved. It is a real shove though an internal one. That some desires, in fact, are just as compelling as physical attacks is a point Simonides makes more clearly in the following lines where profit and the goad of Aphrodite, that is, eros, the subjects of βιᾶται, do attack their victims:

...]ελος, οὐ γὰρ ἐλαφρὸν ἐσθλ[ὸν ἔμμεναι·
ἢ γ]ὰρ ἀέκοντά νιν βιᾶται
κέρ]δος ἀμάχητον ἢ δολοπλ[όκου
με]γασθενὴς οἶστρος Ἀφροδίτ[ας
..].(.)θαλοί τε φιλονικίαι.
(Simon. Fr. 541.7–11 *PMG*)

More difficult to pin down are the ἀεκούσια βίαια that Theognis endures and does not hide.

Αἰαῖ, παιδὸς ἐρῶ ἀπολόχροος, ὅς με φίλοισιν
πᾶσι μάλ' ἐκφαίνει κοὐκ ἐθέλοντος ἐμοῦ.
τλήσομαι οὐ κρύψας ἀεκούσια πολλὰ βίαια·
οὐ γὰρ ἐπ' αἰκελίωι παιδὶ δαμεὶς ἐφάνην.
(Theog. 1341–44)

Carrière following Romagnoli says: "Le poète, en somme, accepte la servitude, prend son parti de la gêne où le met souvent cette liaison qu'il souhaitait discrète, mais qui, malgrè lui, s'affiche publiquement."[14] The βίαια then are "la gêne," difficulties, troubles, uneasiness, inconvenience, the "constraints," as it were, of the relationship imposed by the παῖς. But these βίαια may be more akin to profit; and eros in the passage of Simonides quoted above. Perhaps what Theognis endures is that his desires and feelings, his love for the boy, are made public.[15]

For the most part then, βία consists of actual hands-on force, the force exerted by the threat of such force, or both. In some passages the use of βία can be seen to extend from and to bear a significant residue from βία as hands-on force. The use of βία in the three passages discussed just above, however, shows that βία can also represent internal force or that internal force is treated as βία in the presence of ἑκών group words.

---

[14]J. Carrière, *Théognis Poèmes Élégiaques* (Paris, 1948), 88–90.

[15]Cf. Eur. *Dictys* 339.1–6 *TGF*. I will discuss this passage under ἀνάγκη (iii) since the ἀνάγκη concerns the external constraints on humans set here by the gods rather than the internal constraint exerted by passionate love and disease on humans. Akin to speaking of passion as βία is the use of battle imagery in descriptions of Eros, e.g., the Eros chorus of Sophocles' *Antigone*, 781ff. and the Cypris chorus in his *Trachiniae*, 497ff.

Ἀνάγκη: general description

In the *Lexicon des frühgriechischen Epos*, K. Rüter says of ἀνάγκη:

> Zwang. Notwendigkeit; nicht als göttliche Person oder selbständig wirkende Macht (wie etwa μοῖρα: 'Schicksal'), keine Kraft (wie etwa βίη: 'Gewalt'), sondern ganz allgemein die Ursache eines unvermeidbaren, unfreiwilligen Handelns.[16]

Rüter goes on to say that attention is directed primarily at the acts which depend on ἀνάγκη. He notes that ἀνάγκη does not appear frequently in the nominative. Rather, something happens "unter Zwang," or most frequently, the instrumental dative used adverbially occurs: "etwas geschieht gezwungenermassen."

The ἀνάγκη forms appearing in the passages collected for this study are almost equally divided between circumstantial forms (circumstantial or comitative dative, equivalent prepositional phrases, adverb, or circumstantial participle) and non-circumstantial forms. Rüter's account, which fits the occurrences in circumstantial forms quite well, can be extended equally well to occurrences in non-circumstantial forms. Generally, ἀνάγκη signals that an action or an event is or was inevitable, necessary. It covers circumstances that have culminated in an inevitable situation, but does not by itself specifically identify the circumstances. However, the necessitating circumstances found in the passages collected here can be categorized into a limited number of general types, and these will be described below.[17]

As the passages are discussed, it will become evident that both a strong and a weak sense of "inevitable" are covered by ἀνάγκη. In the strong sense of inevitable, the action is the only physical possibility given the circumstances. There are several passages, however, where the action described as necessary or happening necessarily, under ἀνάγκη, is not the only physical possibility but rather the most acceptable course of action given the circumstances. While there are other possibilities, these are deemed so unreasonable or unworkable that they are treated as though non-existent.[18]

Although not all the circumstances that persist when an action or event is said to take place necessarily are preeminently characterizable in some particular way, e.g., as circumstances of βία, there are some definable circumstances that

---

[16]B. Snell and H. Erbse, *Lexicon des frühgriechischen Epos*, vol. 5, ed. E.M. Voist (Göttingen, 1955), 768.

[17]In two passages, *TrGF* 80.1–4 and Epicharmus 78.1–2 Kaibel, there is insufficient detail to clarify the circumstances underlying the necessity. However, stories relying on the circumstances discussed could be told to account for the ἀνάγκη in each.

[18]These strong and weak uses of ἀνάγκη can be compared with the use of βία to cover both in progress hands-on force as well as threatened force.

do regularly trigger the inevitable, and through them ἀνάγκη is manifested and accounted for. I will discuss these first.[19]

---

[19] In the discussion which follows, I do not, nor do I think it possible, to rely on H. Schreckenberg's treatment of ἀνάγκη (*Ananke: Untersuchungen zur Geschichte des Wortgebrauchs*, Zetemata, 36, Munich, 1964). My specific interest is to set out for those passages in which ἀνάγκη is related to the use of ἑκών group words, those circumstances which persist in actions or events said to occur by necessity. The relationship between ἀνάγκη and ἑκών group words, however, is not an object of study per se in Schreckenberg; in fact, he has very little to say on the subject. (See below p. 78 on Schreckenberg and the FOV.) For example, the frequency with which βία and ἀνάγκη appear in relationship to ἑκών group words is by itself enough to require a discussion in my study of the relationship between βία and ἀνάγκη. Schreckenberg, however, is uninterested in the relationship between βία and ἀνάγκη. (A. Wooley, in fact, mentions this omission as well as Schreckenberg's bare comments on the relationship between ἀνάγκη and ἑκών/ἐθέλω in his review of Schreckenberg: *AJP* 88 (1967) 228–30.) Furthermore, Schreckenberg's particular interest in what he argues is the etymology of ἀνάγκη, "yoke/fetter," and his interest in the progressive history of this word, lead him to speak about the "meaning" of ἀνάγκη in ways I do not and to produce different groupings of uses. For example, Schreckenberg talks of ἀνάγκη "as torture" (p. 44: "Als 'Folter' ist Ananke seit Herodot bekannt") or "meaning torture" (p. 45: "Wie kommt es zu dieser Bedeutung?" The explanation includes the following development: "Man wird danach ἀνάγκη als 'Folter' im Sinne der konkreten physischen Pressur zu verstehen haben."), relates this "meaning" to the basic etymological meaning he posits for ἀνάγκη, and then develops the meaning "torture" into another meaning, "physical pain" (pp. 45ff.). In my view, "torture" would count as but one form or expression of βία which itself is one of the more characterizable types of circumstances in which actions or events are said to take place under ἀνάγκη (See e.g., my discussion of Gorgias B.11a.11DK). I would not say either that βία or ἀνάγκη means "torture" or that ἀνάγκη means βία. As many of Schreckenberg's critics have noted, his methodology commits him to asserting that some uses are literal (ἀνάγκη = "fetter") while others are metaphorical, a distinction which lends itself to arbitrariness. A prime example has been his discussion of ἀνάγκη in *Od.* 1.154 (literal: Odysseus fettered his men and led them away) and *Od.* 22.353 (metaphorical: Phemius was constrained to sing). In my discussion of the second passage (which also contains an ἑκών group word) what counts as or underlies the use of ἀνάγκη is at least the threat of βία, but ἀνάγκη does not therefore mean βία or the threat of βία. However, despite our serious differences over the issue of semantic identity, it should be noted that the kinds of circumstances I gather under ἀνάγκη do come up in Schreckenberg's discussion. For example, in his chapter, "Situationsgegebene Bindung," see pp. 31ff. on orders (cf. p. 137 for ἀνάγκη as νόμος developing from ἀνάγκη as order); pp. 72ff. (cf. p. 33) on fate; on die Zwangslage, pp. 36ff., and cf. my ἀνάγκη (iii); cf. my ἀνάγκη (ia) with ch. 3, "Naturbindung," passim; cf. pp. 65ff. with my ἀνάγκη (ii), e.g., *xenia*. Those critical of Schreckenberg's methodology include Wooley, A.W.H. Adkins (rev. in *CR* 16 [1966] 68–70), H. Vos (rev. in *Mnemos.* 20 [1967] 76–78), and H.B. Gottschalk (rev. in *JHS* 86 [1966] 213–14); the last three also express skepticism about Schreckenberg's underlying views on semantic identity.

Ἀνάγκη (i): βία

One of the more definable types of circumstances in which actions take place under ἀνάγκη are circumstances of βία.[20] In the following three passages, both βία and ἀνάγκη appear, and the necessity marked by ἀνάγκη appears to rely on and be accounted for by the presence of βία. Βία is of the hands-on variety in each. In the first passage, an attendant, explaining to Alcmene why Iolaus did not kill Eurystheus, refers to the king's defeat and capture by a rejuvenated Iolaus:

> τὸ σὸν προτιμῶν, ὥς νιν ὀφθαλμοῖς ἴδοις
> †κρατοῦντα† καὶ σῇ δεσποτούμενον χερί.
> οὐ μὴν ἑκόντα γ' αὐτόν, ἀλλὰ πρὸς βίαν
> ἔζευξ' ἀνάγκη· καί γὰρ οὐκ ἐβούλετο
> ζῶν ἐς σὸν ἐλθεῖν ὄμμα καὶ δοῦναι δίκην.
> (Eur. *Heracl.* 883–87)

Next, Demeter, who heard only the cries of her daughter, Persephone, asks Helios if he saw who abducted Persephone:

> κούρην τὴν ἔτεκον γλυκερὸν θάλος εἴδει κυδρὴν
> τῆς ἀδινὴν ὄπ' ἄκουσα δι' αἰθέρος ἀτρυγέτοιο
> ὥς τε βιαζομένης, ἀτὰρ οὐκ ἴδον ὀφθαλμοῖσιν.
> ἀλλὰ σὺ γὰρ δὴ πᾶσαν ἐπὶ χθόνα καὶ κατὰ πόντον
> αἰθέρος ἐκ δίης καταδέρκεαι ἀκτίνεσσι,
> νημερτέως μοι ἔνισπε φίλον τέκος εἴ που ὄπωπας
> ὅς τις νόσφιν ἐμεῖο λαβὼν ἀέκουσαν ἀνάγκῃ
> οἴχεται ἠὲ θεῶν ἢ καὶ θνητῶν ἀνθρώπων.
> (*HDem.* 66–73)

In the third passage, Demeter tells the daughters of Celeus a tale of her abduction by pirates:

> Δωσὼ ἐμοί γ' ὄνομ' ἐστί· τὸ γὰρ θέτο πότνια μήτηρ·
> νῦν αὖτε Κρήτηθεν ἐπ' εὐρέα νῶτα θαλάσσης
> ἤλυθον οὐκ ἐθέλουσα, βίῃ δ' ἀέκουσαν ἀνάγκῃ
> ἄνδρες ληιστῆρες ἀπήγαγον.
> (*HDem.* 122–25)

---

[20] A circumstantial form of ἀνάγκη appears with a form of βία in Eur. *Heracl.* 883–87, Thuc. 4.98.1–6/#1 and 3, *HDem.* 66–73 and 122–25. In the passages from Euripides and the *Homeric Hymn*, βία is also circumstantial in form. In the passage from Thucydides, βία appears in a verb form. Βία and ἀνάγκη appear together in two other passages, *PrB* 663–72/#2 and *HDem.* 407–13. In both of these passages βία is circumstantial (πρὸς βίαν and βίῃ) and ἀνάγκη appears in verb form.

In these passages we understand that Eurystheus, Persephone, and Demeter, respectively, are compelled because they have been physically subdued.

In the following passage from Thucydides, Brasidas addresses the Acanthian assembly which received him out of fear for the harvest (4.84). Here too, destruction to be achieved through hands-on force defines ἀνάγκη:

> Εἰ δ' ἐμοῦ ταῦτα προϊσχομένου ἀδύνατοι μὲν φήσετε εἶναι, εὖνοι δ' ὄντες ἀξιώσετε μὴ κακούμενοι διωθεῖσθαι καὶ τὴν ἐλευθερίαν μὴ ἀκίνδυνον ὑμῖν φαίνεσθαι, δίκαιόν τε εἶναι, οἷς καὶ δυνατὸν δέχεσθαι αὐτήν, τούτοις καὶ ἐπιφέρειν, ἄκοντα δὲ μηδένα προσαναγκάζειν, μάρτυρας μὲν θεοὺς καὶ ἥρως τοὺς ἐγχωρίους ποιήσομαι ὡς ἐπ' ἀγαθῷ ἥκων οὐ πείθω, γῆν δὲ τὴν ὑμετέραν δῃῶν πειράσομαι βιάζεσθαι, καὶ οὐκ ἀδικεῖν ἔτι νομιῶ.
> (Thuc. 4.87.2)

Brasidas, working to "liberate" Thrace from the control of the Athenians, imagines what the Acanthians will say in response to his arguments for breaking from the Athenians. In particular, he supposes they will say he ought not compel anyone (μηδένα προσαναγκάζειν) to accept freedom. In his response, he spells out the form this compulsion will take; that is, he will try to force them (πειράσομαι βιάζεσθαι) by wasting their land.

In another passage from Thucydides, the Athenians explain their behavior in regard to the charge of the Boeotians that they had transgressed the customs of the Hellenes by their occupation and use of resources in the holy places of Delium:

> τοσαῦτα τοῦ κήρυκος εἰπόντος οἱ Ἀθηναῖοι πέμψαντες παρὰ τοὺς Βοιωτοὺς ἑαυτῶν κήρυκα τοῦ μὲν ἱεροῦ οὔτε ἀδικῆσαι ἔφασαν οὐδὲν οὔτε τοῦ λοιποῦ ἑκόντες βλάψειν·... ὕδωρ τε ἐν τῇ ἀνάγκῃ κινῆσαι, ἣν οὐκ αὐτοὶ ὕβρει προσθέσθαι, ἀλλ' ἐκείνους προτέρους ἐπὶ τὴν σφετέραν ἐλθόντας ἀμυνόμενοι βιάζεσθαι χρῆσθαι. πᾶν δ' εἰκὸς εἶναι τὸ πολέμῳ καὶ δεινῷ τινι κατειργόμενον ξύγγνωμόν τι γίγνεσθαι καὶ πρὸς τοῦ θεοῦ. καὶ γὰρ τῶν ἀκουσίων ἁμαρτημάτων καταφυγὴν εἶναι τοὺς βωμούς, παρανομίαν τε ἐπὶ τοῖς μὴ ἀνάγκῃ κακοῖς ὀνομασθῆναι καὶ οὐκ ἐπὶ τοῖς ἀπὸ τῶν ξυμφορῶν τι τολμήσασιν.
> (Thuc. 4.98.1–6/#1,3)

The disturbance of sacred waters is described as a case of necessity (ἐν τῇ ἀνάγκῃ) which is immediately explained as something the Athenians were forced to do (βιάζεσθαι) when defending themselves from attack. The hands-on βία of the attackers created the situation of ἀνάγκη.[21] Similarly, in the passage quoted earlier from the *Prometheus Bound* (663-72/#2) where circumstantial πρὸς βίαν appears with the verb form ἐπηνάγκαζε, Zeus' threat of force to destroy his progeny is surely what necessitated that Inachus drive out his daughter, Io. Βία accounts for the necessity.

On the basis of these five passages, I would argue that we should also expect βίη in the remaining passage in which a form of βία and a form of ἀνάγκη appear together, to provide the basis for the necessity. In this passage from the *Hymn to Demeter* it was necessary that Persephone taste the pomegranate seed:

εὐτέ μοι Ἑρμῆς ἢ[λθ]' ἐριούνιος ἄγγελος ὠκὺς
πὰρ πατέρος Κρονίδαο καὶ ἄλλων οὐρανιώνων
ἐλθεῖν ἐξ Ἐρέβευς, ἵνα μ' ὀφθαλμοῖσιν ἰδοῦσα
λήξαις ἀθανάτοισι χόλου καὶ μήνιος αἰνῆς,
αὐτὰρ ἐγὼν ἀνόρουσ' ὑπὸ χάρματος, αὐτὰρ ὁ λάθρῃ
ἔμβαλέ μοι ῥοιῆς κόκκον, μελιηδέ' ἐδωδήν,
ἄκουσαν δὲ βίῃ με προσηνάγκασσε πάσασθαι.
(*HDem.* 407-13)

Without βίῃ we might conclude that circumstances arose that necessitated Persephone to taste the pomegranate seed. So much is expressed by προσηνάγκασσε: it was unavoidable that Persephone taste the seed. However, the presence of βίῃ signals that further characterization is at hand. Given the frequency with which βία refers to hands-on force, it is likely that hands-on force is to be seen in Hades' behavior as he tossed the seed into Persephone's mouth, or perhaps in the more general threat of force to which Persephone was subject when taken away by Hades. Without further information it would be inappropriate to posit some other undescribed act of βία on his part.[22]

---

[21] Another way to view this pasagge is not to construe ἀνάγκη and βιάζεσθαι so closely together. In this way ἀνάγκη may refer rather to the human need to drink as the circumstances compelling the Athenians. I am inclined to understand ἀνάγκη closely with βιάζεσθαι since the whole passage concentrates on the aggressors and the immediate explanation of the necessity to use the sacred water is the aggression of the Boeotians. The rhetorical emphasis of the passage is not the necessity to drink *per se*, but the necessity to drink this particular water.

[22] Commentators on this passage (e.g., N.J. Richardson, ed., *The Homeric Hymn to Demeter* [Oxford, 1974], and T.W. Allen, W.R. Halliday, & E.E. Sikes, eds., *The Homeric Hymns* [Oxford, 1936]) consider ἄκουσαν βίῃ a traditional pleonasm so that there is no need to take βίῃ at face value. Since there is no description of any compulsion, they conclude there was none. Here ἄκουσαν, the internal descriptor of the pair, is privileged and the external βίῃ disregarded. I disagree. Cf. my earlier remarks on this so-called pleonasm pp. 11-13. Richardson adds, "Does she (Persephone) perhaps 'protest too much' in self-defence?" But given the range of what counts as βία, there is no need to deny its literal potential. Cf. also *PrB* 663-72/#2 discussed on pp. 8-9.

In a passage from Herodotus, ἀναγκαίως and βία occur in the same passage, but unlike the passages just discussed, the circumstances of βία here are not what triggers ἀνάγκη.

> κάτισον τῶν δορυφόρων ἐπὶ πάσῃσι τῇσι πύλῃσει φυλάκους, οἳ λεγόντων πρὸς τοὺς ἐκφέροντας τὰ χρήματα ἀπαιρεόμενοι ὥς σφεα ἀναγκαίως ἔχει δεκατευθῆναι τῷ Διί. καὶ σύ τέ σφι οὐκ ἀπεχθήσεαι βίῃ ἀπαιρεόμενος τὰ χρήματα, καὶ ἐκεῖνοι συγγνόντες ποιέειν σε δίκαια ἑκόντες προήσουσι.
> (Hdt. 1.89.3)

The soldiers in this passage would pay their tithe to Zeus ἀναγκαίως but there would be no βία. Βία has the usual sense of hands-on force, but the action does not take place ἀναγκαίως because of these circumstances. This passage is not an exception to the finding that where βία and ἀνάγκη appear together βία delimits the circumstances that trigger ἀνάγκη since there is no conjunction of βία and ἀνάγκη here, but rather a disjunction: ἀνάγκη but no βία. This only implies that there are other circumstances besides βία under which actions are said to happen necessarily. This passage will be discussed later under ἀνάγκη (ii).

The relationship between the βία and ἀνάγκη words is more problematic, however in the following passage from Thucydides:[23]

> οὐ γὰρ αἰσχρὸν εἶναι Ἀθηναίους ναυτικῷ μετὰ καιροῦ ὑποχωρῆσαι, ἀλλὰ καὶ μετὰ ὁτουοῦν τρόπου αἴσχιον ξυμβήσεσθαι ἢν ἡσσηθῶσιν· καὶ τὴν πόλιν οὐ μόνον τῷ αἰσχρῷ, ἀλλὰ καὶ τῷ μεγίστῳ κινδύνῳ περιπίπτειν, ᾗ μόλις ἐπὶ ταῖς γεγενημέναις ξυμφοραῖς ἐνδέχεσθαι μετὰ βεβαίου παρασκευῆς καθ' ἑκουσίαν, ἢ πάνυ γε ἀνάγκῃ, προτέρᾳ ποι ἐπιχειρεῖν, ἢ που δὴ μὴ βιαζομένῃ γε πρὸς αὐθαιρέτους κινδύνους ἰέναι.
> (Thuc. 8.27.3)

Andrewes and Dover suggest that ἢ πάνυ γε ἀνάγκῃ may be a gloss on μὴ βιαζομένῃ.[24] On this view, even though the phrase is not a part of the text, it is in line with the pattern already discussed: circumstances of βία tend to trigger actions that happen necessarily, i.e., under ἀνάγκη. The problem is to make sense of the passage maintaining the disputed phrase.

If the text is read as printed, we can understand Phrynichus' remarks to have contained first a general statement and then a more particular one. In the general

---

[23] The MSS do not all read the text as printed: C omits καθ' ἑκουσίαν and B omits ἀνάγκῃ.

[24] A.W. Gomme, A. Andrewes, and K.J. Dover, *A Historical Commentary on Thucydides*, vol. 5 (Oxford, 1981), 64. (Hereafter, *Com. Thuc.*)

statement there is a constrast between καθ' ἑκουσίαν and ἀνάγκη; in the more particular statement there is a comparable contrast: μὴ βιαζομένῃ is parallel to ἀνάγκη and καθ' ἑκουσίαν is parallel to αὐθαιρέτους κινδύνους (self-chosen dangers). The point of the general statement is that in light of recent disastrous events, it would be foolish to attack first even with good preparation whether καθ' ἑκουσίαν (γνώμην?) or under ἀνάγκη; that is, they should not attack with preparation and ἑκόντες or even with preparation and necessarily. In this general remark, ἀνάγκη may indicate a wide variety of circumstances that can necessitate engagement, e.g., weather, enemy tactics, location, etc. (This sort of ἀνάγκη [type iii] is discussed below.) Generally then, attacking first under any conditions is foolish in light of recent losses. To this general remark is added a more specific and currently applicable scenario in which it would be foolish to attack: risking self-chosen dangers without being subject to force (μὴ βιαζομένῃ) and having inadequate preparation. Here βιαζομένῃ is likely to refer to the imminent threat of an actual attack by the enemy. Thus, like the tithe passage from Herodotus discussed above (Hdt. 1.89.3), a form of ἀνάγκη and βία appear in the same passage, but βία is not conjoined with ἀνάγκη as the specific trigger of the ἀνάγκη.

Actions or events that happen under circumstances of superior hands-on force, are one of the more definable kinds of circumstances in which actions or events take place under ἀνάγκη. Most passages which contain ἑκών group words and circumstantial forms of βία do not also have a form of ἀνάγκη; but generally, even where there is no ἀνάγκη form, actions that take place under circumstances of βία can be construed as inevitable in either the strong or weak sense.[25]

In the four passages discussed earlier (Eur. *Heracl.* 883–87 and *HDem.* 66–73, 122–25, 407–13), where βία is actual and in progress, we would judge that the necessity is strong. There was no alternative to going with their captors for Eurystheus, Persephone, or Demeter. But in the passage from the *Prometheus Bound* (663–72/#2), e.g., where Inachus is threatened with βία, and the passage from Thucydides (4.98.1–6/#1&3) where the Athenians, under attack, use sacred waters, there are other possibilities. Inachus could have chosen Io over his progeny or even killed himself and thereby avoided the order of Zeus; the Athenians could have chosen to die of thirst rather than use sacred waters. The passages neither point out nor deny these possibilites. While these alternatives are, strictly speaking, possibilities, they are treated as non-existent because they are ordinarily unacceptable alternatives. Thus, both Inachus and the Athenians in fact, do what seems most reasonable but not the only thing possible in the strictest sense. Suicide is not a *choice* on a par with most choices we make. We

---

[25]Passages like *Il.* 1.428–30 and Eur. *Ion*, 369–80, where the βία involved is an extension of hands-on force, may be an exception. The residue of βία may not be enough to import inevitability.

often claim that someone *has no choice* but to act as he does, although an abhorrent possibility, like suicide, is physically possible. So too the alternatives available to Inachus and the Athenians are strictly speaking possibilities; but because of some deeper values, they are not acceptable enough to be counted as viable alternatives. Thus, the actions of Inachus and the Athenians are necessary but in a weaker sense than strict physical possibility.

Some passages which contain a form of ἀνάγκη but no accompanying βία form are also best categorized under ἀνάγκη (i), since physical force or the threat of it is most likely what underlies the necessity.[26] Hands-on force or at least the threat of it is clearly what Phemius has in mind in the *Odyssey* (22.330–31, 344–53) when he speaks of singing for the suitors who, he says, were greater in both numbers and strength. Subjection to actual or threatened hands-on force is the most likely explanation of the action of the Phocians in Herodotus (9.17.1) who are said to have medized ὑπ' ἀναγκαίης.[27] Likewise, many of those who fought in Sicily "by necessity" (ἀνάγκη) did so, according to Thucydides (7.57.1–10), because they were subject to the superior strength of Athens. Some (7.57.4) were actual subjects (ὑπήκοοι); others, like the Cephallenian and Zacynthian islanders (7.57.7), were de facto subjects since Athens was in total command of the sea.[28] In Thucydides' account of the embassy to Athens after the Athenian success at Pylos (4.19.4), when the Spartan envoys sued for peace, they contrasted their current situation with one in which a completely victorious enemy compels its opponent (κατ' ἀνάγκην) to swear to treaty terms. The compulsion they have in mind is surely the possibility of being subjected to the superior physical force of the enemy army. Likewise, when Herodotus expresses what he expects will be an unpopular opinion about how the war against the Persians would have gone if the Athenians had abandoned their land or submitted to the Persians (7.139.3–4), he presumes the allies of the Lacedaemonians would have deserted them ὑπ' ἀναγκαίης because they would have been subject to the superior military power of the Persians, now masters of their territories. Cassandra, a war prize in Aeschylus' *Agamemnon* (1069–71), is pitied by the Chorus who speak to her in the following passage, but she must obey and step down from the cart which has brought her to the palace of Agamemnon:

---

[26]ἀνάγκη (i): Eur. *Heracl.* 403–14/#1, *Il.* 6.450–61, Thuc. 3.39.7; 1.32.4; 6.87.4; 7.81.3; 8.3.1, *Theog.* 467–72/#1, and Hdt. 7.104.3: if "ἤ" is understood as conjunctive and μέγας τις ὁ ἐποτρύνων ἀγών is understood to refer to some sort of βία, ἀνάγκη is probably of the βία variety; however, if the "ἤ" is disjunctive, ἀνάγκη could be compelling circumstances other than βία—perhaps ἀνάγκη (iii).

[27]See Hdt. 8.30. Presumably the Phocians capitulated to the Persians after their lands had been ravaged despite their initial resistance.

[28]See *Com. Thuc.* vol. 4, (Oxford, 1970), 433–34.

> ἐγὼ δ', ἐποικτίρω γάρ, οὐ θυμώσομαι·
> ἴθ', ὦ τάλαινα, τόνδ' ἐρημώσασ' ὄχον;
> ἑκοῦσ' ἀνάγκῃ τῇδε καίνισον ζυγόν.
> (Aesch. Ag. 1069-71)

The yoke of the slavery she must endure as well as the immediate order she has been given are grounded in physical force.[29]

Finally, hands-on force can also account for δι' ἀνάγκην in this passage from Gorgias' *Defense of Palamedes*:

> δούλοις δὲ πῶς οὐκ ἄπιστον; ἑκόντες τε γὰρ ἐπ' ἐλευθερίαι χειμαζόμενοί τε δι' ἀνάγκην κατηγοροῦσιν.
> (Gorg. B.11a.11DK)

If historical practices concerned with eliciting information from slaves are seen to underlie the passage, Palamedes' point is that slaves make accusations because they are tortured until they do so. Only then are they free of the torture.[30]

In these passages too the presence of actual or threatened hands-on force appears to account for the designation of actions occurring necessarily. Even where there is only a threat of force so that there are other alternatives, the agents act under ἀνάγκη. Because details are lacking, it is not clear whether these alternatives include only extreme choices like those of Inachus (*PrB* 663-72) and the Athenians while occupying the temple and precincts of Delium (Thuc. 4.98.1-6).

Ἀνάγκη (ii): compelling social practices

In another group of passages, acts or events designated as occurring by ἀνάγκη appear to be based on the binding power of certain social practices. Consider the following passage from Sophocles' *Philoctetes*:

> ὄλοιο· καί σοι πολλάκις τόδ' ηὐξάμην.
> ἀλλ' οὐ γὰρ οὐδὲν θεοὶ νέμουσιν ἡδύ μοι,
> σὺ μὲν γέγηθας ζῶν, ἐγὼ δ' ἀλγύνομαι
> τοῦτ' αὖθ' ὅτι ζῶ σὺν κακοῖς πολλοῖς τάλας,
> γελώμενος πρὸς σοῦ τε καὶ τῶν Ἀτρέως
> διπλῶν στρατηγῶν, οἷς σὺ ταῦθ' ὑπηρετεῖς.
> καίτοι σὺ μὲν κλοπῇ τε κἀνάγκῃ ζυγεὶς

---

[29] Reading ἑκοῦσ' with the manuscripts rather than Robortello's εἴκουσ'. If Casaubon's ἀνάγκης τῇδε is read instead of ἀνάγκῃ τῇδε (which, like ἑκοῦσ', Page suspects is correct), this non-circumstantial form would still be grouped under (i).

[30] See D. MacDowell, *The Law in Classical Athens* (Ithaca, 1978), 245-47, on the βάσανοι. Cf. Arist. *Rh.* 1376b-1377a.

ἔμπλεις ἅμ' αὐτοῖς, ἐμὲ δὲ τὸν πανάθλιον
ἑκόντα πλεύσανθ' ἑπτὰ ναυσὶ ναυβάτην
ἄτιμον ἔβαλον, ὡς σὺ φῄς, κεῖνοι δὲ σέ.
(Soph. *Ph.* 1019–28)

In line 1025, Philoctetes charges Odysseus sailed to Troy "by deceit and yoked by necessity" (κλοπῇ τε κἀνάγκῃ ζυγείς). Generally, commentators understand this phrase to refer to Odysseus' attempt to feign madness, which was uncovered by Palamedes. Readers are referred to the tale of Odysseus' madness and the oath taken by Helen's suitors.[31] However, there is disagreement about whose deceit (κλοπή) is meant, Odysseus' or Palamedes', and little attempt to be more specific about the reference of ἀνάγκη.

Kamerbeek says the phrase refers "to Palamedes' ruse and the ensuing necessity for Odysseus to give up his madness." If the phrase is taken as a hendiadys, he recommends interpreting it: "brought by means of ruse under the yoke of necessity."[32] Matthaei takes ἀνάγκῃ ζυγείς (yoked by necessity) as equivalent to ἀναγκασθείς (compelled) but is not concerned to spell out the grounds of the ἀνάγκη. Rather, puzzled about whose κλοπή is meant and thinking that neither Palamedes nor Odysseus fit, he recommends emending κλοπή to κλοπεύς (one who acts with deceit).[33] I presume that he intends the change to refer to Odysseus' general reputation since he simply cannot imagine how Odysseus' failed attempt at deceit could count as κλοπή.

In my view, since Philoctetes speaks to Odysseus specifically about their respective statuses when the ships first set sail, it is unlikely that Philoctetes would refer to Odysseus generally as a κλοπεύς. Instead, he makes reference to the well-known tale of Odysseus' attempt to avoid going to Troy. In Aeschylus' *Agamemnon* (841–42), Agamemnon alludes to the story even as he sincerely worries about Odysseus' safety.

Concerning the question of whose κλοπή is meant, I am inclined to understand it as referring to both Odysseus and Palamedes. The fact that Odysseus intended his deceit to avoid service does not disqualify him as a referent as Matthaei thinks. He can be understood to have been "yoked by his own κλοπή," like one who has been "hoisted by his own petard." Although I hesistate to refer

---

[31] *Cypria* (Proclus' *Chrestomathia* 103.25–28 Allen), Soph. *Odysseus Mainomenos* (462–69 Radt), Ps.-Apollod. 3.10.9, Eur. *IA* 53–71, Cic. *Off.* III.26 (quotes Pacuvius).

[32] J.C. Kamerbeek, *The Plays of Sophocles: Commentaries*, pt. 6, *The Philoctetes* [Leiden, 1980]). R Jebb, (*Sophocles, The Plays and Fragments*, pt. 4, *The Philoctetes*, 2d ed., [Cambridge, 1898]) too understands these words to mean that Odysseus was compelled to join the army by the ruse of Palamedes.

[33] I.P. Matthaei, *Sophocles: Philoctetes* (Altonae, 1822), 212.

to Palamedes' insightfulness as κλοπή, it is possible.[34] However, since Palamedes' trick was not conceived apart from Odysseus' but rather in response to it, the κλοπή can be seen as a single event involving both Odysseus' initial deceit and Paladmedes' clever ruse. The story of the κλοπή is about both Odysseus' feigning madness by ploughing with an ass yoked to an ox, and Palamedes' ruse, placing Odysseus' son in the way.

In any event, it remains to explain what is meant by ἀνάγκη; or if the phrase is taken as a hendiadys, to explain what constitutes the "yoke of necessity." Kamerbeek understands the necessity as the "necessity for Odysseus to give up his madness." Presumably, Odysseus' actions showed he was not mad, and thus Odysseus had no alternative but to give up his feint. If Kamerbeek is right to take ἀνάγκη as the unavoidable conclusion of the preceding event, the κλοπή, then this passage fits my category ἀνάγκη (iii) which will be discussed below. However, this interpretation leaves out the oath sworn by Helen's suitors. The suitors' oath and Odysseus' feigned madness are parts of the same story. For Odysseus' feigned madness was his attempt to avoid the terms of the oath he swore as one of Helen's suitors.[35]

I propose that the ἀνάγκη by which Odysseus was yoked is constituted by his oath as a suitor. His plot having failed, Odysseus was constrained by his oath to go to Troy. The extant versions of the story mention no persuasion or force, only the oath.

The following passage from Euripides' *Phoenissae* also falls under ἀνάγκη (ii) and the compelling power of an oath:

> δισσοῖς Ἄδραστος ὤμοσεν γαμβροῖς τόδε,
> [Τυδεῖ τε κἀμοί· σύγγαμος γάρ ἐστ' ἐμός·]
> ἄμφω κατάξειν ἐς πάτραν, πρόσθεν δ' ἐμέ.
> πολλοὶ δὲ Δαναῶν καὶ Μυκηναίων ἄκροι
> πάρεισι, λυπρὰν χάριν, ἀναγκαίαν δ', ἐμοὶ
> διδόντες· ἐπὶ γὰρ τὴν ἐμὴν στρατεύομαι
> πόλιν. Θεοὺς δ' ἐπώμοσ' ὡς ἀκουσίως
> τοῖς φιλτάτοις ἑκοῦσιν ᾑράμην δόρυ.
> (Eur. *Phoen.* 427–34/#1–2)

Here Polyneices and his relatives are caught up in the inevitable events that follow on Adrastus' oath to return his sons-in-law to their respective homelands: δισσοῖς Ἄδραστος ὤμοσεν γαμβροῖς τόδε (427). Adrastus' oath explains why the Danaans and Mycenaeans are present and underlies Polyneices' description of

---

[34]Cf. Pacuvius' view of the matter: *quod ni Palamedi perspicax prudentia / istius percepset malitiosam audaciam.* Cic.*Off.* III.26.

[35]The extant evidence about the *Cypria* does not mention the oath, but it also does not explain why Odysseus should be expected to go.

the "painful favor" (λυπρὰν χάριν) they give him as "necessary" (ἀναγκαῖαν). Polyneices' description of this favor (χάριν) as painful (λυπράν) is explained in the following line (432): "for I march against my own city." This large context of ἀνάγκη established by Adrastus' oath is that in which Polyneices swears his own oath in lines 433–34. Swept up in the inevitability stemming from the first oath, Adrastus', Polyneices swears that he makes war ἀκουσίως with "those who are closest being ἑκόντες" (τοῖς φιλτάτοις ἑκοῦσιν).[36] Thus, the ἑκών words can be linked to the necessity stemming from Adrastus' oath: Polyneices and his adversaries are both subject to it.

Another social practice, the lottery, underlies ἀνάγκη in the following passage from Euripides' *Heraclidae*:

οὐκ ἂν θάνοιμι τῇ τύχῃ λαχοῦσ' ἐγώ·
χάρις γὰρ οὐ πρόσεστι· μὴ λέξῃς, γέρον.
ἀλλ', εἰ μὲν ἐνδέχεσθε καὶ βούλεσθέ μοι
χρῆσθαι προθύμω, τὴν ἐμὴν ψυχὴν ἐγὼ
δίδωμ' ἑκοῦσα τοῖσδ', ἀναγκασθεῖσα δ' οὔ.
(Eur. *Heracl.* 547–51)

Demophon is prepared to fight the Argives for the sake of the children of Heracles. However, according to the oracles, their success depends on the sacrifice of a maiden to Persephone. Macaria refuses to die if chosen by lot (οὐκ ἂν θάνοιμι τῇ τύχῃ λαχοῦσ' ἐγώ). Being chosen by lot is the circumstance she refers to in ἀναγκασθεῖσα δ' οὔ (but not compelled). Although one could imagine further physical forms of compulsion being called on once the lot has been drawn, nevertheless, it is the lot that would stimulate such action. It is the lot that Macaria rejects and refers to as acting ἀναγκασθεῖσα. The social practice delimits without appeal who is to act.[37]

---

[36] Reading ἑκοῦσιν with γρ Σ instead of τοκεῦσιν codd. et Σ.

[37] Compare the guard in Sophocles' *Antigone*, 223ff. He is certainly a reluctant messenger and clearly considered not going to Creon at all. The soldiers decided to draw lots when they determined Creon must be told of the burial:

ἦν δ' ὁ μῦθος ὡς ἀνοιστέον
σοὶ τοὔργον εἴη τοῦτο κοὐχὶ κρυπτέον.
καὶ ταῦτ' ἐνίκα, κἀμὲ τὸν δυσδαίμονα
πάλος καθαιρεῖ τοῦτο τἀγαθὸν λαβεῖν (272–75).

It is understood that the lot will determine without further recourse who is to go to Creon. The soldier who "won" the lottery does not question his position as determined by the lottery, however uncomfortable he is with his task. The question he asks himself during his delay:

κεἰ τάδ' εἴσεται Κρέων
ἄλλου παρ' ἀνδρός, πῶς σὺ δῆτ' οὐκ ἀλγυνῇ; (229–30)

Another compelling social practice is that of giving orders. The ultimate foundation of an order may well be physical force.[38] However, where a legitimate authority gives an order, the socially accepted response is to comply with the order. The lottery example just discussed could be seen as a type of order. There too physical compulsion may be the ultimate foundation of the lottery's efficacy. But the lot itself is the focus of necessity. An order itself, whatever other source of compulsion may underlie it, is a form of ἀνάγκη, the sort of thing from which an action follows necessarily. Thus, in Book 20 of the *Odyssey* (339–43) where Telemachus discusses ordering his mother to marry, the order is what he refers to by μύθῳ ἀναγκαίῳ:

οὐ μὰ Ζῆν', Ἀγέλαε, καὶ ἄλγεα πατρὸς ἐμοῖο,
ὅς που τῆλ' Ἰθάκης ἢ ἔφθιται ἢ ἀλάληται,
οὔ τι διατρίβω μητρὸς γάμον, ἀλλὰ κελεύω
γήμασθ' ᾧ κ' ἐθέλῃ, ποτὶ δ' ἄσπετα δῶρα δίδωμι.
αἰδέομαι δ' ἀέκουσαν ἀπὸ μεγάροιο δίεσθαι
μύθῳ ἀναγκαίῳ· μὴ τοῦτο θεὸς τελέσειεν.
(*Od.* 20.339–343)

In another example from the *Prometheus Bound*, Hephaestus says:

πάντως δ' ἀνάγκη τῶνδέ μοι τόλμαν σχεθεῖν·
εὐωριάζειν γὰρ πατρὸς λόγους βαρύ.
(*PrB* 16–17)

The "words of my father" can also be construed as orders, specifically the order of Zeus (12:ἐντολή). Hephaestus in this passage is particularly cognizant of the consequences of disobeying Zeus. This testifies to what I have already said is likely, viz., that physical force is the ultimate foundation of the practice of ordering. This foundation, however, may be more or less present to those who are ordered. The order itself, an identifiable social practice, takes on the role of the proximate compelling circumstance under which the ἑκών group word occurs.

Demands or requests are a weaker version of the compelling social practice of orders. In the following passage from the Theognidean corpus, the poet admonishes a Simonides about proper behavior at a symposium:

Μηδένα τῶνδ' ἀέκοντα μένειν κατέρυκε παρ' ἡμῖν,
μηδὲ θύραζε κέλευ' οὐκ ἐθέλοντ' ἰέναι,
μηδ' εὕδοντ' ἐπέγειρε, Σιμωνίδη, ὅντιν' ἂν ἡμῶν
θωρηχθέντ' οἴνωι μαλθακὸς ὕπνος ἕλῃ,

---

may be prompted by his certainty to be punished if found not to have performed the task imposed on him by lot.

[38]Cf. Plato Com. 24.1–2 Kock and Hdt. 3.72.5.

μηδὲ τὸν ἀγρυπνέοντα κέλευ' ἀέκοντα καθεύδειν.
'πᾶν γὰρ ἀναγκαῖον χρῆμ' ἀνιηρὸν ἔφυ.'
(Theog. 467-72)

I understand the last line of this passage to summarize all four actions prohibited in the lines above. Each is somehow a "necessary thing" (ἀναγκαῖον χρῆμα). A form of ἄκων appears in two of the actions. The first, detaining someone (μηδένα ἀέκοντα μένειν κατέρυκε παρ' ἡμῖν), I include as an instance of ἀνάγκη (i) where force or the threat of force is implied by the verb κατέρυκε. Since the setting is a symposium, the force may be more playful than serious. Nonetheless, it is likely to contain an element of physical coercion. In the second occurrence, ordering the wakeful to sleep (μηδὲ τὸν ἀγρυπνέοντα κέλευ' ἀέκοντα καθεύδειν), I understand the demand (κέλευ'...καθεύδειν) to be what constitutes the "necessary thing" (ἀναγκαῖον χρῆμα).

An institutionalized order of some kind, a liturgy or even a statute, is probably the circumstance under which, in addition to the fighting vessels, a hundred smaller vessels (πλοῖα) sailed ἐξ ἀνάγκης with the supply ships (ὁλκάδες) in Thucydides' description of the forces sent to Sicily:[39]

Τοσαύτη ἡ πρώτη παρασκευὴ πρὸς τὸν πόλεμον διέπλει. τούτοις δὲ τὰ ἐπιτήδεια ἄγουσαι ὁλκάδες μὲν τριάκοντα σιταγωγοί, καὶ τοὺς σιτοποιοὺς ἔχουσαι καὶ λιθολόγους καὶ τέκτονας καὶ ὅσα ἐς τειχισμὸν ἐργαλεῖα, πλοῖα δὲ ἑκατόν, ἃ ἐξ ἀνάγκης μετὰ τῶν ὁλκάδων ξυνέπλει· πολλὰ δὲ καὶ ἄλλα πλοῖα καὶ ὁλκάδες ἑκούσιοι ξυνηκολούθουν τῇ στρατιᾷ ἐμπορίας ἕνεκα·
(Thuc. 6.44.1)

An alliance or other formal tie between cities is another compelling social practice to be included under ἀνάγκη (ii). Whether or not there was any difference beyond a difference in title between Athens' "subjects" (ὑπήκοοι) and her "autonomous allies" (ἀπὸ ξυμμαχίας αὐτόνομοι) is doubted by scholars. Dover writes that "the formalities of alliance are subordinated to the reality, which is the extent to which an ally is free to fight or not."[40] Thus, the Cephallenians and Zacynthians, though autonomous, were compelled to fight in the Sicilian campaign by Athens' superior strength, according to Thucydides (7.57.7). However, whatever the *de facto* situation might have been for the autonomous allies, it was possible and presumably credible to claim to be fighting along with Athens under ἀνάγκη because of formal ties or alliances.

---

[39] Andrewes and Dover render ἐξ ἀνάγκης, "requisitioned" (*Com. Thuc.*, vol. 4, 311). We do not know precisely by what formal institution or mechanism the requisitioning took place. See MacDowell, *Law*, 161ff., on "liturgies."

[40] *Com. Thuc.*, vol. 4, 433-34.

According to Thucydides (3.58.2–3), this is what the Plataeans claim in their defense after they surrendered to the Spartans: κατ' ἀνάγκην πολεμήσαντες.[41] They explain they were reluctant to fight against Sparta but were bound to Athens for her help against the Thebans and by formal ties. For the Athenians not only helped the Plataeans in their war, but at the Plataeans' request made them "allies" (ξύμμαχοι) and gave them a share of Athenian citizenship (3.55). In his description of the motivations of the various parties aligned with Athens in the Sicilian campaign (7.57.1–10), what Thucydides says Corcyra could claim as an outwardly fitting explanation, that she was compelled to fight (ἀνάγκη μὲν ἐκ τοῦ εὐπρεποῦς), although Corcyra actually wanted to fight alongside the Athenians because she bore hatred for the Corinthians, is also likely to be a reference to a formal tie of alliance:[42]

> Κερκυραῖοι δὲ οὐ μόνον Δωριῆς, ἀλλὰ καὶ Κορίνθιοι σαφῶς ἐπὶ Κορινθίους τε καὶ Συρακοσίους, τῶν μὲν ἄποικοι ὄντες, τῶν δὲ ξυγγενεῖς, ἀνάγκη μὲν ἐκ τοῦ εὐπρεποῦς, βουλήσει δὲ κατὰ ἔχθος τὸ Κορινθίων οὐχ ἧσσον εἵποντο.
> (Thuc. 7.57.7)

Finally, in the passage from Herodotus discussed earlier, where Croesus gives advice to Cyrus about how to recover some booty from his soldiers (Hdt. 1.89.3), the practice of giving a tithe to Zeus is spoken of as holding ἀναγκαίως. Dedicating booty to a god after a war was customary.[43] This too then can be regarded as a compelling social practice.

Ἀνάγκη (iii): unavoidable prevailing circumstances

In the passages discussed so far ἑκών group words are used to describe persons, characters, or their acts under certain identifiable circumstances which are recognized as triggering ἀνάγκη. For example, what takes place in the presence of hands-on force or under order is recognized as occurring necessarily, under ἀνάγκη. In the passages I collect under (iii) too what follows from the circumstances at hand is considered to happen necessarily, and one or more of these identifiable triggers may also pertain. However, it is not any particular trigger so much that is under scrutiny but the more general recognition that on occasion actions are necessitated by the circumstances that currently pertain. This for example, is Pericles' message to the Athenians in response to the Spartan ultimatum in Book 1 of Thucydides (1.144.3): "you must know that it

---

[41] Thuc. 3.58.2–3 should be read with 3.63.2. In their reply to the Plataean speech, the Thebans recount the Plataean claim that they forced the Plataeans ἄκοντες.

[42] Cf. *Com. Thuc.*, vol. 4, 433–34.

[43] W.W. How and J. Wells, *A Commentary on Herodotus*, vol. 2 (1912; Oxford, 1968), 177–78, for the dedication of a tithe of spoils.

is necessary to go to war" (εἰδέναι δὲ χρὴ ὅτι ἀνάγκη πολεμεῖν). In Book 3 (3.27.1, 47.3–5), the compelling circumstances faced by the Mytilenians, a food shortage, are not as complex as those behind Pericles' remark. Nevertheless, it is the circumstances in which the Mytilenians find themselves, that compel them to surrender to the Athenians.

Humans and gods are always engaging circumstances. It is impossible to be without them, but neither we nor the gods continuously take note of them. Occasionally we do take stock of them, particularly when some trouble or good is upon us or within reach, and recognize not just the truism that they have been there all along but that their presence is limiting. At such times our ability to deal with an imminent good or ill is assessed in terms of the circumstances—those things relevant to us that simply are the case and must be taken into account as we seek to act in relation to the good or ill at hand. In some cases, for example, where necessitating circumstances are attributed to supernatural influence, the circumstances themselves are deemed necessary even beyond the necessity imposed by the unavoidability of what is past or present.[44]

There are five other passages among those that contain ἀνάγκη words that I include in this group. In Sophocles' *Philoctetes*, part of Neoptolemus' message to Philoctetes reads:

ἀνθρώποισι τὰς μὲν ἐκ θεῶν
τύχας δοθείσας ἔστ' ἀναγκαῖον φέρειν.
(Soph. *Ph.* 1316–17)

The happenings or chances of life (τύχαι) must be endured. Among the τύχαι Philoctetes endures are his physical affliction and the hands-on force of his fellow Greeks. These are among the recognizable triggers of ἀνάγκη already discussed. But here the message is not that some particular circumstance triggers necessary action, but that it is the human condition to be subject to and constrained by circumstances which come from the gods. What is necessary is not only bearing τύχαι, but insofar as these τύχαι come from the gods, the τύχαι themselves are necessary. In a fragment from the *Dictys* of Euripides, in fact, what can be construed as τύχαι, passions and disease (ἔρωτες and νόσος), are referred to in the words θεῶν ἀνάγκας (necessities of the gods):

πατέρα τε παισὶν ἡδέως συνεκφέρειν
φίλους ἔρωτας ἐκβαλόντ' αὐθαδίαν,
παῖδάς τε πατρί· καὶ γὰρ οὐκ αὐθαίρετοι
βροτοῖς ἔρωτες οὐδ' ἑκουσία νόσος.

---

[44]See R. Sorabji, *Necessity, Cause, and Blame: Perspectives on Aristotle's Theory* (Ithaca, 1980), 223. This sort of necessity is recognized by Aristotle. For references to Aristotle, see Sorabji, 223 n. 43.

σκαιόν τι δὴ τὸ χρῆμα γίγνεσθαι φιλεῖ,
θεῶν ἀνάγκας ὅστις ἰᾶσθαι θέλει.
(Eur. *Dictys* Fr. 339 *TGF*)

In these passages and several of those to be discussed in Chapter 2, which I will also include in group (iii), persons and characters find themselves in necessitating circumstances attributed to supernatural influence. But that the gods are sometimes made the authors of human circumstances need not obscure the prominence of circumstances themselves and the general recognition that circumstances (even where one of the identifiable triggers of ἀνάγκη is absent) can be such that certain events or actions take place necessarily. The gods are only an intermediate stratum in a hierarchy. The divine and human conditions are succinctly described by the New Comedy poet Philemon:

δοῦλοι βασιλέων εἰσίν, ὁ βασιλεύς θεῶν,
ὁ θεὸς ἀνάγκης.
(Philem. 31.4–5 Kock)

Recognition that one is in the midst of necessitating circumstances is not limited to those circumstances the gods influence.[45] In fact, as Simonides puts it, "not even the gods fight necessity" (Simon. Fr. 542.29–30 *PMG*· ἀνάγκᾳ/ δ' οὐδὲ θεοὶ μάχονται). The gods too are subject to necessitating circumstances.

In this famous poem of Simonides (Simon. Fr. 542 *PMG*) ἀνάγκη is not limited to the particular triggering circumstances distinquished so far. It reflects the necessity of what happens to be the case, circumstances themselves. Here too the gods may supply or influence circumstances for mortals who depend on the gods to be "good" (ἀγαθοί). However, though the gods do not depend on circumstances to be ἀγαθοί,[46]

θεὸς ἂν μόνος τοῦτ' ἔχοι γέρας, ἄνδρα δ' οὐκ
ἔστι μὴ οὐ κακὸν ἔμμεναι,
ὃν ἀμήχανος συμφορὰ καθέλῃ·
πράξας γὰρ εὖ πᾶς ἀνὴρ ἀγαθός,
κακὸς δ' εἰ κακῶς.
(Simon. Fr. 542.14–18 *PMG*)

still they too come up against circumstances. Understanding ἀνάγκη closely with ἀμήχανος συμφορά (16), "irresistible misfortune," has the advantage of explaining why even the gods do not fight it. For even if the goddess Ἀνάγκη is meant here, as some scholars hold, there needs to be an explanation of what it

---

[45] Other examples of ἀνάγκη (iii) that are of natural origin are discussed in ch. 2.

[46] This depends on accepting as at least centrally Simonidean the lines given in Plato which are bracketed in lines 19–20.

is about her the gods cannot fight. I understand Simonides to be saying that the gods, like humans, find themselves in necessitating circumstances that are themselves necessary at least insofar as what is past or presently the case is unavoidable.[47] In this poem there is no need to conjure some personified force (e.g. Fate),[48] comparable to the gods in their relationship to mortals, in order to account for the double aspect of ἀνάγκη in circumstances, which are themselves necessary and necessitating.

A fragment from the *Cresphontes* of Euripides and another passage from Thucydides fit this context too:

γ τοῦτον κατακτὰς δῶμα Πολυφόντης [ἔ]χει.
ΚΡ. πότερα βιαίως ἢ τύχαις ἀκουσίοις;
γ βίαι δολώσας, ὡς τυραννεύοι χθονός.
(Eur. *Cres.* Fr. 66.20–22 Harder)

ἐν μὲν γὰρ εἰρήνῃ καὶ ἀγαθοῖς πράγμασιν αἵ τε πόλεις καὶ οἱ ἰδιῶται ἀμείνους τὰς γνώμας ἔχουσι διὰ τὸ μὴ ἐς ἀκουσίους ἀνάγκας πίπτειν· ὁ δὲ πόλεμος ὑφελὼν τὴν εὐπορίαν τοῦ καθ' ἡμέραν βίαιος διδάσκαλος καὶ πρὸς τὰ παρόντα τὰς ὀργὰς τῶν πολλῶν ὁμοιοῖ·
(Thuc. 3.82.2)

In the first passage βιαίως and τύχαις ἀκουσίοις are disjuncts. I understand the alternatives to be force of arms or existing circumstances that unavoidably resulted in power being assumed where those subject to this power are ἄκοντες. The existing circumstances may have been of the sort that are regularly associated with ἀνάγκη, apart from βία, or unrestricted as in the poem of Simonides discussed above (Simon. Fr. 542 *PMG*). Although the frequency with which persons are ἄκοντες (or their acts ἀκούσιοι) when subject to ἀνάγκη may contribute to how the phrase; τύχαις ἀκουσίοις approaches what is elsewhere ἀνάγκη, I would emphasize the close association between τύχη and ἀνάγκη shown in three of the passages discussed under ἀνάγκη (iii) to support the alternative to βιαίως I offer above.[49] θεῶν ἀνάγκας in the *Dictys* fragment (339.1–6 *TGF*) is comparable to ἐκ θεῶν τύχας δοθείσας ἔστ'

---

[47]M. Dickie, "The Argument and Form of Simonides 542 *PMG*" *HSCP* 82 (1978), 23 n. 7, rightly argues against the view of W. Donlan, "Simonides, Fr. 4D and *P.Oxy*.2432" *TAPA* 100 (1969), 84, who says that συμφορά (16) means "a force or passion over which the subject has no control."

[48]This is H.W. Smyth's view in *Greek Melic Poets* (London, 1900), 316.

[49]Cf. A. Harder, *Euripides' Kresphontes and Archelaos: Introduction, Text and Commentary* (Leiden, 1985), 66, on τύχαις ἀκουσίοις. In the next chapter I will begin to argue against the view that ἀνάγκη and ἄκων are simply interchangeable or pleonastic when combined. Even though ἀκουσίοις may contribute to the alternative I see in this passage, I would maintain it has its own distinct perspective.

ἀναγκαῖον φέρειν in the passage from Sophocles' *Philoctetes* (1314–24), and ἀμήχανος συμφορά may well be what ἀνάγκη refers to in Simonides' poem (Fr. 542 *PMG*).

Finally, in the passage from Book 3, Thucydides idealizes peacetime and hyperbolizes the absence of compelling circumstances in times of peace. His emphasis is on war, βίαιος διδάσκαλος, "a forceful teacher," and a particularly powerful source of necessary and necessitating circumstances. Βία is an obvious factor that underlies ἀκουσίους ἀνάγκας. But here too it is not βία that is emphasized but the necessary and necessitating quality of its circumstances.

Summary

The range of necessity and the inevitable exemplified by these groups of ἀνάγκη is striking. There is on the one hand the strongest case of actual, in progress physical force to which no one would object as a bona fide case of necessity; and then there is a variety of arguable cases.

The first of these is threatened physical force. While we may sympathize with the seemingly realistic point of view that often enough there is no significant difference (at least in terms of what will happen anyway) between applied and threatened physical force and thereby understand the use of βία to cover both, still there are occasions when we simply are unsatisfied with a plea of force when it is only threatened.[50] We are likely to be more empathetic with the necessity of complying with certain social practices, especially where the fabric of society is at stake, for example the necessity of keeping oaths. The fact that foreswearing was not an indictable offense or one punished by law, despite the pervasiveness of oaths even in legal matters, should not be taken to minimize the importance of oaths or the perceived necessity in keeping them.[51] We should not let our own cynicism about the efficacy of leaving the gods to handle their own affairs affect our evaluation of the practice.[52]

---

[50]Cf. Arist. *NE* 3.1 and *EE* 2.8. In his summary of types of necessity recognized by Aristotle, Sorabji, *Necessity*, 224, notes that Aristotle is not definitive about the threat of force. He both rejects the mere threat of force as constituting βία and accepts some cases of acting under threat of force as cases of being necessitated. I take up this issue in more detail in ch. 4.

[51]For the use of oaths in legal proceedings, see A.R.W. Harrison, *The Law of Athens* (Oxford, 1971); D.M. MacDowell, *Law*, as well as *Athenian Homicide Law in the Age of the Orators* (Manchester, 1962)

[52]Such a cynicism may, for example, lie beneath the unwillingness of scholars to take Euripides' Medea as a serious avenger of forsworn oaths. Cf. Hesiod on Oath, Ὅρκος, begotten of Ἔρις. Oath's siblings include a host of evils, and about Oath the poet writes: Ὅρκον θ', ὃς δὴ πλεῖστον ἐπιχθονίους ἀνθρώπους / πημαίνει, ὅτε κέν τις ἑκὼν ἐπίορκον ὀμόσσῃ (*Th.* 231–32).

The part of the Greek view of necessity which we are likely to find particularly debatable is that necessity under which decisions to act in a certain way are deemed necessary even where alternatives are possible. But whatever the ultimate judgment about any of these necessities within a context of plea or excuse making, the point to be attended here is that usage allows these designations, and that this itself reflects not only Greek views about the world, but in situations of ethical import may reflect a sensitivity to the human condition that we might otherwise overlook in favor of more obvious and perhaps harsh practices.

2. The Functional Opposite View

This chapter begins to determine and describe the relationship between ἑκών group words and the circumstances of βία and other forms of ἀνάγκη detailed in Chapter 1. In addition to those passages discussed in the first chapter, that is, those which contained some form of the words βία or ἀνάγκη related to an ἑκών group word, this chapter will also include examples from the large number of passages which do not contain any βία or ἀνάγκη words, but which can be sorted nonetheless into the three basic ἀνάγκη groups determined in Chapter 1: (i) hands-on force, βία; (ii) compelling social practices; and (iii) unavoidable prevailing circumstances. Three-fourths of the passages collected for this study can be sorted into these groups. However, the large number of passages not containing βία or ἀνάγκη words precludes individual discussion and documentation of this claim. Therefore each section of this chapter which discusses the relationship between a type of ἀνάγκη and ἑκών group words will have two parts: Part One will contain examples drawn from the passages discussed in Chapter 1; Part Two will contain examples from the remaining passages which I infer represent the groups already determined.[1]

The large number of passages in which ἑκών group words are related to some form of ἀνάγκη demands that some view of this relationship be established. To get at this relationship, the first view I will develop is an extreme view I call the Functional Opposite View (FOV). This view is one way of explaining the use of ἑκών group words that can be derived from gross observation of the data.[2] The FOV is based on the consistency with which ἄκων and negative forms are conjoined with circumstances of ἀνάγκη, and ἑκών and positive forms are opposed to such circumstances. What counts as ἀνάγκη has been shown to include, for the most part, circumstances which are external and recognizable or observable by others (the hands-on force of other agents [i], social practices [ii], etc.). There are also some compelling circumstances which

---

[1]Those passages that are not used as examples can be found in the Index Locorum which lists all the passages and their categories.

[2]It must be kept in mind that the FOV is an extreme view based on the most striking features of the usage of ἑκών group words and the particular articulation of the FOV discussed in this study is my own. Its usefulness is primarily as an heuristic device. However, its fundamental principle or particular features related to its fundamental principle, can be found in a variety of discussions, translations or comments on ἑκών group words (especially the negative form, ἄκων). See the Appendix at the end of this chapter for specific examples.

seem better described as internal, e.g., ἔρως and νόσος (ia); but in these too there is ordinarily a rather high degree of observability which is itself a common topos.³ One simply looks at what circumstances are at hand to determine whether a person or character is ἑκών or ἄκων. Either one acts under ἀνάγκη and is ἄκων or one is ἑκών.

Ἑκών and ἄκων are themselves circumstantial participles that personally describe an agent, and the forms ἑκούσιος and ἀκούσιος describe the acts of an agent who is ἑκών or ἄκων.⁴ Thus, the FOV allows the personal and internal circumstances of an agent to be determined on the basis of whether or not the more observable circumstances of ἀνάγκη pertain. The presence or absence of circumstances of ἀνάγκη exhaust, in effect, the significance of the personal descriptions ἑκών and ἄκων. Someone described as ἑκών is not acting in any particular way but rather is acting in any way at all when no circumstances of ἀνάγκη pertain; someone described as ἄκων is subject to circumstances of ἀνάγκη.

This chapter will set out the common patterns that are the basis of the Functional Opposite View and exceptions to this view. It will conclude by suggesting that while circumstances of ἀνάγκη may be the occasion for the occurrences of ἑκών group words, another more subtle story must be sought to capture the significance of these words while still accommodating the frequency of the patterns on which the FOV is based. Those passages which contain forms

---

³The more obvious exceptions to circumstances of ἀνάγκη being decidedly external as well as observable are the cases of internal force included under ἀνάγκη (ia). But even in these cases a significant role is played by what is at least an externally compelling stimulant: the object of one's passion. Likewise, an argument could be made to emphasize the internal component of compelling circumstances which are more obviously external. E.g., the necessity of an order involves not only an external component, the order and the authority from which it is issued, but also an internal component, the ordered person's feelings of obligation to respond to the order. The relationship and interaction between the external and internal components of compelling circumstances and any determination of the strict locus of compulsion in any particular type of case are difficult matters open to a wide range of explanations. As one would expect, the passages do not directly address these issues, however much an implicit view may be contained in them. (For one ancient view, see Gorgias' *Encomium of Helen*, especially sections 8–12.) But even though internal and external features are not mutually exclusive and both may be involved ultimately even in a case that seems predominantly of just one sort, the FOV emphasizes that it is especially the recognizable, observable, and external aspect of these circumstances that is most prominent in relationship to the use of ἑκών group words.

⁴Sometimes ἑκούσιος and ἀκούσιος describe not the acts of an agent but the agent himself, especially in Thucydides.

of βία or ἀνάγκη (i) will be discussed first; then passages categorized as ἀνάγκη (ii) and (iii).[5]

The FOV and ἀνάγκη (i): Part One

In those passages where an ἑκών group word is related to actual or potential force signalled by a form of βία or ἀνάγκη (i), two broad groups can be distinguished: (A) contains negative forms, ἄκων and οὐχ ἑκών, conjoined with hands-on force; (B) contains positive forms, ἑκών and οὐκ ἄκων, generally opposed to hands-on force.[6]

---

[5] In two passages there is not enough information to determine the circumstances of the ἀνάγκη:

εἴπερ γὰρ οὐδὲ τοῖς κακῶς δεδρακόσιν
ἀκουσίως δίκαιον εἰς ὀργὴν πεσεῖν,
οὐδ' ἣν ἀναγκασθείς τις εὖ δράσῃ τινά,
προσῆκον εἶναι τῷδ' ὀφείλεσθαι χάριν.
(*TrGF* 80.1–4)

ἀλλὰ μὰν ἐγὼν ἀνάγκαι ταῦτα πάντα ποιέω·
οἴομαι δ' οὐδεὶς ἑκὼν πονηρὸς οὐδ' ἄταν ἔχων.
(Epicharm. 78.1–2 Kaibel)

However, there is no evidence that the triggering circumstances already distinguished could not account for the ἀνάγκη in these passages. In the first, I understand ἀναγκασθείς to apply to the protagonists of both clauses: someone who does another good, and someone who does another ill. Thus, this is another example of an agent victim acting ἄκων under circumstances of ἀνάγκη. The second passage, whatever the trigger for ἀνάγκη, adds to the examples where acting under ἀνάγκη appears to be opposed to being ἑκών. These passages should also be counted among the general statements discussed in ch. 3.

[6] Although the privative form, ἄκων, occurs more frequently than the negated form οὐχ ἑκών, and ἑκών more frequently than the negated privative, οὐκ ἄκων, I detect no apparent difference between ἄκων and οὐχ ἑκών or ἑκών and οὐκ ἄκων. I expect that in poetry, at least, the forms would be used indiscriminately anyway, however the metrics of the line demanded. Moreover, in Thucydides there is an example of a form of ἑκούσιος used to refer back to an earlier remark where a form of οὐκ ἄκων occurs. The Thebans first refer to particular events in Plataean collaboration with Athens with the words ταῦτα οὔτε ἄκοντες, and a few lines later they summarize their remarks as τὸν ὑμέτερον ἑκούσιον ἀττικισμόν (Thuc. 3.64.2–65.1). I detect no difference between the negated privative and the positive form. The choice of οὔτε ἄκοντες rather than ἑκόντες provides both clarity and a fine parechesis; the whole phrase reads; ταῦτα οὔτε ἄκοντες ἔχοντές τε τοὺς νόμους. Cf. Thuc. 4.98.1–6/#1&3 where the Athenians claimed about their behavior at Delium that they neither did anything unjust nor in the future would they do harm ἑκόντες (οὔτε ἀδικῆσαι ἔφασαν οὐδὲν οὔτε τοῦ λοιποῦ ἑκόντες βλάψειν) and a few lines later would include themselves in the same category as those who seek refuge at altars when fleeing τῶν ἀκουσίων ἁμαρτημάτων. This issue will be discussed again in ch. 4 in connection with some examples that are relevant to the technical distinction Aristotle draws between ἄκων and οὐχ ἑκών.

Ἄκων or οὐχ ἑκών conjoined with ἀνάγκη (i) and (ia): description

In discussing these passages use will be made of two distinctions to be explained below: agent or passive and actual or threatened. These distinctions will not only shed light on the variety of circumstances encompassed by βία and ἀνάγκη (i) but will also help to isolate persons or characters who regularly tend to be ἄκοντες. Even if the designations ἑκών and ἄκων are not exhausted by the presence of particular circumstances, it will be of use to know if any subset of the victims of βία do regularly tend to be ἄκοντες.

The persons or characters affected by hands-on force in this group of passages range from being totally passive victims to agent victims. By a totally passive victim I mean that the victim directly experiences and is completely subjected to physical force. Something happens to this victim, but the victim does not do anything beyond what is involved in the application of the force itself. By an agent victim I mean that the victim performs actions other than those directly involved with the exertion of the force that is suffered. The force itself can range from being actually in progress to threatened. In many passages where there is insufficient evidence to make a definite characterization, the force could be characterized as actual and/or threatened. In some, what is actual force initially changes to threatened force over time.

Examples of totally passive victims suffering in progress force include victims who are taken away bodily (e.g., HDem. 66–72; HDem. 122–25); restrained (e.g., PrB 12–20/#1; Theog. 467–72); harmed (e.g., HDem. 407–13); and raped (e.g., Bacchyl. 17.39–46). A paradigm of the passive victim is Persephone in the *Hymn to Demeter*:

βίῃ δ' ἀέκουσαν ἀνάγκῃ
ἄνδρες ληιστῆρες ἀπήγαγον.
(HDem. 122–25)

Agent victims act in a variety of ways: some victims join forces with their aggressors (e.g., Hdt. 9.17.1; Thuc. 3.64.2–65.1/#2; 4.87.2); in a passage from Thucydides the victims show self-control (σωφρονεῖν: 6.87.4); some victims simply walk (e.g., Il. 7.191–98/#2; 1.345–48); and in the *Prometheus Bound* (663–72/#2) Inachus performs an act of violence on someone else, Io. Ordinarily, the aggressor's violence aims to provoke the victim's act. But in Thucydides' description of the Athenians at Delium (4.98.1–6/#1&3), the Athenian use of sacred waters was a consequence of circumstances of violence but not an intended one.

Since agent victims not only suffer the effects of violence but perform some action, it is not surprising that if the force which affects them is not merely threatened, it is not as direct or continuous as the violence suffered by totally passive victims. For example, even where actual force may have been endured initially, it must have been supplanted by threatened force in order for the agent victims in Herodotus (9.17.1) and Thucydides (3.64.2–65.1/#2) to have medized, for Briseis (*Il.* 1.345–48) to go with the heralds (i.e. she is not "dragged away"), and for Ajax (*Il.* 7.191–98/#2) to imagine what he denies, being frightened off. Moreover, in his description of Athenian behavior at Delium (4.98.11–6/#1&3), Thucydides depicts a combat situation where violence is engaged in generally by the group but presumably not directly suffered by individuals at the times they are using the sacred waters. A paradigm case of the agent victim is that of Inachus in *Prometheus Bound*:

> ἐξήλασέν με κἀπέκληισε δωμάτων
> ἄκουσαν ἄκων· ἀλλ' ἐπηνάγκαζέ νιν
> Διὸς χαλινὸς πρὸς βίαν πράσσειν τάδε.
> (*PrB* 670–72)

One reason I have said that victims "range" from being passive to being agents is that the status of some changes over time. In *Iphigenia in Aulis* (1148–52) Clytemnestra is unlike other victims who are raped and taken away bodily in that she is also married (ἔγημας: 1149). This implies activity on her part that goes beyond being taken away and made a sexual partner. At first a passive victim, she becomes an agent victim. Helen in Euripides' *Trojan Women* (959–60, 1010–22), and Andromache in his *Andromache* (32–40/#1–2) have similar experiences. Furthermore, in all three cases, since the victimization is long term, the threat of violence probably replaces initial actual force.

In some passages it is unclear whether actual or threatened force is operative.[7] If we assume that actual βία applies in such passages, then they too are clear cases where the victims are passive. The experiences of the victims are

---

[7]Examples include *Il.* 15.178–88: Poseidon restrained; Soph. *OC* 932–36: Creon restrained; *Od.* 21.344–53: Telemachus restrained from giving; Ar. *Lys.* 223–28: Lysistrata and Kalonike raped; *Od.* 4.645–56/#1, 1.397–404, and 9.403–12: Noëmon, Telemachus, and Polyphemus, respectively, have something taken away from them; Eur. *Heracl.* 403–14: a citizen kills or gives up for sacrifice his daughter; and Hdt. 7.139.3–4: Spartan allies restrained. (This last passage seems to straddle the passive or agent distinction for another reason too. The allies of the Lacedaimonians are passive victims. Insofar as their cities have been captured [κατὰ πόλις ἁλισκομένων] they are in effect restrained by their enemies. However, the Lacedaimonians are described as betrayed by them [προδοθέντες] which suggests an activity on the part of the allies. But this betrayal is a logical consequence of the situation of the allies and not a direct act on their part. Rather, it is "as if" they betrayed the Lacedaimonians.) In those passages where the event in question is prospective, threatened force seems more likely than actual in progress force: e.g., Soph. *OC* 932–36, *Il.*15.178–88, *Od.* 1.397–404, 21.344–53, Ar. *Lys.* 223–28/#2, and Hdt. 7.139.3–4. In others, e.g., *Od.* 4.645–56/#1 and 9.403–12, although the events are not prospective and the verbs ἀπηύρα and βιάζεται probably express actual βία, there is insufficient detail to determine for sure whether the βία is actual.

such that something happens to them, and they do not do anything beyond what is involved by the application of the force they suffer. But if the force is only threatened, the victims seem to straddle the passive/agent distinction. What happens to them, e.g., being restrained or having something taken away from them, is akin to what happens to totally passive victims, but would also involve some agency on the victims' part. Consider again this passage from the *Iliad* where βίη is taken to apply to Achilles (as well as or instead of Briseis):

Ὣς ἄρα φωνήσασ' ἀπεβήσετο, τὸν δὲ λίπ' αὐτοῦ
χωόμενον κατὰ θυμὸν ἐϋζώνοιο γυναικός,
τὴν ῥα βίη ἀέκοντος ἀπηύρων·

(*Il.* 1.428–30)

I have argued that there is no actual force applied to Achilles in this transaction, although Agamemnon has threatened force. If Achilles is subject to force here, then it is only the threat of force. He is in effect "restrained" or one could say he "does nothing," i.e., his act is not to act. Not acting, of course, can at times be to act. We can, I think, distinguish such an act from the behavior of one who is restrained. In the case of Achilles, no one is holding his arms or blocking his movement. He is not restrained in the way that the totally passive victim is restrained. Within the context of the passages described here, Achilles is akin to passive victims who are restrained or have something taken away from them; but he is unlike the agent victims because he does not engage in an activity (fighting, going, forcing, taking) that goes beyond what is involved in the direct application of force.

Two of the passages in which circumstances of internal force, βία (ia), are conjoined with victims described by negative forms of ἑκών group words can also be included here:[8]

Μή μ' ἀέκοντα βίηι κεντῶν ὑπ' ἄμαξαν ἔλαυνε
εἰς φιλότητα λίην, Κύρνε, προσελκόμενος.

(Theog. 371–72)

...]ελος, οὐ γὰρ ἐλαφρὸν ἐσθλ[ὸν ἔμμεναι·
ἢ γ]ὰρ ἀέκοντά νιν βιᾶται
κέρ]δος ἀμάχητον ἢ δολοπλ[όκου
με]γασθενὴς οἶστρος Ἀφροδίτ[ας
..].(.)θαλοί τε φιλονικίαι.

(Simon. 541.7–11 *PMG*)

---

[8]If Κύπρις is demythologized in Eur. *Hipp.* 358–61, then this passage should be added to (ia). Otherwise, it fits in (iii). For the other (ia) passage, Theog. 1341–44, see the discussion below in *The FOV and ἀνάγκη (iii), Part One*, on passages where the ἑκών group word does not describe the victim or his acts but rather the force which afflicts the victim.

In both passages the victim is ἄκων, subject to force, and an agent. In the passage from Theognis, where βία may represent the speaker's passions, the victim anticipates his participation in a torrid love affair. Since the speaker demands of Kurnus that he not goad the speaker, it may be that the speaker is not yet moved by his own passions but sees the threat of these passions. In the passage from Simonides, the victim, attacked by profit and eros, is imagined to be driven to actions through which he ceases to be good. This agent is the victim of actual internal force. Although both of these agents are ἄκοντες and subject to internal βία, there are too few examples to draw any conclusions about whether a person or character is predictably ἄκων when such βία is present.[9]

Discussion

The passages in group (A) have two features in common: persons or characters are victims of force and are described by negative forms of ἑκών group words. This fact is the basis of the FOV. However, beneath this superficial collocation of ἄκων and βία there lies a considerable difference in behavior ranging from passive to active, and considerable variation in the imminence of βία. This variety itself suggests that the frequency of the collocation of forms of ἄκων and circumstances of βία may be misleading if it is taken to imply a pleonastic combination, or that the import of describing a character or person as ἄκων is exhausted by the recognition that circumstances of βία persist. The regularity with which victims of force are ἄκοντες could be accounted for by other views in other ways. Chapters 4 and 5 will take up Aristotle's explanations and my own.

Furthermore, there are some cases where force is conjoined not with the usual ἄκων form but with a ἑκών form. In two passages an agent victim of threatened force is ἑκών. In the following passage from the *Agamemnon*, the chorus recognizes the ἀνάγκη of Cassandra's position even if it is now only the threat of force, but bids her to be ἑκοῦσα:[10]

---

[9]Cf. Aristotle on desire and *akrasia NE* 3.1.20–27, *EE* 2.8.10, and *MM* 1.14: he does not count the passions under βία.

[10]*Ag.* 1071: Page reads εἴκουσ' (Robortello) ἀνάγκῃ τῇδε but in Denniston and Page, *Aeschylus: Agamemnon* (Oxford, 1957), we find: "ἑκοῦσ' (codd.) ἀνάγκης τῆσδε (Casaubon) is as likely to be the correct reading." Reluctance to accept ἑκοῦσ' may be the result of not recognizing what I stress here, that one can be subject to ἀνάγκη but ἑκών. Cf. Schreckenberg, *Ananke*, p.33, who reads ἑκοῦσ' (codd.) ἀνάγκης τῆσδε (Casaubon), but does not comment on the relationship between ἑκοῦσ' and ἀνάγκης. He is interested in ἀνάγκης ζυγόν, which he considers a paraphrase for δούλιον ζυγόν, and the theme of subjugation. He does not connect ἀνάγκη in this passage with force per se but thinks it has a more abstract meaning here while maintaining what he thinks is its basic sense, ζυγόν. See the reviews of Adkins (*CR* 16 [1966] 68–70) and Gottschalk

ἐγὼ δ', ἐποικτίρω γάρ, οὐ θυμώσομαι·
ἴθ', ὦ τάλαινα, τόνδ' ἐρημώσασ' ὄχον;
ἑκοῦσ' ἀνάγκης τῆσδε καίνισον ζυγόν.
(Aesch. *Ag.* 1069-71)

In Book 3 of the *Odyssey*, Telemachus describes the suitors as committing outrages against him (ὑβρίζοντες) and Nestor, saying he has heard the suitors are in Telemachus' house plotting evil while Telemachus is ἄκων (ἀέκητι σέθεν), questions whether Telemachus is overpowered (by the suitors) ἑκών or through the hatred of the people following some word of a god.[11] Nestor then wonders aloud whether Odysseus will return to avenge the βία present in his household. Even if the βία is only a threat that hangs over Telemachus, Nestor's question implies Telemachus could be subject to it and still act ἑκών:[12]

αἲ γὰρ ἐμοὶ τοσσήνδε θεοὶ δύναμιν περιθεῖεν,
τίσασθαι μνηστῆρας ὑπερβασίης ἀλεγεινῆς,
οἵ τέ μοι ὑβρίζοντες ἀτάσθαλα μηχανόωνται.
ἀλλ' οὔ μοι τοιοῦτον ἐπέκλωσαν θεοὶ ὄλβον,
πατρί τ' ἐμῷ καὶ ἐμοί· νῦν δὲ χρὴ τετλάμεν ἔμπης."
Τὸν δ' ἠμείβετ' ἔπειτα Γερήνιος ἱππότα Νέστωρ·
"ὦ φίλ', ἐπεὶ δὴ ταῦτά μ' ἀνέμνησας καὶ ἔειπες,
φασὶ μνηστῆρας σῆς μητέρος εἵνεκα πολλοὺς
ἐν μεγάροις ἀέκητι σέθεν κακὰ μηχανάασθαι.
εἰπέ μοι ἠὲ ἑκὼν ὑποδάμνασαι, ἦ σέ γε λαοὶ
ἐχθαίρουσ' ἀνὰ δῆμον, ἐπισπόμενοι θεοῦ ὀμφῇ·
τίς δ' οἶδ' εἴ κέ ποτέ σφι βίας ἀποτίσεται ἐλθών,
ἢ ὅ γε μοῦνος ἐών, ἦ καὶ σύμπαντες Ἀχαιοί;"
(*Od.* 3.205-17/#2)

(*JHS* 86 [1966] 213-14) for succinct and convincing critiques of Schreckenberg's use of the phrase ζυγόν ἀνάγκης as a confirmation of his view about the literal meaning of ἀνάγκη.

[11] See Stanford, ed., *The Odyssey of Homer*, 2d ed., vol.1 (London, 1959), on line 215. He prefers to explain θεοῦ ὀμφῇ (word of a god) as "a deposing oracle such as demanded the deposition of Oedipus," but he cites others who think it means "a vague impulse which, having no clear rational source, was attributed to divine prompting." If besides or in addition to the βία of the suitors, "overpowered ἑκών" is to be understood by either of these explanations of "word of a god," then Telemachus is ἑκών while subject to an oracle, ἀνάγκη (ii), or subject to ἀνάγκη (iii), here compelling circumstances of supernatural origin. In either case, the passage would still be an exception to the FOV.

[12] Cf. *Od.* 16.91-98 where Odysseus asks Telemachus the same question but does not mention βία.

Since the FOV recognizes as βία actual and threatened βία, these cases of threatened βία conjoined with positive ἑκών forms are significant and count against the adequacy of the FOV.

Finally, one passage can be understood as an exception to the very core of the FOV, the reliable pattern that passive victims of actual hands-on force are ἄκοντες:

δούλοις δὲ πῶς οὐκ ἄπιστον; ἑκόντες ⟨τε⟩ γὰρ ἐπ' ἐλευθερίαι χειμαζόμενοί τε δι' ἀνάγκην κατηγοροῦσιν.
(Gorg. B.11a.11DK)

In this passage, the slaves who, I have suggested, are to be thought of as subjected to torture within the course of legal proceedings, are described as making accusations ἑκόντες. Insofar as the description of the slaves as ἑκόντες is relevant to their accusing activity and not their experience of βία, they seem more like agent victims. Totally passive victims of βία are regularly ἄκοντες when the focus of our attention to them as ἄκοντες is related directly to their experience of βία.[13] However, the accusations of the slaves take place nonetheless under circumstances of actual in progress βία, torture, as well as the threat of more torture. Severe circumstances of this sort are usually the kind under which agents tend to be ἄκοντες. Moreover, even if the actual βία is taken as interrupted (at least long enough for the slaves to speak), it is still more violent than the βία suffered by many agent victims. My point is that the imminence of βία for these slaves is more like that associated with passive victims of βία. But despite their circumstances of actual βία, the slaves are ἑκόντες. The extreme circumstances of βία in this case do not render these victims ἄκοντες as the Functional Opposite View would lead us to expect.

The preceeding passage from Gorgias' *Defense of Palamedes* will be discussed again in Chapters 4 and 5 in relationship to other views. For now it is important because, like the passages where victims of threatened βία are ἑκόντες, it too drives a wedge between circumstances of βία and being ἄκων. Even under circumstances of βία which is severe and in progress, it is possible to be ἑκών. Whatever relationship there is between βία and being ἄκων, it is not as automatic as the mere collocation of force and ἄκων forms (and, as I shall show, the opposition of force and ἑκών forms) might suggest. Generally, the passivity of the victim is related to the actuality of the βία he suffers, and when hands-on force is in progress the passive victim tends to be ἄκων. It may also be the case that victims who straddle the passive or agent distinction but

---

[13]In some cases, although other descriptions which do not suggest constraint are possible, they are not appropriate. For example, when Prometheus (Aesch. *PrB* 12–20/#1) is described as ἄκων, he is properly described as experiencing the βία of being nailed to a rock and not as experiencing the outcome of his humanitarian exploits.

seem akin to the more passive victim tend to be ἄκων under circumstances of only threatened βία. But this regularity cannot be relied on to the extent that where βία is not such that the victim is passive, he is predictably ἑκών, since the agent victim of threatened βία can be ἄκων or ἑκών.

Ἑκών or οὐκ ἄκων opposed to ἀνάγκη (i): description and discussion

In these passages, where positive forms of the ἑκών group (or in one case a negated privative) seem opposed to physical force, the opposition is often expressed by one or the other of two formulas: a person or character is ἑκών or subject to physical force; or ἑκών and not subject to physical force.

When these passages are examined to determine the force to which the persons or characters are subject, they provide further examples of the range of victims, passive to agent, subjected to actual or threatened force or both, which has already been discussed in some detail. There are victims of actual force, e.g., Philoctetes who would probably be fetched bodily (ἢ στελοῦσί σε) if he were to go with Odysseus βίᾳ or ἐκ βίας:

> Φι. ἀπόδος, ἄφες μοι, παῖ, τὰ τόξα.   Οδ. τοῦτο μέν,
> οὐδ' ἢν θέλῃ, δράσει ποτ'. ἀλλὰ καὶ σὲ δεῖ
> στείχειν ἅμ' αὐτοῖς, ἢ βίᾳ στελοῦσί σε.
> Φι. ἔμ', ὦ κακῶν κάκιστε καὶ τόλμης πέρα,
> οἵδ' ἐκ βίας ἄξουσιν;   Οδ. ἢν μὴ ἕρπῃς ἑκών.
> Φι. ὦ Λημνία χθὼν καὶ τὸ παγκρατὲς σέλας
> Ἡφαιστότευκτον, ταῦτα δῆτ' ἀνασχετά,
> εἴ μ' οὗτος ἐκ τῶν σῶν ἀπάξεται βίᾳ;
> (Soph. *Ph*. 981-88)

agent victims subject to threatened force, e.g., the actual subjects (ὑπήκοοι) and the de facto subjects of Athens (Thuc. 7.57.1–10) fighting in Sicily;[14] and victims of more ambiguous status, who might be passive or agent victims of actual and/or threatened force, e.g., the suppliants whom King Pelasgus tells the herald will never by force "go" with their Egyptian cousins:

> τί σοι λέγειν χρὴ τοὔνομ'; ἐν χρόνωι μαθὼν
> εἴσῃι σύ τ' αὐτὸς χοἰ ξυνέμποροι σέθεν.
> ταύτας δ' ἑκούσας μὲν κατ' εὔνοιαν φρενῶν
> ἄγοις ἄν, εἴπερ εὐσεβὴς πίθοι λόγος·
> τοιάδε δημόπρακτος ἐκ πόλεως μία
> ψῆφος κέκρανται, μήποτ' ἐκδοῦναι βίαι
> στόλον γυναικῶν· τῶνδ' ἐφήλωται τορῶς

---

[14]To summarize Thuc. 7.57.1–10, Thucydides contrasts the Athenians who went ἑκόντες to Sicily and others who went ἑκόντες for the sake of profit, with those who went under compulsion.

γόμφος διαμπάξ, ὡς μένειν ἀραρότως.
ταῦτ' οὐ πίναξίν ἐστιν ἐγγεγραμμένα
οὐδ' ἐν πτυχαῖς βίβλων κατεσφραγισμένα,
σαφῆ δ' ἀκούεις ἐξ ἐλευθεροστόμου
γλώσσης. κομίζου δ' ὡς τάχιστ' ἐξ ὀμμάτων.
(Aesch. *Supp.* 938-49)

The more interesting feature of these passages appears when the persons or characters are conceived of as being ἑκόντες. In some cases the circumstances suggest that being ἑκών or being subject to physical force are totally exclusive disjuncts. No force, not even the threat of force, pertains when the persons or characters are conceived of as being ἑκόντες. Like those passages in which ἄκων and other negative forms are conjoined with βία, these passages are basic to the FOV. Three of these passages will serve as examples of this sort of disjunction.[15]

In the passage from the *Suppliants* just quoted (938-49), King Pelasgus' characterization of the suppliants going with their cousins ἑκοῦσαι in contrast with their going by force leaves no obvious place for even the threat of physical force attending them. Furthermore, given that Pelasgus is firmly entrenched in the city's vote and is also ready to fight for the women (944ff., 950ff.), it is unlikely that even a threat of force which affected the suppliants would be tolerated. Likewise, in the following passage in which Pindar addresses Peace, profit (κέρδος) taken from the home of one who gives it ἑκών is clearly contrasted with the eventual overthrow of what is gained through βία:

τὺ δ' ὁπόταν τις ἀμείλιχον
καρδίᾳ κότον ἐνελάσῃ,
τραχεῖα δυσμενέων
ὑπαντιάξαισα κράτει τιθεῖς
ὕβριν ἐν ἄντλῳ· τὰν οὐδὲ Πορφυρίων μάθεν
παρ' αἶσαν ἐξερεθίζων. κέρδος δὲ φίλτατον,
ἑκόντος εἴ τις ἐκ δόμων φέροι.
βία δὲ καὶ μεγάλαυχον ἔσφαλεν ἐν χρόνῳ.
(Pind. *Pyth.* 8.8-15)

The ἑκών in this case has no shadow of βία hanging over him. Finally, in this passage from Euripides' *Trojan Women*, Cassandra describes Helen, the woman for whose sake Agamemnon has led so many to death:

ὁ δὲ στρατηγὸς ὁ σοφὸς ἐχθίστων ὕπερ
τὰ φίλτατ' ὤλεσ', ἡδονὰς τὰς οἴκοθεν

---

[15]Other examples include: Eur. *Heracl.* 883-87, *Hel.* 391-96, *Cyc.* 253-60/#1-2; *Od.* 22.330-31 with 344-53; Hdt. 1.89.3, 7.104.3; Thuc. 3.39.7, 6.92.5.

τέκνων ἀδελφῶι δοὺς γυναικὸς οὕνεκα,
καὶ ταῦθ' ἑκούσης κοὐ βίαι λεληισμένης.
(Eur. *Tro.* 370–73)

The most likely implication of Cassandra's description of Helen is that she thinks Helen's "rape" was no rape at all and involved not even a trace of threatened βία.[16]

A few other passages may also belong to the exclusive disjunct group. However, the persons or characters conceived of as ἑκόντες in these passages may still be subject to the threat of βία even though actual βία is absent and disjoined with acting ἑκών. In some passages there is not enough information to be sure whether or not there is in fact an imminent and operating threat of βία even though actual βία is denied. For example, in the passage from *Iphigenia in Aulis* discussed earlier (356–69), when Menelaus says that Agamemnon sent for Iphigenia ἑκών and not by force (βίᾳ), this may mean that actual force was not applied to Agamemnon and still leave room for the threat of force pertaining even as Agamemnon acted ἑκών.[17]

The situations in other passages, however, are clear enough to show that when the relevant persons or characters in them are conceived of as ἑκόντες in the absence of actual in progress βία, they are still clearly subject to the threat of βία. Consider the situations in the following passages from Sophocles' *Philoctetes* and Thucydides:[18]

Φι. ἀπόδος, ἄφες μοι, παῖ, τὰ τόξα.   Οδ. τοῦτο μέν,
οὐδ' ἢν θέλῃ, δράσει ποτ'. ἀλλὰ καὶ σὲ δεῖ
στείχειν ἅμ' αὐτοῖς, ἢ βίᾳ στελοῦσί σε.
Φι.   ἔμ', ὦ κακῶν κάκιστε καὶ τόλμης πέρα,
οἵδ' ἐκ βίας ἄξουσιν;   Οδ. ἢν μὴ ἕρπῃς ἑκών.
Φι.   ὦ Λημνία χθὼν καὶ τὸ παγκρατὲς σέλας
Ἡφαιστότευκτον, ταῦτα δῆτ' ἀνασχετά,
εἴ μ' οὗτος ἐκ τῶν σῶν ἀπάξεται βίᾳ;
(Soph. *Ph.* 981–88)

Here Odysseus is still determined to bring Philoctetes along with his bow back to Troy. It is not likely that if Philoctetes were to creep along without being physically prodded by Odysseus' lackeys that he would do so without any threat of βία as well.

---

[16] Compare Eur. *Tro.* 370–73 with *El.* 1065–68 discussed in ch. 4 pp. 109–10 and ch. 5 pp. 129–31, and Aesch. *Ag.* 803 with Eur. *Tro.* 1037.

[17] Other examples include: *Od.* 4.645–56/#2–3, Thuc. 3.63.2/#2, 3.64.2–3 with 65.1/#1 and 3, 1.32.4, and Eur. *Ion* 369–80/#3.

[18] Other examples include: Thuc. 3.82.2, 4.19.4, 7.57.1–10, and 8.27.3.

In Thucydides' account of the Plataean surrender, the Plataeans, who had run out of provisions and were no longer able to resist the siege (3.52.1, 57.3), describe themselves as having surrendered ἑκόντες:

> οὐκ ἐχθροὺς γὰρ ἡμᾶς εἰκότως τιμωρήσεσθε, ἀλλ' εὔνους, κατ' ἀνάγκην πολεμήσαντας. ὥστε καὶ τῶν σωμάτων ἄδειαν ποιοῦντες ὅσια ἂν δικάζοιτε καὶ προνοοῦντες ὅτι ἑκόντας τε ἐλάβετε καὶ χεῖρας προϊσχομένους (ὁ δὲ νόμος τοῖς Ἕλλησι μὴ κτείνειν τούτους), ἔτι δὲ καὶ εὐεργέτας γεγενημένους διὰ παντός.
> (Thuc. 3.58.2–3)

This view of the surrender corresponds to that of the Spartan commander who interrrupted the siege and invited the Plataeans to surrender ἑκόντες:

> προσπέμπει δὲ αὐτοῖς κήρυκα λέγοντα, εἰ βούλονται παραδοῦναι τὴν πόλιν ἑκόντες τοῖς Λακεδαιμονίοις καὶ δικασταῖς ἐκείνοις χρήσασθαι, τούς τε ἀδίκους κολάζειν, παρὰ δίκην δὲ οὐδένα.
> (Thuc. 3.52.2–3)

Nevertheless, the Plataeans are surely no less threatened by Spartan force (and their own lack of provisions as well). The Spartan commander is determined to take the city. It is taking it by storm that he hopes to avoid because of speculation about the terms of an expected treaty:

> γνοὺς δὲ ὁ Λακεδαιμόνιος ἄρχων τὴν ἀσθένειαν αὐτῶν βίᾳ μὲν οὐκ ἐβούλετο ἑλεῖν (εἰρημένον γὰρ ἦν αὐτῷ ἐκ Λακεδαίμονος, ὅπως, εἰ σπονδαὶ γίγνοιντό ποτε πρὸς Ἀθηναίους καὶ ξυγχωροῖεν ὅσα πολέμῳ χωρία ἔχουσιν ἑκάτεροι ἀποδίδοσθαι, μὴ ἀνάδοτος εἴη ἡ Πλάταια ὡς αὐτῶν ἑκόντων προσχωρησάντων)
> (Thuc. 3.52.2)

The commander supposes that because he has stopped short of actually taking Plataea by force, Plataea would not have to be returned. It would be included with those who ἑκόντες joined the Peloponnesians.

The agents in these passages remain victims of threatened physical violence even though the disjunction between acting ἑκών and acting under βία excludes actual in-progress force. The disjunction is not as strong as it is in the examples discussed from Aeschylus, Pindar, and Euripides, because only actual βία and not also threatened βία is disjoined with acting ἑκών. Since the FOV counts as βία actual in-progress force as well as the threat of such force, these passages detract from the simple regularity on which the FOV is based. Like the exceptional passages described in (A), these passages drive a wedge between the relationship of circumstances of βία with ἑκών group words as set out by the FOV.

The FOV and ἀνάγκη (i): Part Two

Many of the passages I would add to this group where the prevailing circumstance is hands-on force, are not controversial. Physical force is blatant in the action and the vocabulary that depicts it or can be easily inferred. For example, Diomedes drags from their chariot two of Priam's sons:

ὣς τοὺς ἀμφοτέρους ἐξ ἵππων Τυδέος υἱὸς
βῆσε κακῶς ἀέκοντας

(Il. 5.163-164)

They are clearly passive victims of βία. Likewise, in Euripides' *Iphigenia in Aulis* (1360-66/#3), Clytemnestra's concern is that Iphigenia will be taken away under force (ἄξει δ' οὐχ ἑκοῦσαν ἁρπάσας;). In the *Odyssey*, although Athena in the guise of Mentes describes no particular act of violence, she implies by her words that Odysseus is being physically restrained in the manner of a passive victim of βία. This is most likely what would be expected of "fierce and dangerous men":

χαλεποὶ δέ μιν ἄνδρες ἔχουσιν,
ἄγριοι, οἵ που κεῖνον ἐρυκανόωσ' ἀέκοντα.

(Od. 1.198-99)

Other passages provide examples of agent victims of threatened force or straddle the agent or passive victim distinction. For example, in Herodotus, Scythian strategy is to draw their neighbors into the war against Darius by having a division of Scythian soldiers retreat in the direction of these neighbors while the Persians are in pursuit.

πρῶτα μέν νυν ὑπάγειν σφέας ἰθὺ τῶν χωρέων τῶν ἀπει-
παμένων τὴν σφετέρην συμμαχίην, ἵνα καὶ τούτους ἐκπο-
λεμώσωσι· εἰ γὰρ μὴ ἑκόντες γε ὑπέδυσαν τὸν πόλεμον τὸν
πρὸς Πέρσας, ἀλλ' ἀέκοντας ἐκπολεμῶσαι·

(Hdt. 4.120.4/#2)

Though the neighbors are not directly under attack, the nearness of the Persian threat is expected to draw them ἀέκοντες into the war. In Book 8, Herodotus comments on the distress of the Ionians in the Persian forces, who supposed the smaller Athenian force of ships would be overwhelmed by the Persian fleet in an engagement off Euboea:

ὅσοι μέν νυν τῶν Ἰώνων ἦσαν εὔνοοι τοῖσι Ἕλλησι, ἀέκοντές
τε ἐστρατεύοντο συμφορήν τε ἐποιεῦντο μεγάλην ὁρῶντες
περιεχομένους αὐτοὺς καὶ ἐπιστάμενοι ὡς οὐδεὶς αὐτῶν

ἀπονοστήσει· οὕτω ἀσθενέα σφι ἐφαίνετο εἶναι τὰ τῶν Ἑλλήνων πρήγματα.
(Hdt. 8.10.2)

Since the Ionians who march ἀέκοντες along with the Persians may have been pressed into service by actual or threatened force or some combination, this passage, like others already discussed, straddles the agent or passive victim distinction. All these passages can be accommodated by the FOV.

There are also more passages where being ἑκών appears opposed to acting under physical force. There are examples which suggest strong opposition between acting ἑκών and under force, both actual and threatened. But there are also more examples where there is still an imminent threat of force for those described by ἑκών group words, and two more passage in which actual force is conjoined with a positive form of ἑκών. These latter passages then can be added to those which count against the FOV.

In the following example there is a strong implication that performing some act ἑκών is in strong opposition to performing that act under force. This passage and others like it are easily accommodated by the FOV. In *Iliad* 13 (219–34), when Poseidon in the guise of Thoas stirs the Greeks to battle, he curses "whoever this day ἑκών holds back from the fighting": ὅς τις ἐπ' ἤματι τῷδε ἑκὼν μεθίῃσι μάχεσθαι (234). In a war there are many circumstances that would compel someone to abandon the fighting, not the least of which is being severely wounded, the result of an opponent's actual superior hands-on force. The passage implies a strong opposition between the agent leaving the battle ἑκών and doing so under such force and most likely under the threat of such force as well. Here I have in mind the threat of force within the limitations of a particular engagement of the enemy. The overarching threat of force constituted by the context of the war itself is not relevant to Poseidon's threat.

In a passage taken from Athenagoras' speech to the Syracusean assembly, there is a direct opposition between performing an action ἑκών and performing it under actual force:

> ὑμεῖς δὲ ἢν εὖ βουλεύησθε, οὐκ ἐξ ὧν οὗτοι ἀγγέλλουσι σκοποῦντες λογιεῖσθε τὰ εἰκότα, ἀλλ' ἐξ ὧν ἂν ἄνθρωποι δεινοὶ καὶ πολλῶν ἔμπειροι, ὥσπερ ἐγὼ Ἀθηναίους ἀξιῶ, δράσειαν. οὐ γὰρ αὐτοὺς εἰκὸς Πελοποννησίους τε ὑπολιπόντας καὶ τὸν ἐκεῖ πόλεμον μήπω βεβαίως καταλελυμένους ἐπ' ἄλλον πόλεμον οὐκ ἐλάσσω ἑκόντας ἐλθεῖν, ἐπεὶ ἔγωγε ἀγαπᾶν οἴομαι αὐτοὺς ὅτι οὐχ ἡμεῖς ἐπ' ἐκείνους ἐρχόμεθα, πόλεις τοσαῦται καὶ οὕτω μεγάλαι.
> (Thuc. 6.36.3–4)

The issue is whether the Athenians are likely to plot a first strike against Sicily without being forced to attack by some explicit military maneuvre or even the near threat of such a maneuvre, while still embroiled in a great war with the Peloponnesians. A first strike seems to be treated as an ἑκούσιος act. Any overarching constraint of the general hostility between enemies or opponents seems irrelevant to the strong opposition between the first strike ἑκούσιος action and reacting to an attack that is actual or clearly threatened.

Although the absence of all constraint, including all of the ἀνάγκη (iii) variety, may seem somewhat exaggerated, the FOV accommodates passages of this sort: the agents are ἑκόντες in the absence of force within the more narrow limitations of time and place. The irrelevance of overarching necessity in these passages distinguishes them from those passages discussed earlier (Soph. *Ph.* 981–88, Thuc. 3.52.2–3; 58.3) where acting ἑκών is strongly opposed only to actual βία but the threat of βία is not remote but imminent and significant.

In contrast, the following passages involving ἀνάγκη (i) add to those already discussed in which the disjunction between acting under force and acting ἑκών is not totally exclusive. Even though actual in-progress force is not in effect when the agents are conceived of as acting ἑκόντες, the agents are still subject to the threat of such force. These passages then are also exceptions to the FOV and count against it. In Euripides' *Bacchae*, Pentheus' attendant reports that Dionysus surrendered οὐκ ἄκων:

> Πενθεῦ, πάρεσμεν τήνδ' ἄγραν ἠγρευκότες
> ἐφ' ἣν ἔπεμψας, οὐδ' ἄκρανθ' ὡρμήσαμεν.
> ὁ θὴρ δ' ὅδ' ἡμῖν πρᾶος οὐδ' ὑπέσπασεν
> φυγῇ πόδ', ἀλλ' ἔδωκεν οὐκ ἄκων χέρας
> οὐδ' ὠχρός, οὐδ' ἤλλαξεν οἰνωπὸν γένυν,
> γελῶν δὲ καὶ δεῖν κἀπάγειν ἐφίετο
> ἔμενέ τε, τοὐμὸν εὐτρεπὲς ποιούμενος.
> (Eur. *Bacch.* 434–40)

That even actual force would be ineffective against the god is unimportant. It is clear that the attendant's task is to fetch Dionysus by force if necessary. We are reminded of the scene in the *Philoctetes* (981–88) where Philoctetes is told he is to come ἑκών or be dragged off by force, βίᾳ. In both cases a threat of force remains even as the agent acts ἑκών. Likewise, in Euripides' *Hecuba*, when Polyxena declares she will die ἑκοῦσα the contrast is between offering her neck to the executioner and being taken to him by force:

> τοσαῦτ' ἔλεξε, πᾶς δ' ἐπηύξατο στρατός.
> εἶτ' ἀμφίχρυσον φάσγανον κώπης λαβὼν
> ἐξεῖλκε κολεοῦ, λογάσι δ' Ἀργείων στρατοῦ
> νεανίαις ἔνευσε παρθένον λαβεῖν.
> ἡ δ', ὡς ἐφράσθη, τόνδ' ἐσήμηνεν λόγον·

> Ὦ τὴν ἐμὴν πέρσαντες Ἀργεῖοι πόλιν,
> ἑκοῦσα θνῄσκω· μή τις ἅψηται χροὸς
> τοὐμοῦ· παρέξω γὰρ δέρην εὐκαρδίως.
> ἐλευθέραν δέ μ', ὡς ἐλευθέρα θάνω,
> πρὸς θεῶν, μεθέντες κτείνατ'· ἐν νεκροῖσι γὰρ
> δούλη κεκλῆσθαι βασιλὶς οὖσ' αἰσχύνομαι.
> (Eur. *Hec.* 542–52)

Here too it is clear that even as Polyxena acts ἑκοῦσα she is subject to the threat of imminent force. The character addressed in a fragment of Plato Comicus is also threatened with violence if he does not comply with a demand:

> εἰ μὲν οὖν ταύτην σὺ τὴν θάλατταν ἀποδώσεις ἑκών,
> εἰ δὲ μή γε, ταῦτα πάντα συντριαινῶν ἀπολέσω.
> (Plato Com. 24.1–2 Kock)

Again, it is likely he would still be subject to this threat even if he were to act ἑκών. Finally, in Herodotus' account of Darius' bold plan for entering the palace to attack the Magi, Darius says that any guard who ἑκών stands aside and lets them into the palace will be rewarded later, but that they will force passage if anyone tries to stand in their way:

> ὃς ἂν μέν νυν τῶν πυλουρῶν ἑκὼν παρίῃ, αὐτῷ οἱ ἄμεινον ἐς
> χρόνον ἔσται· ὃς δ' ἂν ἀντιβαίνειν πειρᾶται, διαδεικνύσθω
> ἐνθαῦτα ἐὼν πολέμιος, καὶ ἔπειτα ὠσάμενοι ἔσω ἔργου
> ἐχώμεθα.
> (Hdt. 3.72.5)

The threat of force to which the guards are subject in this passage comes from two sources. First, Darius supposes the guards will not refuse the seven entry out of the ordinary fear of reprisal which Darius supposes will affect the behavior of the guards:

> ὑμεῖς δὲ ἴστε φυλακὰς τὰς κατεστεώσας ἐούσας οὐδὲν
> χαλεπὰς παρελθεῖν. τοῦτο μὲν γὰρ ἡμέων ἐόντων τοιῶνδε
> οὐδεὶς ὅστις οὐ παρήσει, τὰ μέν κου καταιδεόμενος ἡμέας, τὰ
> δέ κου καὶ δειμαίνων·
> (Hdt. 3.72.2–3)

Secondly, in regard to the threat of an immediate attack by the conspirators, it is significant that it is Darius who uses ἑκών to describe any of the guards and not a guard. For if all goes well with the ploy, no guard would have any reason to suspect any immediate attack from Darius and the others. Darius, however, prepared to use force immediately, pictures the guards acting ἑκόντες while subject to this threat.

Finally, consider the following two passages in which a character described as undergoing what ordinarily would be understood to constitute actual force, is nonetheless ἑκοῦσα. In the first, Electra describes the disgraceful acts of the sisters Helen and Clytemnestra:

ἡ μὲν γὰρ ἁρπασθεῖσ' ἑκοῦσ' ἀπώλετο,
σὺ δ' ἄνδρ' ἄριστον Ἑλλάδος διώλεσας,
σκῆψιν προτείνουσ' ὡς ὑπὲρ τέκνου πόσιν
ἔκτεινας· οὐ γάρ ⟨σ'⟩ ὡς ἔγωγ' ἴσασιν εὖ.
(Eur. *El.* 1065–68)

Helen is described as raped and ruined ἑκοῦσα.[19] In the second passage, Alcmeon, who has just claimed to have killed his mother, is asked whether he did so ἑκών with his mother ἑκοῦσαν:

⟨Α.⟩ μητέρα κατέκταν τὴν ἐμήν, βραχὺς λόγος.
⟨Φ.⟩ ἑκὼν ἑκοῦσαν ἢ ⟨οὐ⟩ θέλουσαν οὐχ ἑκών;
(Eur. *Alcm.* Fr. 68/#2 *TGF*)

The actions of both passages, rape and killing, typify actions which occur under actual force. But each of the victims is nonetheless described as ἑκοῦσα. In the second passage, even if Alcmeon's answer is that his mother was not killed ἑκοῦσα, the question itself implies the description is possible.

The FOV and ἀνάγκη (ii)

Part One

In those passages collected under ἀνάγκη (ii), persons or characters are subject to compelling social practices. The nature of these practices is such that the distinctions made for victims of hands-on force, i.e. agent or passive and actual or threatened, do not provide much insight into these passages. All the victims would be agents subject to actual compelling practices. An aim of the social practice in question is for those subject to them to do certain things. Thus all those subject to ἀνάγκη (ii) practices are agents. Even if an action required by such a practice were passive, e.g., remaining in a certain place, the nonphysical nature of these practices prohibits the kind of passivity and behavior peculiar to the restrained victim of βία who remains in a certain place. Also, it is peculiar to βία that both actual and threatened force count as βία. Although one could conceive of someone threatening a command, e.g., as opposed to an actually issued command, there is no example of this distinction in the texts. Moreover, even if there were examples, they would not generate the same inter-

---

[19]Cf. Eur. *Tro* 370–73 where there is a clear exclusive disjunction between describing Helen as ἑκοῦσα and her abduction as rape.

est since the immaterial manner in which a social practice compels actually is already akin to the power of merely threatened force to compel.

What is still of interest is to determine whether a person or character subject to these practices can be ἑκών or ἄκων, or whether, as the FOV would lead us to expect, the necessitating circumstances are always conjoined with a person or character designated ἄκων and opposed to a person or character designated ἑκών. What we find is that although the FOV can accommodate most of the ἀνάγκη (ii) passages, there are exceptions in this group too.

As the FOV would lead us to expect, compelling circumstances of social practices are found conjoined with negative forms of ἑκών group words. There are five examples from the passages discussed in Chapter 1. Penelope (*Od.* 20.339–343), Hephaestus (*PrB* 12–20), and the speaker admonishing Simonides about appropriate symposiastic behavior (Theog. 467–72/#2) are all subject to orders or demands and are ἄκοντες; in Euripides' *Phoenissae* (427–34/#1), Polyneices acts ἀκουσίως while subject to the oath of Adrastus; and the Plataeans fought alongside the Athenians subject to their alliance with them and ἄκοντες (Thuc. 3.63.2/#1 [read with 3.58.2–3]). The FOV easily accommodates such passages.

Among the passages discussed in Chapter 1, there are also examples of positive forms of ἑκών opposed to compelling social practices. Since the disjunction in these passages seems exclusive, the FOV has no difficulty accommodating them. In Euripides' *Heraclidae* (547–51) the disjunction between acting ἑκών and the compelling practice seems exclusive because Macaria will give her life ἑκοῦσα but not if chosen by lot In Thucydides (6.44.1), the supply ships that sailed to Sicily ἐξ ἀνάγκης also seem exclusively contrasted with those that went ἑκούσιοι for commercial reasons and under no obligation to Athens (πολλὰ δὲ καὶ ἄλλα πλοῖα καὶ ὁλκάδες ἑκούσιοι ξυνηκολούθουν τῇ στρατιᾷ ἐμπορίας ἕνεκα).

Passages discussed in Chapter 1 which are exceptions to the FOV are discussed below.[20] These passages provide examples of someone being ἑκών

---

[20] Also, reading Thuc. 3.67.4–5 where the Thebans describe the Plataeans as ἑκόντες joining the Athenians (recalled at 3.64.5/#2), closely with Thuc. 3.58.2–3 where the Plataeans claim they fought against Sparta because they were compelled by their alliance with Athens (and 3.63.2/#1 where the Thebans recall this claim and describe the Plataeans as ἄκοντες), the Thebans can be taken to reject the claim of the Plataeans that they fought with the Spartans, compelled by the alliance formed during the Persian wars, that is, a case of acting ἑκών opposed to acting under ἀνάγκη; or this may be another exceptional case of acting ἑκών while subject to the ἀνάγκη of the alliance. See also Eur. *Phoen.* 427–34/#2 and discussion in ch. 1 pp. 25–26. If ἑκοῦσι is accepted as a reading, Eteocles et al. would fall in with this group—they act ἑκόντες but subject to the ἀνάγκη stemming from Adrastus' oath.

while subject to a compelling social practice and not ἄκων in accordance with the FOV.

In his description of the participants in the campaign against Sicily, Thucydides does contrast those who came ἑκόντες, e.g., the Athenians themselves and others who came for profit, and those who came under ἀνάγκη, those subject to Athenian might or bound by alliance. However, not all those who sailed under compelling ties to Athens did so ἄκοντες. The Argives, e.g., though allies of Athens, are not mentioned along with the subjects and autonomous allies who came under ἀνάγκη, but with the profiteers, those mentioned under a new heading of those who came ἑκούσιοι:

> τῶν δὲ ἄλλων ἑκούσιος μᾶλλον ἡ στρατεία ἐγίγνετο ἤδη. Ἀργεῖοι μὲν γὰρ οὐ τῆς ξυμμαχίας ἕνεκα μᾶλλον ἢ τῆς Λακεδαιμονίων τε ἔχθρας καὶ τῆς παραυτίκα ἕκαστοι ἰδίας ὠφελίας Δωριῆς ἐπὶ Δωριᾶς μετὰ Ἀθηναίων Ἰώνων ἠκολούθουν.
> (Thuc. 7.57.9)

In Herodotus' tale of Croesus' advice to Cyrus about recovering some booty already in the hands of the soldiers, the soldiers would give their tithe to Zeus ἀναγκαίως and ἑκόντες:

> κάτισον τῶν δορυφόρων ἐπὶ πάσῃσι τῇσι πύλῃσι φυλάκους, οἳ λεγόντων πρὸς τοὺς ἐκφέροντας τὰ χρήματα ἀπαιρεόμενοι ὥς σφεα ἀναγκαίως ἔχει δεκατευθῆναι τῷ Διί. καὶ σύ τέ σφι οὐκ ἀπεχθήσεαι βίῃ ἀπαιρεόμενος τὰ χρήματα, καὶ ἐκεῖνοι συγγνόντες ποιέειν σε δίκαια ἑκόντες προήσουσι.
> (Hdt. 1.89.3)

Circumstances of necessity do not render these victims ἄκοντες. Since the absence of βία is rather explicit in this passage, it should be mentioned that on the Functional Opposite View this absence of βία could be seen as responsible for rendering the soldiers ἑκόντες. However, since there is evidence that drives a wedge between βία and descriptions of persons or characters as ἑκόντες or ἄκοντες, there may be some other explanation for the soldiers being ἑκόντες while subject to the necessary practice and despite the absence of βία.

The contrast Philoctetes draws between himself and Odysseus (Soph. *Ph.* 1019–28) also speaks against the Functional Opposite View, and here there is no lurking βία. Although being ἑκών and circumstances of ἀνάγκη are opposed on the surface in this passage, they are also conjoined. The opposition is created by the contrast between Odysseus who went to Troy yoked by ἀνάγκη and Philoctetes who sailed ἑκών. I have argued that the ἀνάγκη of this passage is likely to be the oath of the suitors. If so, Philoctetes, also a suitor of

Helen, was also bound by the oath.[21] Philoctetes too then went to Troy under ἀνάγκη but ἑκών.

Part Two

Further examples of compelling social practices include a few passages where lottery or election bear on agents as well as examples of an oath, laws, and hospitality. But most of the examples to be added to this group are passages where agents described by ἑκών group words are subject to orders or requests or demands. Here too there are passages which the FOV cannot accommodate. The following examples will show that an agent subject to compelling social practices may be ἄκων or ἑκών. The presence of the social practice does not automatically render the agent ἄκων.

Lottery or election are the compelling social practices that bear on agents in the following passages. The FOV readily accommodates those in which the compelling social practices are conjoined with a negative form, ἄκων. The guard who goes ἄκων to Creon to tell him of the burial of Polyneices does so under the compulsion of the lot (πάλος καθαιρεῖ):

καὶ ταῦτ' ἐνίκα, κἀμὲ τὸν δυσδαίμονα
πάλος καθαιρεῖ τοῦτο τἀγαθὸν λαβεῖν.
πάρειμι δ' ἄκων οὐχ ἑκοῦσιν, οἶδ' ὅτι·
στέργει γὰρ οὐδεὶς ἄγγελον κακῶν ἐπῶν.
(Soph. *Ant.* 274–77/#1)

Two passages in Thucydides refer to Nicias who was elected ἄκων to lead the expedition to Sicily. In the first, Thucydides describes Nicias just before reporting his speech against sending the expedition: καὶ ὁ Νικίας ἀκούσιος μὲν ᾑρημένος ἄρχειν (Thuc. 6.8.4). The second is from the speech of Hermocrates to the Syacusean assembly. He has heard that the Athenian commander is not eager for the expedition: ἄλλως τε καὶ τοῦ ἐμπειροτάτου τῶν στρατηγῶν, ὡς ἐγὼ ἀκούω, ἄκοντος ἡγουμένου (Thuc. 6.34.6).

There is at least one passage involving election that counts against the FOV. In this excerpt from Euripides' *Iphigenia in Aulis*, Achilles answers Clytemnestra's questions about who will come for Iphigenia:

Κλ. ἥξει δ' ὅστις ἄψεται κόρης;
Αχ. μυρίοι γ', ἄξει δ' Ὀδυσσεύς.
Κλ. ἆρ' ὁ Σισύφου γόνος;
Αχ. αὐτὸς οὗτός.

---

[21] See ch. 1 n. 31 for some ancient sources. For variations in the list of suitors see Sir J.G. Frazer, ed. and trans., *Apollodorus: The Library*, vol. 2 (Cambridge, 1921), 26.

Κλ. ἴδια πράσσων, ἢ στρατοῦ ταχθεὶς ὕπο;
Αχ. αἱρεθεὶς ἑκών.

(Eur. *IA* 1361–64)

Odysseus too has undergone some sort of election (αἱρεθείς) to his task of fetching Iphigenia. But he is ἑκών despite the imposition:

There are several passages where ἑκών group words describe those acting under orders or in response to requests or demands. The following are examples of those who act ἄκοντες under orders. In Euripides' *Bacchae*, Pentheus' attendant explains to Dionysus that he acts οὐχ ἑκών under Pentheus' orders:

κἀγὼ δι' αἰδοῦς εἶπον· Ὦ ξέν', οὐχ ἑκὼν
ἄγω σε, Πενθέως δ' ὅς μ' ἔπεμψ' ἐπιστολαῖς.

(Eur. *Bacch.* 441–42)

The heralds Talthybius and Eurybates go ἀέκοντε to Achilles' ship under Agamamnon's orders:

Ὣς εἰπὼν προίει, κρατερὸν δ' ἐπὶ μῦθον ἔτελλε·
τὼ δ' ἀέκοντε βάτην παρὰ θῖν' ἁλὸς ἀτρυγέτοιο,
Μυρμιδόνων δ' ἐπί τε κλισίας καὶ νῆας ἱκέσθην.

(*Il.* 1.326–28)

Likewise, in Book 18 the verb πέμψεν (sent) implies that Helios was ordered to set by Hera, and Helios did so ἀέκων:

Ἥλιον δ' ἀκάμαντα βοῶπις πότνια Ἥρη
πέμψεν ἐπ' Ὠκεανοῖο ῥοὰς ἀέκοντα νέεσθαι·
ἠέλιος μὲν ἔδυ, παύσαντο δὲ δῖοι Ἀχαιοὶ
φυλόπιδος κρατερῆς καὶ ὁμοιΐου πολέμοιο.

(*Il.* 18.239–42)

In *Odyssey* 5 acting ἑκών and acting under orders are opposed and the opposition appears to be strong. In answer to Calypso's questions, Hermes says that Zeus ordered him to come to her island (Ζεὺς ἐμέ γ' ἠνώγει), and he asks rhetorically who would come ἑκών:

Ζεὺς ἐμέ γ' ἠνώγει δεῦρ' ἐλθέμεν οὐκ ἐθέλοντα·
τίς δ' ἂν ἑκὼν τοσσόνδε διαδράμοι ἁλμυρὸν ὕδωρ
ἄσπετον;

(*Od.* 5.99–101)

The FOV accommodates all of these examples.

In some passages "order" may be too strong or formal to describe the demands or requests made. For example, when Teiresias tells Oedipus, σὺ γάρ μ' ἄκοντα προυτρέψεν λέγειν, Oedipus is certainly urging Teiresias to say what he knows, and he does use imperatives: λέγ' and φράσον (Soph. *OR*

354–62). But the demand may fall short of an outright order when compared, for example, to the commands of a king to an underling like the attendant in the passage from the *Bacchae* discussed above (Eur. *Bacch.* 441–42). Since ἄκων is conjoined with the compelling social practice, the FOV accommodates this passage too.

There are also several passages that count against the FOV, where agents are ἑκόντες while acting under orders or in response to demands.[22] When Philoctetes orders the Chorus to leave him saying, ἀπό νύν με λείπετ' ἤδη, the Chorus responds, φίλα μοι, φίλα ταῦτα παρήγγειλας ἑκόντι τε πράσσειν (Soph. *Ph.* 1177–80). In the *Prometheus Bound* the Chorus responds, οὐκ ἀκούσαις ἐπεθώυξας τοῦτο, Προμηθεῦ, to Prometheus' request that they alight from their chariots to listen to him (277–78). In the *Odyssey*, Eurykleia too obeys οὐκ ἀέκουσα an order from Penelope to wash the feet of Odysseus: ἐμὲ δ' οὐκ ἀέκουσαν ἄνωγε/κούρη Ἰκαρίοιο, περίφρων Πηνελόπεια (19.374–75). In the *Agamemnon*, Clytemnestra works at persuading Agamemnon to comply to her request or demand that he tread on the now infamous tapestries (943). Though part of the line is corrupt, the command πιθοῦ and ἑκὼν ἐμοί are secure:[23] πιθοῦ, †κράτος μέντοι πάρες γ'† ἑκὼν ἐμοί.

Two passages where Pindar speaks of himself in the first person also belong to this group and count against the FOV:

τὸ δὲ πὰρ ποδὶ ναὸς ἑλισσόμενον αἰεὶ κυμάτων
λέγεται παντὶ μάλιστα δονεῖν
θυμόν. ἑκόντι δ' ἐγὼ νώ-
τῳ μεθέπων δίδυμον ἄχθος
ἄγγελος ἔβαν
πέμπτον ἐπὶ εἴκοσι τοῦτο γαρύων
εὖχος ἀγώνων ἄπο, τοὺς ἐνέποισιν ἱερούς,
Ἀλκίμιδα, σέ γ' ἐπαρκέσαι
κλειτᾷ γενεᾷ·
(Pind. *Nem.* 6.55–61)

ἐμὲ δ' εὐθὺν ἀκόντων
ἱέντα ῥόμβον παρὰ σκοπὸν οὐ χρή
τὰ πολλὰ βέλεα καρτύνειν χεροῖν.

---

[22]Other examples include Soph. *Ph.* 769–73/#1–2, Eur. *El.* 669–70, *Supp.* 857–59, *Il.* 11.714–17, Epicharm. Fr. 37/#2 Kaibel, and in *Il.* 14.103–8 with 128 we could infer from Agamemnon's remark that he does not order the men ἀέκοντας to go, that he thinks they would follow an order to go ἑκόντες.

[23]Ar. *Cl.* 865–69 also shows an ambiguity between persuasion and obedience. Strepsiades wants his son to obey him (861–2) but tells Socrates: ἄγω γάρ σοι τὸν υἱὸν τουτονὶ / ἄκοντα ἀναπείσας. In the preceding line εὖ γ' ὅτι ἐπείσθης is ambiguous.

Μοίσαις γὰρ ἀγλαοθρόνοις ἑκών
'Ολιγαιθίδαισίν τ' ἔβαν ἐπίκουρος.
(Pind. Ol. 13.93–97)

Through a poetic conceit, he fashions himself a messsenger, ἄγγελος ἔβαι, in the first passage, and an ally of the Muses, ἔβαν ἐπίκουρος, in the second. Both roles present him as subject to orders and demands. Nonetheless, the poet bears his burden ἑκόντι νώτῳ and ἑκών, respectively.

Although there is no example of ξενία (the practice of hospitality) in the passages of Chapter 1, there should be no hesitation for readers of Homer to accept ξενία as a compelling social practice.[24] Being subject to the constraints of Nestor's hospitality is what Telemachus wishes to avoid in the *Odyssey* : μὴ μ' ὁ γέρων ἀέκοντα κατάσχῃ ᾧ ἐνὶ οἴκῳ ἱέμενος φιλέειν (19.124–33). The FOV seems to accommodate this passage since the agent is ἄκων and subject to the practice. This particular social practice, however, should cause us to pause and reconsider whether the conjunction of ἄκων and the compelling social practice is ordinary, as the FOV holds, or unusual. Although the practice of hospitality makes demands of guests as well as hosts, it would be odd to suppose that the response of Telemachus is usual and regularly associated with being subject to the practice of ξενία. It would be very odd to suppose that being subject to the practice would automatically render someone ἄκων, as the FOV holds. In Euripides' *Iphigenia in Tauris*, we see the constraints of ξενία are born by the hosts of Orestes:

ἐλθὼν δ' ἐκεῖσε πρῶτα μέν ⟨μ'⟩ οὐδεὶς ξένων
ἑκὼν ἐδέξαθ' ὡς θεοῖς στυγούμενον·
οἳ δ' ἔσχον αἰδῶ, ξένια μονοτράπεζά μοι
παρέσχον
(Eur. *IT* 947–50)

No one ἑκών received him, but he was given a meal at a table by himself. Here too, if the FOV is correct, subject to the constraints of ξενία we should expect a host always to be ἄκων. But this passage gives the impression that it is unusual for a host to act the way these hosts do. Superficially, the FOV seems to accommodate these passages; but the larger sense of the passages does not readily support the FOV.

In two passages from Aristophanes, acting ἑκών is opposed to acting under the force of laws. In the *Wasps*, Philocleon, having been summoned by an accuser (κατήγορος) on a charge of *hybris* declares he will settle the matter ἑκών:

---

[24]See E. Benveniste, *Le vocabulaire des institutions indo-européennes*, 6th ed., vol. 1 (Paris, 1969), 87ff.

> ἐγὼ μὲν οὖν αὐτῷ διαλλαχθήσομαι
> ἑκών· ὁμολογῶ γὰρ πατάξαι καὶ βαλεῖν.
> ἀλλ' ἐλθὲ δευρί. πότερον ἐπιτρέπεις ἐμοὶ
> ὅ τι χρή μ' ἀποτείσαντ' ἀργύριον τοῦ πράγματος
> εἶναι φίλον τὸ λοιπόν, ἢ σύ μοι φράσεις;
>   (Ar. *Wasps* 1421-25)

He admits the beating and seeks to pay compensation without going to trial. His accuser is also eager to avoid the courtroom: δικῶν γὰρ οὐ δέομ' οὐδὲ πραγμάτων (1426). Similarly, in the *Clouds*, Pheidippides' explanation of "the old and new day" contrasts settling debts ἑκόντες with settling them in court:

> Φε. ἐκεῖνος οὖν τὴν κλῆσιν ἐς δύ' ἡμέρας
> ἔθηκεν, εἴς γε τὴν ἕνην τε καὶ νέαν,
> ἵν' αἱ θέσεις γίγνοιντο τῇ νουμηνίᾳ·
> Στ. ἵνα δὴ τί τὴν ἕνην προσέθηκεν;   Φε. ἵν', ὦ μέλε,
> παρόντες οἱ φεύγοντες ἡμέρᾳ μιᾷ
> πρότερον ἀπαλλάττοινθ' ἑκόντες. εἰ δὲ μή,
> ἕωθεν ὑπανιῷντο τῇ νουμηνίᾳ.
>   (Ar. *Cl.* 1189-95)

In both cases, even as the accused acts ἑκών he is still subject to the threat of legal action.

One passage, akin to the situation in Sophocles' *Philoctetes* (1019-28) which was discussed in Chapter 1,[25] links acting οὐχ ἑκών and acting under the necessity imposed by an oath. In the *Agamemnon*, Agamemnon tells the Chorus that Odysseus sailed οὐχ ἑκών and describes him as "yoked" (ζευχθείς):

> εἰδὼς λέγοιμ' ἄν, εὖ γὰρ ἐξεπίσταμαι
> ὁμιλίας κάτοπτρον, εἴδωλον σκιᾶς,
> δοκοῦντας εἶναι κάρτα πρευμενεῖς ἐμοί·
> μόνος δ' Ὀδυσσεύς, ὅσπερ οὐχ ἑκὼν ἔπλει,
> ζευχθεὶς ἑτοῖμος ἦν ἐμοὶ σειραφόρος·
> εἴτ' οὖν θανόντος εἴτε καὶ ζῶντος πέρι
> λέγω.
>   (Aesch. *Ag.* 838-44)

I understand this "yoke," like the yoking necessity of the *Philoctetes* passage, to be a reference to the oath sworn by Helen's suitors. Odysseus, subject to this oath, was compelled to go and did so οὐχ ἑκών. In the *Philoctetes* too we could infer Odysseus sailed ἄκων from the contrast Philoctetes makes between himself (he went ἑκών) and Odysseus who went to Troy yoked by necessity.

---

[25] See ch. 1 pp. 23-25. The ἀνάγκη by which Odysseus was yoked was the oath of the suitors.

Superficially then, the FOV seems to accommodate the passage from the *Agamemnon*. But it has already been argued about the passage from the *Philoctetes* that since both men were bound by the oath, merely being subject to an oath does not render an agent ἄκων. One man goes ἄκων, the other ἑκών; but both are bound by the oath.

Summary

These passages show that an agent caught up in the circumstances included under ἀνάγκη (ii) (laws or orders, alliances, oaths, lotteries, elections, hospitality, and religious practices like the tithe) is not automatically rendered ἄκων. One cannot simply identify these circumstances as pertaining and predict whether an agent affected by them is ἄκων or ἑκών. The most one can conclude at this point is that these circumstances are particularly relevant to the designation of a person or character as ἑκών or ἄκων.

The FOV and ἀνάγκη (iii)

Part One

The following passages are unusual in that the ἑκών group words in them do not modify the victim of force or necessity or his acts but rather the afflicting force of necessity itself.[26] In Euripides' *Dictys*, disease, one of the compulsions sent by the gods, is denied to be ἑκουσία:[27]

καὶ γὰρ οὐκ αὐθαίρετοι
βροτοῖς ἔρωτες οὐδ' ἑκουσία νόσος.
σκαιόν τι δὴ τὸ χρῆμα γίγνεσθαι φιλεῖ,
θεῶν ἀνάγκας ὅστις ἰᾶσθαι θέλει.
(Eur. *Dictys* 339.3–6*TGF*)

In the *Cresphontes* (66.20–22 Harder), chance events are labelled ἀκούσιαι (πότερα βιαίως ἢ τύχαις ἀκουσίοις;). Similarly, Thucydides describes the compelling circumstances which arise in war as themselves ἀκούσιοι:

ἐν μὲν γὰρ εἰρήνῃ καὶ ἀγαθοῖς πράγμασιν αἵ τε πόλεις καὶ οἱ ἰδιῶται ἀμείνους τὰς γνώμας ἔχουσι διὰ τὸ μὴ ἐς ἀκουσίους ἀνάγκας πίπτειν·
(Thuc. 3.82.2)

---

[26]Cf. Theog. 1341–44 where the force is internal (i/a):
Αἰαῖ, παιδὸς ἐρῶ ἀπαλόχροος, ὅς με φίλοισιν
πᾶσι μάλ' ἐκφαίνει κοὐκ ἐθέλοντος ἐμοῦ.
τλήσομαι οὐ κρύψας ἀεκούσι(α) πολλὰ βίαια·
οὐ γὰρ ἐπ' αἰκελίωι παιδὶ δαμεὶς ἐφάνην.

[27]See ch. 1 n. 15.

It is not a particularly large step to go from describing the agent (or his acts) under ἀνάγκη as ἑκών (or ἑκούσιος) or ἄκων (or ἀκούσιος) to describing the circumstances themselves that precipitate such acts by ἑκών group words, especially since ἀνάγκη covers not only the circumstances but what issues from them. These passages provide more evidence of ἀνάγκη conjoined with negative ἑκών group words. But there is no need to conclude that all ἀνάγκαι are automatically ἀκούσιοι. The particular ἀνάγκαι (e.g., βία, passion, disease) relevant to these passages, however, may represent those that regularly do afflict victims who are ἄκοντες thereby facilitating the transfer of the ἑκών group word to the circumstances themselves.

In the following two passages, there appears to be a strong opposition between acting ἑκών and acting under ἀνάγκη:

ἥσθην πατέρα τὸν ἁμὸν εὐλογοῦντά σε
αὐτόν τ' ἔμ'· ὧν δέ σου τυχεῖν ἐφίεμαι
ἄκουσον. ἀνθρώποισι τὰς μὲν ἐκ θεῶν
τύχας δοθείσας ἔστ' ἀναγκαῖον φέρειν·
ὅσοι δ' ἑκουσίοισιν ἔγκεινται βλάβαις,
ὥσπερ σύ, τούτοις οὔτε συγγνώμην ἔχειν
δίκαιόν ἐστιν οὔτ' ἐποικτίρειν τινά.
(Soph. Ph. 1314–20)

πάντας δ' ἐπαίνημι καὶ φιλέω,
ἑκὼν ὅστις ἔρδῃ
μηδὲν αἰσχρόν· ἀνάγκᾳ
δ' οὐδὲ θεοὶ μάχονται.
(Simon. Fr. 542.27–30 *PMG*)

The first passage is part of Neoptolemus' admonition to Philoctetes. He goes on to rebuke Philoctetes for being savage in his anger and rejecting advice from one who is kindly disposed to him and not the enemy Philoctetes thinks him to be. Philoctetes' refusal to give up his present hardships by returning to Troy with the Greeks, even now when Neoptolemus has returned the bow, is an example of the kind of behavior Neoptolemus says it is right neither to forgive nor to pity. There is an opposition between the τύχαι (chance) given by the gods to humans who must endure them (ἔστ' ἀναγκαῖον φέρειν), ἀνάγκη (iii), and involving oneself in ἑκουσίοισιν βλάβαις harm that is ἑκούσιος). In the second passage, the poet appears to contrast one who does shameful deeds ἑκών with one who is compelled to do such things (ἀνάγκῃ). If we approach these passages relying on the FOV, we automatically consider as strong and exclusive the opposition between acting under ἀνάγκη and acting ἑκών.

However, two cases in which a positive form of ἑκών is related to ἀνάγκη (iii) show the view that one can act ἑκών under ἀνάγκη (iii):

εἰδέναι δὲ χρὴ ὅτι ἀνάγκη πολεμεῖν, ἢν δὲ ἑκούσιοι μᾶλλον
δεχώμεθα, ἧσσον ἐγκεισομένους τοὺς ἐναντίους ἕξομεν, ἔκ τε
τῶν μεγίστων κινδύνων ὅτι καὶ πόλει καὶ ἰδιώτῃ μέγισται
τιμαὶ περιγίγνονται·

(Thuc. 1.144.3)

In this excerpt from the speech in which Pericles urges the Athenians not to make any concessions to the Peloponnesians, the Athenians are told it is necessary for them to go to war: ἀνάγκη πολεμεῖν. But here we see agents who find themselves in the midst of compelling prevailing circumstances but who are urged to undertake their task ἑκούσιοι.

In Book 3, the Mytilenians are described as compelled (ἀναγκάζονται) to surrender because of their lack of supplies:

Οἱ δὲ Μυτιληναῖοι ἐν τούτῳ, ὡς αἵ τε νῆες αὐτοῖς οὐχ ἧκον
ἀπὸ τῆς Πελοποννήσου ἀλλὰ ἐνεχρόνιζον καὶ ὁ σῖτος
ἐπελελοίπει, ἀναγκάζονται ξυμβαίνειν πρὸς τοὺς Ἀθηναίους
διὰ τάδε.

(Thuc. 3.27.1)

Later, after a reconsideration of the fate of Mytilene, Diodotus describes at least some of the Mytilenians, the demos as opposed to those in authority, as surrendering ἑκόντες:

εἰ δὲ διαφθερεῖτε τὸν δῆμον τὸν Μυτιληναίων, ὃς οὔτε
μετέσχε τῆς ἀποστάσεως, ἐπειδή τε ὅπλων ἐκράτησεν, ἑκὼν
παρέδωκε τὴν πόλιν, πρῶτον μὲν ἀδικήσετε τοὺς εὐεργέτας
κτείνοντες, ἔπειτα καταστήσετε τοῖς δυνατοῖς τῶν
ἀνθρώπων ὃ βούλονται μάλιστα·

(Thuc. 3.47.3)

Although, at the very least, Diodotus exaggerates the action of the Mytilenians in his efforts to save them, it is also the case that the Athenians knew about the compelling circumstances under which the Mytilenians surrendered. It would have to make sense to them that the demos could both be compelled to surrender and do so ἑκών.[28] Being subject to ἀνάγκη does not automatically render the Athenians in Pericles' speech, or the Mytilenians ἄκοντες. These passages too are not accommodated by the FOV.

---

[28]It may be thought that the speech of Diodotus is too far removed from the actual surrender of the Mytilenians for the connection I draw between ἀναγκάζονται and ἑκούσιοι. If so, the use of ἑκούσιοι in this passage could be categorized with those passages in which ἑκών group words appear when circumstances of Harm or Wrong pertain. These passages are discussed in ch. 3.

Part Two

Constraining circumstances with supernatural influence

There are enough passages to be added to this category to be able to discern a subgroup in which the prevailing constraining circumstances under which agents are described by ἑκών group words are brought about by supernatural influence. The following are examples of those passages where there is direct interference of a god or gods, and the agents are ἄκοντες. Others are included in the Index Locorum.[29]

In Euripides' *Heraclidae*, Eurystheus contends that he, οὐχ ἑκών, took on the quarrel with his cousin Heracles, and that Hera imposed the problem which he thinks of as a "disease" (τὴν νόσον):

ἐγὼ δὲ νεῖκος οὐχ ἑκὼν τόδ' ἠράμην·
ἤδη γε σοὶ μὲν αὐτανέψιος γεγώς,
τῷ σῷ δὲ παιδὶ συγγενὴς Ἡρακλέει.
ἀλλ' εἴτ' ἔχρῃζον εἴτε μή—θεὸς γὰρ ἦν—
Ἥρα με κάμνειν τήνδ' ἔθηκε τὴν νόσον.
(Eur. *Heracl.* 986-90)

Following this explanation, θεὸς γὰρ ἦν, Eurystheus goes on to more specifically detail the machinations of Hera. In the *Oedipus at Colonus* (960-99/#1,2,4), Oedipus, who tells Creon he experienced all his misfortunes ἄκων (962-64), also refers to the killing of his father as τὸ ἆκον πρᾶγμα (977), and says he ἄκων married his mother (987). He too ascribes to the gods responsibility for the unavoidable circumstances on which he reflects:[30]

ὅστις φόνους μοι καὶ γάμους καὶ συμφορὰς
τοῦ σοῦ διῆκας στόματος, ἃς ἐγὼ τάλας
ἤνεγκον ἄκων· θεοῖς γὰρ ἦν οὕτω φίλον·
(Soph. *OC* 962-64)

The madness of Ajax brought on by Athena in Sophocles' *Ajax* is another example:

---

[29] At *Od.* 18.125-42 Odysseus, speaking of the human condition, says ἄνθρωπος endures ἀεκαζόμενος the λυγρά accomplished by the gods. The passage is reminiscent of the type (iii) ἀνάγκη passages already discussed. While the gods are said to be the source of human τύχαι, the remarks are more generalized than the specific interventions of an individual god (e.g., Athena's interventions in the life of Ajax: Soph. *Aj.* 447-56). These gifts of the gods are unavoidable in the strong sense and so is the human response to them: humans must endure. Cf. Eur. *Ion* 642-45 and *Andr.* 977-84.

[30] That Oedipus ascribes responsibility to the gods need not, of course, detract from his own responsibility. For "over-determined" acts see E.R. Dodds, *The Greeks and the Irrational* (Berkeley, 1971), 28-50; and R.P. Winnington-Ingram, *Sophocles: An Interpretation* (Cambridge, 1980), 173-78.

> νῦν δ' ἡ Διὸς γοργῶπις ἀδάματος θεὰ
> ἤδη μ' ἐπ' αὐτοῖς χεῖρ' ἐπευθύνοντ' ἐμὴν
> ἔσφηλεν ἐμβαλοῦσα λυσσώδη νόσον,
> ὥστ' ἐν τοιοῖσδε χεῖρας αἱμάξαι βοτοῖς·
> κεῖνοι δ' ἐπεγγελῶσιν ἐκπεφευγότες,
> ἐμοῦ μὲν οὐχ ἑκόντος· εἰ δέ τις θεῶν
> βλάπτοι, φύγοι τἂν χὠ κακὸς τὸν κρείσσονα.
> (Soph. Aj. 447–56)

Once Ajax was afflicted by Athena, the escape of his intended victims followed inevitably. Both the madness and its effects then were necessary in the stronger sense of there being no other possibilities at all for Ajax because of the interference of the goddess. His enemies escape and Ajax says of himself, "ἐμοῦ μὲν οὐχ ἑκόντος."

Other circumstances involving supernatural influence in which agents find themselves, include oracles, prophecies, or prophetic dreams. The agents respond to these circumstances as fixed necessitating factors. But under these circumstances an agent may act ἑκών or ἄκων. In Aristophanes' *Knights*, Cleon, declaring that his oracle has been fulfilled by the Sausage Seller, gives up ἄκων the crown to his rival:

> οἴμοι πέπρακται τοῦ θεοῦ τὸ θέσφατον.
> κυλίνδετ' εἴσω τόνδε τὸν δυσδαίμονα.
> ὦ στέφανε χαίρων ἄπιθι, κεἴ σ' ἄκων ἐγὼ
> λείπω· σὲ δ' ἄλλος τις λαβὼν κεκτήσεται,
> κλέπτης μὲν οὐκ ἂν μᾶλλον, εὐτυχὴς δ' ἴσως.
> (Ar. Kn. 1248–52)

But in other cases the agent acts ἑκών. For example, In Herodotus, King Sabacos, after a disturbing dream that suggested some disaster was nigh, left Egypt ἑκών in accordance with an oracle that he was to rule there only fifty years:

> οὐκ ὦν ποιήσειν ταῦτα, ἀλλὰ γὰρ οἱ ἐξεληλυθέναι τὸν χρόνον ὁκόσον κεχρῆσθαι ἄρξαντα Αἰγύπτου ἐκχωρήσειν. ἐν γὰρ τῇ Αἰθιοπίῃ ἐόντι αὐτῷ τὰ μαντήια τοῖσι χρέωνται Αἰθίοπες ἀνεῖλε ὡς δέοι αὐτὸν Αἰγύπτου βασιλεῦσαι ἔτεα πεντήκοντα. ὡς ὦν ὁ χρόνος οὗτος ἐξήιε καὶ αὐτὸν ἡ ὄψις τοῦ ἐνυπνίου ἐπετάρασσε, ἑκὼν ἀπαλλάσσετο ἐκ τῆς Αἰγύπτου ὁ Σαβακῶς.
> (Hdt. 2.139.2–3)

In Euripides' *Heraclidae*, King Demophon, preparing to defend the Heraclidae, reports that all the oracles, however varied in other ways, order the sacrifice of a maiden to Demeter's daughter:

> χρησμῶν δ' ἀοιδοὺς πάντας εἰς ἓν ἁλίσας
> ἤλεγξα καὶ βέβηλα καὶ κεκρυμμένα
> [λόγια παλαιά, τῇδε γῇ σωστήρια]·
> καὶ τῶν μὲν ἄλλων διάφορ' ἐστὶ θεσφάτοις
> πόλλ'· ἓν δὲ πᾶσι γνῶμα ταὐτὸν ἐμπρέπει·
> σφάξαι κελεύουσίν με παρθένον κόρῃ
> Δήμητρος, ἥτις ἐστὶ πατρὸς εὐγενοῦς.
> (Eur. *Heracl.* 403–09)

Even though the death is necessitated by oracles, Macaria, goes ἑκοῦσα to her death:

> ἡγεῖσθ' ὅπου δεῖ σῶμα κατθανεῖν τόδε
> καὶ στεμματοῦτε καὶ †κατάρχεσθ', εἰ δοκεῖ†·
> νικᾶτε δ' ἐχθρούς· ἥδε γὰρ ψυχὴ πάρα
> ἑκοῦσα κοὐκ ἄκουσα, κἀξαγγέλλομαι
> θνήσκειν ἀδελφῶν τῶνδε κἀμαυτῆς ὕπερ.
> εὕρημα γάρ τοι μὴ φιλοψυχοῦσ' ἐγὼ
> κάλλιστον ηὕρηκ', εὐκλεῶς λιπεῖν βίον.
> (Eur. *Heracl.* 528–34)

Euripides' Iphigenia also goes ἑκοῦσα to her death because of the word of a god:

> ἔλεξε τοιάδ'· Ὦ πάτερ, πάρειμί σοι·
> τοὐμὸν δὲ σῶμα τῆς ἐμῆς ὑπὲρ πάτρας
> καὶ τῆς ἁπάσης Ἑλλάδος γαίας ὕπερ
> θῦσαι δίδωμ' ἑκοῦσα πρὸς βωμὸν θεᾶς
> ἄγοντας, εἴπερ ἐστὶ θέσφατον τόδε.
> (Eur. *IA* 1552–56)

The curse too under which Polyneices acts in Euripides' *Suppliants* is prophetic in power, and the fratricide it includes is accepted as a fixed event:

> Θη. ἦλθον δὲ δὴ πῶς πατρίδος ἐκλιπόνθ' ὅρους;
> Αδ. Τυδεὺς μέν αἷμα συγγενὲς φεύγων χθονός.
> Θη. ὁ δ' Οἰδίπου ⟨παῖς⟩ τίνι τρόπωι Θήβας λιπών;
> Αδ. ἀραῖς πατρώιαις, μὴ κασίγνητον κτάνοι.
> Θη. σοφήν γ' ἔλεξας τήνδ' ἑκούσιον φυγήν.
> (Eur. *Supp.* 147–51)

The ἀνάγκη to which Polyneices responds is necessary in the strong sense then, but, as in the case of Sabacos (Hdt. 2.139.2–3), the responsive action of Polyneices is necessary in the weaker sense of what is an acceptable course given the circumstances. But whatever the strength of the ἀνάγκη, Polyneices' flight is called ἑκούσιον.

Persons and characters subject to the necessity of these passages can be ἄκοντες or ἑκόντες. They are not automatically rendered ἄκοντες as the FOV expects.[31]

Other prevailing circumstances

In passages that do not show supernatural influence, some persons or characters finding themselves in the midst of or confronted with unavoidable and constraining circumstances appear to be helpless or victimized by these circumstances. Others are more aggressive. Among the first sort is the inadvertent traveller, described in a simile, who ἀέκων disturbs a nest of wasps by merely passing nearby:

Οἱ δ' ἅμα Πατρόκλῳ μεγαλήτορι θωρηχθέντες
ἔστιχον, ὄφρ' ἐν Τρωσὶ μέγα φρονέοντες ὄρουσαν.
αὐτίκα δὲ σφήκεσσιν ἐοικότες ἐξεχέοντο
εἰνοδίοις, οὕς παῖδες ἐριδμαίνωσιν ἔθοντες,
αἰεὶ κερτομέοντες, ὁδῷ ἔπι οἰκί' ἔχοντας,
νηπίαχοι· ξυνὸν δὲ κακὸν πολέεσσι τιθεῖσι.
τοὺς δ' εἴ περ παρά τίς τε κιὼν ἄνθρωπος ὁδίτης
κινήσῃ ἀέκων, οἱ δ' ἄλκιμον ἦτορ ἔχοντες
πρόσσω πᾶς πέτεται καὶ ἀμύνει οἷσι τέκεσσι.
    (*Il.* 16.257–65)

Children by their taunting have readied these wasps to swarm in defense of their offspring even in response to the traveller's unintentional provocation. The traveller finds himself in the midst of the circumstances from which inevitable consequences follow: he is sure to disturb the wasps, and they are sure to attack.

---

[31]Orestes in Eur. *IT* 511–12 should also considered in this group, (iii S), even if also in group (i). Orestes fled Argos driven out by the Erinyes (and thus he fits in group [i]), but also he went first to Athens and then to Tauris responding to the oracles of Apollo (e.g., 77–94, 105, 929–31, 940–82). At 511–12 Iphigenia asks whether Orestes left Argos as an exile (φυγάς) or by some chance (τύχη). Orestes replies, "In fact I flee (φεύγω) in some way οὐχ ἑκών and ἑκών." It would be difficult not to associate οὐχ ἑκών with the fact that Orestes is hounded by the Erinyes; but how should one explain that he also flees ἑκών? Among plausible explanations is the hope of release from the madness of the Erinyes offered by the oracles of Apollo. On this view Orestes acts ἑκών while subject to the constraining influence of the oracles. Cf. the view of M. Platnauer, ed., *Euripides: Iphigenia in Tauris*, (Oxford, 1938) ad loc: Orestes flees ἑκών because the city did not send him into exile. In my view this explanation is another example of the tendency to interpret ἑκών group words along the lines of the FOV. See the Appendix to this chapter.

The unavoidable and constraining circumstances in which Sophocles' Iole finds herself are more personal, her beauty. According to Deianira, Iole's beauty precipitated Iole's enslavement and the destruction of her country:

τὸ κάλλος αὐτῆς τὸν βίον διώλεσεν,
καὶ γῆν πατρῴαν οὐχ ἑκοῦσα δύσμορος
ἔπερσε κἀδούλωσεν.
(Soph. *Tr.* 465–67)

The fact that the unavoidable and constraining circumstance which affects Iole is a physical characteristic, a natural endowment, intensifies her helplessness.[32] Compare too the old man in Euripides' *Ion* who gives in to his physical limitations, but not ἑκών:[33]

Κρ.   ἀλλὰ μὴ παρῇις κόπωι.
Πρ. οὔκουν ἑκών γε· τοῦ δ' ἄκοντος οὐ κρατῶ.
(Eur. *Ion* 745–46)

Frequently those who find themselves caught up in such circumstances are ἄκοντες as the FOV expects. But there are some who respond ἑκόντες. For example, there is Herodotus' tale of Amasis being crowned king, an event Herodotus says happened οὔ κως ἀεκούσιον:

ὁ δὲ ἐπείτε ἀπικόμενος κατελάμβανε τοὺς Αἰγυπτίους ταῦτα
μὴ ποιέειν, λέγοντος αὐτοῦ τῶν τις Αἰγυπτίων ὄπισθε στὰς
περιέθηκέ οἱ κυνέην καὶ περιτιθεὶς ἔφη ἐπὶ βασιληίῃ περι-
τιθέναι. καὶ τῷ οὔ κως ἀεκούσιον ἐγίνετο τὸ ποιεύμενον, ὡς
διεδείκνυε. ἐπείτε γὰρ ἐστήσαντό μιν βασιλέα τῶν
Αἰγυπτίων οἱ ἀπεστεῶτες, παρεσκευάζετο ὡς ἐλῶν ἐπὶ τὸν
Ἀπρίην.
(Hdt. 2.162.1–2)

While Amasis spoke to the Egyptians in an effort to put down a rebellion, a man standing near placed a helmet on Amasis' head and declared him king. The necessity of this passage is found in the very unavoidableness of the present circumstances in which Amasis found himself. Amasis is a "victim" of circum-

---

[32] In *NE* 3.5 Aristotle discusses things that are and are not "in our power" (ἐφ' ἡμῖν). The beauty and ugliness with which we are born, for example, are not in our power, whereas the beauty or ugliness that result from proper or improper care of our bodies are. Such things are οὐχ ἑκούσια but not necessarily thereby ἀκούσια. (There are some commentators who assume those things which Aristotle says are neither ἐφ' ἡμῖν nor ἑκούσια are thereby ἀκούσια. See ch. 4 n. 4.) Thus, these passages can be read in line with Aristotle's technical category of οὐχ ἑκούσια. But since ἄκων and οὐχ ἑκών are interchangeable in literature, they do not reflect his distinction. The stronger reading of the ODA View (to be discussed in ch. 5) seems more likely in these passages.

[33] 746 ἀπόντος Reiske; ἄκοντος Λ

stance but not ἀέκων. Likewise, the inexperienced youth of Athens who take up the war οὐκ ἀκουσίως, also respond positively to their circumstances:

> ὀλίγον τε ἐπενόουν οὐδὲν ἀμφότεροι, ἀλλ' ἔρρωντο ἐς τὸν
> πόλεμον οὐκ ἀπεικότως· ἀρχόμενοι γὰρ πάντες ὀξύτερον ἀν-
> τιλαμβάνονται, τότε δὲ καὶ νεότης πολλὴ μὲν οὖσα ἐν τῇ
> Πελοποννήσῳ, πολλὴ δ' ἐν ταῖς Ἀθήναις οὐκ ἀκουσίως ὑπὸ
> ἀπειρίας ἥπτετο τοῦ πολέμου, ἥ τε ἄλλη Ἑλλὰς ἅπασα
> μετέωρος ἦν ξυνιουσῶν τῶν πρώτων πόλεων.
> (Thuc. 2.8.1)

Generally, my impression of the victims in these examples is that they are truly struck by their circumstances or are suddenly and unavoidably caught up in them. All of a sudden something has already happened to the victim or all of a sudden the victim has already done something. The victim is frequently ἄκων but contrary to the expectations of the FOV, may be ἑκών.

Persons or characters who more actively engage the unavoidable and constraining circumstances with which they are confronted are best exemplified by those who make decisions while confronted with these circumstances. Even where the decisions or choices have the air of being the "only" possible course, these victims give the impression that they are active rather than that things are just happening to them.[34] These victims are more likely to have reasons for their actions or explanations. For example, in the *Iliad* (4.30–49), confronted with the unrelenting hostility of Hera and the prospect of acting with impunity in the future, Zeus allows Hera the destruction of Troy. Zeus is an unusual case in that he is both ἑκών and ἄκων: καὶ γὰρ ἐγὼ σοὶ δῶκα ἑκὼν ἀέκοντί γε θυμῷ (43).[35] The circumstances that confront Menelaus in his chariot race with Antilochus are more pressing and his action is accordingly a swift one:

> αἱ δ' ἠρώησαν ὀπίσσω
> Ἀτρεΐδεω· αὐτὸς γὰρ ἑκὼν μεθέηκεν ἐλαύνειν,
> μή πως συγκύρσειαν ὁδῷ ἔνι μώνυχες ἵπποι,
> δίφρους τ' ἀνστρέψειαν ἐϋπλεκέας, κατὰ δ' αὐτοὶ
> ἐν κονίῃσι πέσοιεν ἐπειγόμενοι περὶ νίκης.
> (*Il.* 23.433-37)

But the poet describes Menelaus as ἑκών when he slows down his mares, having decided to avoid a disastrous collision of men and horses. In the *Philoctetes* (1047-62), Odysseus, having declared his famous line, οὐ γὰρ

---

[34]This "only" is not to be taken in the strong sense of the only physical possibility, but in the weaker sense of the best course of action. Extreme alternatives, e.g., suicide, are rarely even considered and for all practical purposes are non-existent.

[35]Cf. Eur. *IT* 511-12 where Orestes says he flees οὐχ ἑκὼν ἑκών. See remarks above in n. 31.

τοιούτων δεῖ, τοιοῦτός εἰμ' ἐγώ, and his propensity for winning, announces that ἑκών he will give way to Philoctetes: νῦν δὲ σοὶ γ' ἑκὼν ἐκστήσομαι (1053). Dealing with Philoctetes is not worth the bother. Thus, in what is perhaps another ruse to drive Philoctetes into compliance through fear of another abandonment, Odysseus reckons that he and Teucer have enough skill to accomplish the task without Philoctetes since they have his bow.

Although overtly the FOV does not accommodate such passages, it may seem that a special case is emerging through this evidence, especially those passages where there is a strong contrast between acting on the basis of a decision and being a more passive victim of circumstances.[36] It may be that the agent who acts on a decision, even if it is made under compelling circumstances, regularly does so ἑκών. The emphasis on decision-making may exaggerate its presence and efficacy to the extent that the presence of necessitating circumstances is obscured, indeed, dismissed, so that the FOV can accommodate these passages as cases of acting ἑκών in the absence of ἀνάγκη.

In the Melian Dialogue (Thuc. 5.111.3) the Athenian speaks of those who can still see where they are being carried (ἐς οἷα φέρονται), i.e., the direction circumstances push them, falling ἑκόντες into irremediable disaster (ξυμφοραῖς ἀνηκέστοις ἑκόντας περιπεσεῖν). Greater shame belongs to those who were still able to "see ahead" (προύπτοις κινδύνοις / πολλοῖς προυρωμένοις) but act foolishly (μετὰ ἀνοίας) than to those who suffer by chance (τύχη). Attacking first when circumstances do not warrant attack but a defensive strategy also counts as taking on danger ἑκών in the following two passages from Thucydides. The first is his account of Brasidas' strategy at Megara, and the second his account of Nicias' strategy at Syracuse when he sent a personal letter to Athens describing their desperate situation:

> καλῶς δὲ ἐνόμιζον σφίσιν ἀμφότερα ἔχειν, ἅμα μὲν τὸ μὴ ἐπιχειρεῖν προτέρους μηδὲ μάχης καὶ κινδύνου ἑκόντας ἄρξαι, ἐπειδή γε ἐν φανερῷ ἔδειξαν ἑτοῖμοι ὄντες ἀμύνεσθαι, καὶ αὐτοῖς ὥσπερ ἀκονιτὶ τὴν νίκην δικαίως ἂν τίθεσθαι, ἐν τῷ αὐτῷ δὲ καὶ πρὸς τοὺς Μεγαρέας ὀρθῶς ξυμβαίνειν·
> (Thuc. 4.73.2)

> ὁ δὲ τὰ κατὰ τὸ στρατόπεδον διὰ φυλακῆς μᾶλλον ἤδη ἔχων ἢ δι' ἑκουσίων κινδύνων ἐπεμέλετο.
> (Thuc. 7.8.3)

---

[36]In the section which assesses the FOV at the end of this chapter I will consider other examples which could be construed as special cases within the FOV, but I address this particular case here in order to introduce further passages which count against the FOV.

In all these passages there is a contrast between passively enduring circumstances and more actively engaging them while there is still time to make choices, influence events, and avert a tide of inevitability.[37]

Nonetheless, even if some passages are rescued for the FOV in this way, there are agents who act on decisions but do so ἄκοντες. For example, Zeus, in the passage already discussed (*Il*.4.37–49), acts ἑκών but also ἀέκοντί γε θυμῷ when he grants Hera her request. In the Melian Dialogue, the Melians warn the Athenians of those who when confronted with the facts of Athenian behavior towards Melos will decide it best to make war on Athens albeit ἄκοντες:

> ὅσοι γὰρ νῦν μηδετέροις ξυμμαχοῦσι, πῶς οὐ πολεμώσεσθε αὐτοὺς, ὅταν ἐς τάδε βλέψαντες ἡγήσωνταί ποτε ὑμᾶς καὶ ἐπὶ σφᾶς ἥξειν; κἂν τούτῳ τί ἄλλο ἢ τοὺς μὲν ὑπάρχοντας πολεμίους μεγαλύνετε, τοὺς δὲ μηδὲ μελλήσαντας γενέσθαι ἄκοντας ἐπάγεσθε;
> (Thuc. 5.98)

In Book 2, the Athenians led by Phormio sail into narrow waters ἄκοντες when provoked by circumstances in order to protect Naupactus:[38]

> ὁ δέ, ὅπερ ἐκεῖνοι προσεδέχοντο, φοβηθεὶς περὶ τῷ χωρίῳ ἐρήμῳ ὄντι, ὡς ἑώρα ἀναγομένους αὐτούς, ἄκων καὶ κατὰ σπουδὴν ἐμβιβάσας ἔπλει παρὰ τὴν γῆν·
> (Thuc. 2.90.3)

In *Iliad* Book 11, Ajax, πόλλ' ἀέκων, retreats from battle because of his fear for the ships and presumably a decision to defend them:

> ὣς Αἴας τότ' ἀπὸ Τρώων τετιημένος ἦτορ
> ἤϊε πόλλ' ἀέκων· περὶ γὰρ δίε νηυσὶν Ἀχαιῶν.
> (*Il*. 11.556–57)

Finally, in *Oedipus Rex*, Creon, comparing his life as it is to what it would be like if he were king, supposes he would do many things ἄκων:

> νῦν μὲν γὰρ ἐκ σοῦ πάντ' ἄνευ φόβου φέρω,
> εἰ δ' αὐτὸς ἦρχον, πολλὰ κἂν ἄκων ἔδρων.
> (Soph. *OR* 590–91)

---

[37] Compare these first-strike passages in which the immediate situation does not emphasize the absence of force with Thuc. 6.36.3–4 where it is clear that the absence of force is relevant.

[38] Cf. Thuc. 2.90.1 where the Athenians are seen as ἄκοντες and subject to the compelling circumstances created by the Peloponnesians.

Here too at least some of these things would be the results of decisions, prudential decisions based on fear of unwanted consequences, but decisions nonetheless.

These passages show an agent can act ἑκών or ἄκων when acting on the basis of decisions wrought by a confrontation with compelling circumstances. Actions based on an agent's decision are not automatically ἑκούσιοι.

Summary

The most important inference to be drawn from a consideration of passages where ἑκών group words are associated with βία and ἀνάγκη is that the function of ἑκών group words is not exhausted by the ascription or denial of βία or ἀνάγκη. Individuals or their actions are described with ἑκών group words under circumstances of βία and ἀνάγκη. However, the evidence does not sustain the FOV claim of a strong relationship between ἑκών group words and βία and ἀνάγκη such that a person is automatically ἄκων under circumstances of βία or ἀνάγκη or automatically ἑκών if these circumstances are absent. It is neither pleonastic to say that a victim of βία or ἀνάγκη is ἄκων, nor does the fact that circumstances of βία or ἀνάγκη pertain exclude a person or character from being ἑκών. Because a victim of force and necessity may be ἑκών or ἄκων we can infer that ἑκών group words do something other than reflect the circumstances at hand. Moreover, it cannot be determined solely on the basis of what external or observable circumstances pertain whether a person is ἑκών or ἄκων. The Functional Opposite View is not adequate to account for the use of these words. But any adequate view must still account for the FOV's observation that ἑκών group words appear frequently when circumstances of βία or ἀνάγκη pertain.

The Functional Opposite View: an assessment

The Functional Opposite View as defined in this chapter was fashioned to reflect a fundamental feature of the majority of passages containing ἑκών group words: these words appear in contexts in which they are related to some form of ἀνάγκη, necessity, and what constitutes necessity in these passages can be categorized into three basic types. The FOV is a strong view about the relationship between the ἑκών group words and ἀνάγκη. It holds that an agent is ἄκων (or his act ἀκούσιος) when subject to ἀνάγκη but ἑκών (or his act ἑκούσιος) in the absence of ἀνάγκη. Acting ἑκών functions as the opposite of acting under necessity. When negative forms describe agents subject to ἀνάγκη, or positive forms describe agents in the absence of ἀνάγκη, it is to be understood as merely pleonastic construction. Those passages which do not meet these expectations have been discussed as exceptions which show the inadequacy of the FOV to explain the use of ἑκών group words.

The task ahead is to discover how the exceptions to the FOV can be explained while preserving the fundamental observation on which the FOV is based, that is, there is some relationship between ἀνάγκη and ἑκών group words. One route would preserve the FOV and make room for the apparent exceptions by explaining them as rhetorical uses, that is exaggerations still tied to the FOV, technical uses, developments within the FOV, or even that the FOV is itself a development from some earlier usage. This is not the procedure I will pursue in the remainder of this book, but before taking a different position I will briefly pursue this approach and my objections to it.

Consider the following typical exceptions to the FOV (set out under ἀνάγκη [i]) in which the agents are ἑκόντες though subject to threatened force: Cassandra (Aesch. *Ag.* 1069–71), Telemachus (*Od.* 3.205–17/#2), Philoctetes (Soph. *Ph.* 981–88), the Plataeans (Thuc. 3.58.3, 3.52.2–3), and Polyxena (Eur. *Hec.* 542–52). An argument could be made that these are special cases based on the reliable core of the FOV, the totally passive victim of actual force who is regularly ἄκων. The first two could simply be rhetorical exaggerations. Ordinarily, the FOV counts the force exerted by the threat of force as well as certain social practices and the constraint exerted by circumstances as forms of ἀνάγκη all of which must be absent in order for an agent to be ἑκών. But in these cases, the most severe form of ἀνάγκη, actual force, is privileged and exaggerated so as to stand in for the absence of all ἀνάγκη. If this strategy is followed, one could perhaps deal even with the tortured slaves (Gorg. B.11a.11DK) who are described as ἑκόντες accusing their master. Exaggeration of this magnitude may seem to go well beyond any rhetorical stretching of the FOV and appear to simply undermine it. But perhaps the situation is so extreme that the description is really some sort of cruel or ironic joke.

The other three passages could be explained in the same way, but the passages from the *Philoctetes* and Thucydides suggest an even finer development. While allowing the FOV to remain fundamentally untouched, these passages may be construed as evidence for the development (perhaps specifically a 5th century development) of a technical or even legal usage. Both passages are concerned with meeting technical requirements: in Thucydides, the concern is with satisfying the terms of a future treaty; and at some level Odysseus is concerned to meet the requirements of an oracle. The technical requirement is that the act take place without actual force, and this is sufficient for the act to count as ἑκούσιος. [39]

---

[39]Cf. my discussion of the first-strike and surrender passages in Thucydides (6.36.3–4 and 3.52.2–3/3.58.3 respectively), pp. 49–50 which I allowed as an example of strong opposition between acting ἑκών and acting under force in the

This way of construing the evidence would also be congenial to those passages (discussed earlier under ἀνάγκη [iii]) which suggest that acting on the basis of a decision, however subject an agent may be to some form of ἀνάγκη, renders the agent ἑκών. Not all agents who act on the basis of a decision are ἑκόντες, but this may only mean that this is a special sense or perhaps a sense not fully developed and need not apply in all cases of decision-making. Where decision-making is not so exaggerated a feature of the situation that it in effect denies the presence of compelling circumstances, we would expect, in accordance with the FOV, an agent to be ἄκων. Only in a more limited number of cases would decision-making be treated as having such strong implications that all constraint is in effect denied (or ignored) and the agent considered ἑκών.

Alternatively, one might want to consider whether originally it was the absence of actual force alone that rendered an agent ἄκων with the other sorts of ἀνάγκη developing later. Since from as far back as the Homeric texts there are examples of forms of ἀνάγκη besides actual force related to ἑκών group words, this may not be an especially appealing view. But the Homeric texts could be seen as a *terminus ante quem* so that other types of ἀνάγκη had already been absorbed.[40]

Readers may be disappointed that this is not the route I shall be taking, if even some of these preliminary remarks look promising. But in my view this is a route frequently travelled but fraught with difficulties. My objections begin with qualms about the arbitrariness of supposing one use or sense fundamental and another rhetorical or technical, since arguments could be made to turn upside down which use or sense is fundamental and which is somehow special.

Even more problematic is that such an approach would produce a variety of senses for ἑκών group words and the sort of attendant list of translations so diverse that one ought to wonder if we really understand the word at all.[41] This of course, is exactly the problem which prompted this study in the first place. What I have discussed as exceptions to the FOV, and the further circumstances to be discussed in the next chapter, even if tolerated by that view as special cases or developments, come to have a life of their own. For example, even if in certain passages acting ἑκών in the sense of acting on the basis of a decision, developed from exaggerating decision-making so that it came to count as an absence of ἀνάγκη (what it means according to the FOV to be ἑκών) in

---

absence of actual force. By privileging the role of actual force in these passages, they too could be seen as moving in this technical direction.

[40]On either of these views, the remainder of the passages to be discussed in the next chapter, those which are not easily categorized as involving one or another type of ἀνάγκη, e.g., cases involving ignorance and error, would be reconciled as further special senses or exaggerations of the basic view for rhetorical effect.

[41]Cf. my remarks on Maschke, *Willenslehre*, in the Appendix to this chapter.

these passages it seems that the agent is ἑκών not because ἀνάγκη is denied, but because the agent acted with deliberation. To ἑκών in the sense of "not compelled" or "voluntarily" we can add "deliberately." Other exceptions to the FOV, for example, an agent who is ἑκών though constrained by an order or the practice of hospitality (ξενία), could be treated in a similar way: ἑκών is an exaggeration suggesting the agent acts as though not subject to the constraint of the order or social practice, i.e., he acts "of his own accord" or "according to his desire" or "willingly." With this approach we are on our way to a dictionary list of the many senses of ἑκών group words.[42]

My development of the FOV on the basis of the types of ἀνάγκη related to ἑκών group words might cause some to be more satisfied with this sort of outcome than they would be if they had never heard of the FOV. Having the FOV as a basis from which certain special or rhetorical uses could develop may seem to give such offshoots some respectability. Even a diverse set of senses for a single group of words developing from some common core seems more acceptable than simply gathering different senses with no tie to explain the diversity. Nonetheless, I am no more satisfied with the sense list approach to this word group even in conjunction with an underlying and unifying view. Again, an unappealing arbitrariness arises in determining which uses should be construed as following the pattern of the FOV directly and which should be construed as special cases. One can further object that the sense list approach employs the larger contexts too generously in detecting special or rhetorical uses, and then reads into ἑκών group words the meanings evoked by the larger contexts. Take for example, the suggestion that an agent is ἑκών, though subject to ἀνάγκη, because of an exaggerated view of decision-making. One could argue that decision-making is a feature of the larger context implanted in the difficult ἑκών as though this word were some sort of receptacle to be filled differently from context to context.

Finally, what is for me perhaps the most compelling reason to reject an approach which relies on special senses which develop from the central meaning of the FOV, is that it does not take seriously enough exceptions to the FOV. Rather than try to explain exceptions as special cases one could reject the FOV and begin to look for an explanation that preserves the observation on which it is based, the frequency with which ἑκών group words are related to circumstances of ἀνάγκη, but does not treat ἑκών group words as synonymous with the presence or absence of ἀνάγκη. In fact, the special explanations themselves begin to focus our attention on the ἑκών group words in a different way. It is part of these explanations that the agent's being ἑκών does not mean simply that ἀνάγκη is absent. Being ἑκών no longer says something about what is

---

[42]Of course, in making these comments I am making no claim about the way in which the variety of senses and translations of ἑκών group words actually did come about.

external to the agent, but something internal, e.g., the agent has made a decision or acts in accord with his own desire. This points to a feature of the FOV that even intuitively speaks against it: it equates what goes on within an individual with what goes on outside the individual as though a statement of the latter is sufficient for the former.

Undoubtedly, there is a regularity with which victims of ἀνάγκη are ἄκοντες. But this regularity need not be accounted for as it is by the FOV. Totally passive victims of actual force tend to be described as ἄκόντες and persons or characters can be ἑκόντες in the absence of actual βία even when the threat of βία remains. However, that a person or character can be ἑκών or ἄκων under all the types of ἀνάγκη which appear when ἑκών group words are used, suggests it is not the presence or absence of ἀνάγκη, even actual βία, that determines the designation ἑκών or ἄκων. We can continue to wonder what it is about passive victims of actual force and victims of other types of ἀνάγκη that so frequently renders them ἄκοντες without supposing this designation depends exclusively on the presence of these external circumstances.

As an alternative to the FOV and what I have called the sense list approach, I would like to suggest a new view for explaining ἑκών group words, the Occasions for Describing Attitude View (ODA View). The circumstances of ἀνάγκη set out in these opening chapters (and other related circumstances to be discussed in the next chapter) are the special occasions for designating a person (or his act) ἑκών or ἄκων (or his act, ἑκούσιος or ἀκούσιος). This view accommodates ἑκών group words by maintaining a persistent account of their meaning under a limited variety of related circumstances which occasion their use but are not simply substitutes for them. The ODA View's account of the use of ἑκών group words will be taken up in Chapter 5.

The Functional Opposite View: Appendix

The following is a sampling of the kinds of discussions, comments, or translations which strike me as relying on the fundamental principle of the view I call the Functional Opposite View. Of course, I am in no way claiming that any of the examples relies on an articulated version of that view. In fact it has seemed to me that in general there has been a lack of awareness that any interpretative view rather than a straightforward rendering of ἑκών group words is even involved in discussions, comments, or translations of these words.

For a view which can be seen to rely on the fundamental principle of the view I dub the FOV, see e.g., Maschke, *Willenslehre*, on ἑκών and ἄκων. Since the scope of his work is enormous, I can only indicate here how an analysis of Maschke's discussion reveals the fundamental principle of the FOV. His view of the first stage in the development of the role of will in Greek law relies on the kind of relationship based on opposition and interchangeability between ἑκών group words and compulsion that I have dubbed the FOV. In his chapter on Ionic epic, Maschke explains "Will" is of two varieties, and it is with ἐθέλειν (which comes from the θυμός rather than the φρένες) that ἑκών and ἄκων are associated, never with βούλεσθαι (pp. 2–4). In an extraordinary manipulation of equations and negations of the Greek words on which he focuses and a variety of German words he assumes can be substituted for them, Maschke explains: "Daraus ergibt sich für die Negation (that is of ἐθέλειν) die Bedeutung ungern, widerwillig, widerstrebend, *contre coeur* und zwar auch in Beziehung auf das, was wir technisch als Willensmängel bezeichen, und dementsprechend für die Positive die Umkehrung in gern d.h. freiwillig, so dass ἐθέλειν = ἑκών und die Negation = ἄκων gesetzt wird" (pp. 3–4). From these equations he goes on to explain ἐθέλειν (=ἑκών) is opposed to acting in a compelling situation (holding (as I do that there is much that counts as compelling, e.g., force, a threat, an order, natural phenomena, passion such as sudden anger or terror [pp. 4ff.]): "Hiernach steht ἐθέλειν also im Gegensatz zum Handeln in einer Zwangslage: die Ananke schliesst das Wollen aus" (p. 4). In fact, lack of will (οὐκ ἐθέλειν = ἀέκων) and compulsion are spoken of as though interchangeable because compulsion completely excludes will and also intention. "Schon das ἐθέλειν ist ausgeschlossen durch den Affekt, der zu Taten hinreisst, die man später bereut; das οὐκ ἐθέλειν ist = ἀέκων, das Gegenteil = ἑκών. Willensmängel wie Gewalt, Betrug, Zorn schleissen die Freiwilligheit und damit auch die Absicht aus" (p. 9). For Maschke this explains why, in the early stages of Greek law, there is no difference in the legal consequences for premeditated murder and unpremediated murder, or for different types of unpremediated murder, negligent and accidental. Maschke's analysis of ἑκών group words continues by examining chronologically and through a number of authors, examples which reflect the early view, or variations of it, and development away from it. The view itself is not doubted, though even in his discussion of epic, he points out uses of the pairs ἐθέλειν = ἑκών and οὐκ ἐθέλειν = ἀέκων which differ from his basic conception: "Wenn wir so die Fälle kennen gelernt haben, in denen das ἐθέλειν durch Willensmängel ausgeschlossen und die Handlung deshalb ἄκων wird, so ist nur noch in Kürze auf einige Anwendungen des Worts hinzuweisen, in denen der Keim zu seiner späteren technischen Verwendung sich erkennen lässt als Bezeichnung für die gewollte im Gegensatz zur ungewollten Tat" (p. 6). Like the approach I rejected at the end of ch. 2, Maschke's approach is to handle passages which pose difficulty for his view or seem to be exceptions, as the germ of later development. He does not seem to suspect that there might be something fundamentally wrong with the interpretation from which these developments are said to arise.

The Functional Opposite View: Appendix

For the treatment of combinations of ἄκων and βία or ἀνάγκη as mere pleonasm see e.g.: Leaf, *Iliad*, on βίη ἀέκοντος (*Il.* 1.430); Richardson, *Hymn to Demeter*, on ἀέκουσαν ἀνάγκη (*HDem.* 72) and βίη δ' ἀέκουσαν ἀνάγκη (*HDem.* 124), and Richardson, *Hymn to Demeter*, and Allen, Halliday, & Sikes, *Homeric Hymns*, on ἄκουσαν δὲ βίη (*HDem.* 413); and Jebb's (*Oed. Col.*) translation of Soph. *OC* 935 βίᾳ τε κοὐχ ἑκών: "by no free choice." Pleonasm is also seen by Jebb, *Ph.*, and Kamerbeek, *Ph. Com.*, in the phrase ἑκὼν αὐτός (Soph. *Ph.* 1332): Jebb says it is like "of thy *own* free will." For βία treated as interchangeable with ἄκων, see e.g.: Classen and Steup, *Thucydides* (Berlin, 1919), on Thuc. 1.43.3: βίᾳ ἡμῶν, "ein verstärktes ἀκόντων ἡμῶν." See also Griffith's (*Com. PrB*) reading of πρὸς βίαν (Aesch. *PrB* 672), "in violation of his (Inachus') will" (to which, cf. Griffith on *PrB* 771 where he recognizes that a voluntary act or decision can still be done ἄκων), and Jebb's translation of ἄκουσαν at Soph. *OC* 827 and ἄκοντα Soph. *Ph.* 618: "by force." In relation to the modified FOV's inclusion of ignorance and error (see ch. 3 pp. 79–85), cf. translations mentioned in the Introduction, n. 2.

For interpretations of ἄκων as virtually interchangeable with ἀνάγκη, see, e.g., Kamerbeek on Soph. *Ph.* 987: "the second (ἄκων) means 'forced by necessity'"; Jebb on Soph. *Ph.* 305–6, πολλὰ γὰρ κτλ. (τάχ' οὖν τις ἄκων ἔσχε· πολλὰ γὰρ τάδε/ἐν τῷ μακρῷ γένοιτ' ἂν ἀνθρώπων χρόνῳ): "for such things (viz., such necessities as ἄκων implies) are likely to occur often," and Wecklein, *The Prometheus Bound*, 2d ed., trans. F.D. Allen (Munich, 1878; New York, 1981), on *PrB* 671, ἄκουσαν ἄκων· ἀλλ' ἐπηνάγκαζέ νιν: "ἀλλ' ἐπηνάγκαζέ refers to the notion contained in ἄκων."

The positive form, ἑκών, is commonly translated without special comment as "willingly," "of one's free will," "by choice," "on purpose," "voluntarily" etc. As I have already said in the Introduction, these are not themselves straightforward concepts; and in the absence of discussion about the terms, it is not safe to be too confident about any conjectures concerning the assumptions that underlie them. But in general, although commentators and translators do not usually explain their renderings of positive forms, often it seems that these renderings of the positive form are understood as ruling out what is understood in the negative form, typically, force or necessity. Sometimes translations or statements of meaning show this view clearly. Rogers, *Aristophanes*, e.g., translates ἑκών at *Wasps* 1422 "without compulsion"; and in studies of the Socratic paradox that "no one does wrong ἑκών," O'Brien's interpretation of ἑκών (*Paradoxes*, 218 n. 15) is not unusual, however distinctive his overall treatment of the paradoxes. Distinguishing an earlier and a later Platonic view, he says for the earlier view of the *Protagoras*, "ἑκών means acting without constraint." Sometimes context leads to more specific interpretations of the positive form, ἑκών; e.g., Jebb's (*Oed. Tyr.*) note on Soph. *OT* 1229–30:

"both these horrors were due to conscious acts (ἑκόντα), as distinguished from those acts in which Oedipus and Jocasta had become involved without their knowledge (ἄκοντα)."

Schreckenberg's view on the relationship between ἀνάγκη and ἑκών group words is not clear. See, for instance, *Ananke*, 29–30, 39. In his review (*Mnemos*. 1967), Vos criticizes Schreckenberg's identification of ἀνάγκη and δεσμός arguing that ἀνάγκη and οὐχ ἑκών, ἀέκων, and οὐκ ἐθέλων are semantically identical, but clearly ἀέκων does not equal δεσμός. Although it is typical for Schreckenberg to treat pairings like ἀνάγκη and οὐχ ἑκών as semantically identical, his remarks are not as clear-cut as Vos implies by his argument. (Perhaps it is Vos who thinks ἀνάγκη and οὐχ ἑκών are semantically identical?). The general outline of the FOV is evident in A. Adkin's discussion of ἑκών in Poseidon's threat in *Il*. 13.234 in *Merit and Responsibility* (Oxford, 1960), 11: ἑκών is taken as excluding what happens ἄκων, and ἄκων is taken "in the sense of 'under compulsion,' at all events when that compulsion is exercised by other human beings." Cf. Fraenkel's comment (*Aeschylus: Agamemnon*, vol. 3 [Oxford, 1950]) on *Ag*. 1071: "ἑκοῦσ'", placed emphatically at the beginning, implies 'before she has you forcibly dragged into the house.'" I also want to stress that the FOV is not Aristotle's view, although sometimes his view may seem to be reduced to it: see e.g., Vernant, "Intimations," 34. I discuss differences between Aristotle and the FOV in Chapter 4.

3. Other Occasions

The ἑκών group words discussed so far have been those which appear when persons or characters are confronted with a form of ἀνάγκη. Even where the ἀνάγκη is not further specified as βία or a social practice for example, external circumstances that are compelling bear on those described by ἑκών group words. The remainder of the passages containing ἑκών group words can be sorted into four types: those in which some error is committed, harm or wrong is done, third-party cases, i.e., those in which a person other than the doer or receiver of the action under consideration is described by the ἑκών group word, and finally, passages in which some general remark is made about τὸ ἑκούσιον or τὸ ἀκούσιον.[1]

Agents who err

Although there is no explicit ἀνάγκη vocabulary from which to argue these cases, those passages in which error, including error due to ignorance, is linked to ἑκών group words can be understood as related to the kind of necessity found in ἀνάγκη (iii) passages. Agents who err are also laboring under circumstances which are in some sense compelling.[2] Any action is circumscribed by the facts

---

[1]The Index Locorum ordinarily gives only one type of occasioning circumstance for each passage. But there are cases where several types of occassioning circumstances may pertain to one event. E.g., Deianira's act in *Trachiniae*, falls under error, supernatural influence (see 153ff. on the oracle concerning Heracles' death), and the power of love, a form of βία (see the Ode to Cypris *Trach*. 497–530); and some passages where an ἄκων agent errs have been grouped elsewhere under ἀνάγκη (iii) Supernatural (S) because of the interference of the gods or the supernatural in bringing about the agent's error: Eur. *Hipp*. 1431–36 where Artemis speaks to Theseus about the death of Hippolytus (ἄκων γὰρ ὤλεσάς νιν; ἀνθρώποισι δὲ θεῶν διδόντων εἰκὸς ἐξαμαρτάνειν); and Soph. *OC* 960–99/#1,2,4, where Oedipus discusses the infamous acts which he committed ἄκων.

[2]It is easier to see that one person's or character's error can provide another's ἀνάγκη. An agent can find himself in circumstances generated by the error of another. For example, in Eur. *Hipp*., Phaedra, who (688–94) counts herself among the victims (ἄκοντας φίλους) of those she curses, the nurse and others who fail to do good (μὴ καλῶς εὐεργετεῖν), and who (1305) is described as perishing οὐχ ἑκοῦσα by the machinations (μηχαναῖς) of her nurse, refers to the nurse's disclosure of her secret as her "errors" (σὰς ἁμαρτίας). Phaedra is a victim of the circumstances created by her nurse's error and her understanding of these circumstances is that certain events will follow inevitably from the nurse's action. Hippolytus, telling Theseus and old Pittheus of her passion, will fill the

that obtain at the time of the action. This awareness is the basis of ἀνάγκη (iii). Generally, as agents we interact with these circumstances. However, if the agent is ignorant of some pertinent fact of the circumstances within which he acts or miscalculates or in some other way, not clearly due to ignorance or miscalculation, fails to accomplish what he intends, there is a sense in which the circumstances seem to take over and themselves compel something to happen.[3] In this way error can be considered a relative of ἀνάγκη.

Consider, for example, two cases of error due to ignorance of some pertinent fact. In Sophocles' *Trachiniae*, when Deianira—who is three times described as acting ἄκουσα (τοῖς σφαλεῖσι μὴ 'ξ ἑκουσίας [727-28]; ἄκουσα...ἔρξειεν τάδε [935]; and ἥμαρτεν οὐχ ἑκουσία [1123])—gives Heracles the "love potion," she is ignorant that the drug is actually a poison.[4] But Deianira's action is controlled by this fact, and certain inevitabilities flow from the fact that the potion was a poison.[5] Similarly, in Aristophanes' *Wasps* (990-92 and 999-1002), Philocleon, ignorant of which voting urn is designated to hold ballots for conviction and deceived into misplacing his ballot, acquits the canine defendant whom he intended to convict (κἀπολέλυκεν οὐχ ἑκών [992], and ἄκων γὰρ αὔτ' ἔδρασα [1002]).

In these cases where agents err (either by doing something other than what they intended because of ignorance of circumstantial detail, miscalculation, or by failing to accomplish what they set out to do) they regularly do so ἄκοντες. The FOV then can be emended to include error as a relative of ἀνάγκη in

---

whole land with shameful stories about her. Whether or not Phaedra has actually misjudged Hippolytus is not important; what is, is that she deems herself confronted with compelling circumstances that require action from her: ἀλλὰ δεῖ με δὴ καινῶν λόγων (688).

[3] Passages which could be construed as cases of miscalculation are the poet who failed to win the love of a παῖς (Theog. 1377-80: ἀέκων τῆς σῆς φιλότητος ἁμαρτών); and a soldier who set fire to a woods (Thuc. 4.30: ἐμπρήσαντός τινος κατὰ μικρὸν τῆς ὕλης ἄκοντος καὶ ἀπὸ τούτου πνεύματος ἐπιγενομένου τὸ πολὺ αὐτῆς ἔλαθε κατακαυθέν). The last case may not be a case of error due to miscalculation but rather what Aristotle calls; ἀτύχημα: it was beyond the powers of the agent to predict what actually happened.

[4] At 582ff., after Deianira has told the Chorus about the "gift" she has sent Heracles, she talks about daring κακά. But it is clear that it is the use of charms at all and their power to restore to her the love of Heracles that concerns her, not the evil of poisoning. At 672ff. Deianira explains how she has learned too late of the deception of the centaur.

[5] Cf. the agent victim of βία described in ch. 2, pp. 38-52 passim.

recognition of this regularity with which an error is done ἄκων.⁶ Though the number of examples of error is limited, I would liken this association to the strong association between being ἄκων and being a passive victim of actual force.⁷ For the FOV, making a mistake is something one does because of compelling circumstances; without such circumstances, the utter irrationality of erring precludes occurrence. What it is to be ἄκων then would be exhausted by the presence of circumstances of ἀνάγκη or circumstances in which agents err. Thus, in the case of mistaken action, we expect what we find: a regular association between acting ἄκων and erring. Moreover, the case of Euripides' *Hypsipyle* may provide an example of acting ἑκών in strong opposition with erring, another pattern on which the FOV relies:

[εἶπ]ὲ τῇδε συμφορὰν τέκνου,
παρὼν γὰ[ρ οἶσ]θα· φησὶ δ' ἥδ' ἑκουσίως
κτανεῖν μ[ε π]αῖδα κἀπιβουλεῦσαι δόμοις.
(Eur. *Hyps*. 60.34–36 Bond)

In this fragment of Euripides' play, Hypsipyle tells Amphiarius that Eurydice says she, Hypsipyle, ἑκουσίως killed Eurydice's child as part of a plot against the house of Lycurgus. The circumstances of the child's death, from what we can recover from the fragments, are that Hypsipyle set the child down in a grove while she led Amphiarius to a spring where he could get water needed for a sacrifice. A serpent (δράκων) which guarded the spring killed the child.

It is possible that Hypsipyle knew nothing of the serpent. However, she had been nurse to Opheltes long enough to offer her affection for him as evidence against Eurydice's accusations.⁸ Thus, though Hypsipyle is not a native, she is not newly arrived and can be expected to have known about something as prodigious as the local δράκων. Moreover, although scholars differ about whether or not Fr. 18 is the speech of a messenger or of Hypsipyle, the passage does seem to describe the habits of the creature and the reaction of the shepherds to it. This too suggests the δράκων was a phenomenon known to the community.

---

⁶Although I allow this modification of the FOV, it does not require the variety of senses and corresponding translations tolerated by the sense list approach discussed at the end of ch. 2.

⁷What makes the FOV attractive as an account of ἑκών group words is the regularity with which ἄκων etc. is conjoined with ἀνάγκη and ἑκών etc. opposed to it. The FOV is weakened, however, by its generous view of what counts as ἀνάγκη. We will see that this weakness is avoided in the negative account of τὸ ἑκούσιον offered by Aristotle where the criteria for τὸ ἀκούσιον are limited to superior actual force and ignorance of relevant circumstances accompanied by pain or regret.

⁸See *Euripides' Hypsipyla*, ed. G.W. Bond (Oxford, 1963), Fr. 60.

Since it is likely that Hypsipyle knew of the δράκων, her error was not ignorance of this important detail, but probably some degree of carelessness or miscalculation. The degree and extent of her carelessness in leaving the child unattended, even though she and Amphiarius were close enough to see the child (Fr. 60.75ff.), would be heightened if Fr.18 was spoken by Hypsipyle as part of an earlier dialogue with Amphiarius when she agrees to lead him to the spring.[9] Thus, even though the passage in which ἑκουσίως appears does not directly disjoin acting ἑκουσίως and acting in error, the details of the play suggest that there may be a disjunction between acting ἑκών and acting in error.[10]

There are also five passages in which an agent is ἑκών when the verb is a form of ἁμαρτάνειν, "to err" or "miss the mark." Thus, the question must be asked whether these passages count against the FOV in conjoining rather than opposing acting ἑκών with error. In what follows I will argue that these passages do not offer evidence against the regularity with which error is conjoined with acting ἄκων, or in strong opposition to acting ἑκών. For in these cases the agent misses the mark since he fails to perform according to accepted or expected social norms; but he does not act out of miscalculation or ignorance or fail to do what he intends. What the agents do in these passages may well be the sorts of things that ordinarily do happen only under the workings of ἀνάγκη or when agents err. But it is not true of the particular acts in these passages that personal error disrupted action that was meant to be in accord with accepted or expected behavior. Since what is normally an error is not an error in these particular circumstances, these passages are better understood as cases of acting ἑκών in opposition to acting in error, a usage which reflects one of the typical patterns on which the FOV is based, acting ἑκών in opposition to acting under ἀνάγκη.

Ἡμάρτανε in *Iliad* 10.369–75 is an instance of the so-called "original" meaning of ἁμαρτάνειν, "to miss," found frequently in Homer. As Bremer writes, "the battlefield in the *Iliad* provides an admirable background for numerous cases of hitting and missing: τυγχάνειν and ἁμαρτάνειν."[11] But in all the hitting and missing, this is the only case where someone misses ἑκών (Ἦ ῥα, καὶ ἔγχος ἀφῆκεν, ἑκὼν δ' ἡμάρτανε φωτός). The sense of the passage makes it very clear that Diomedes' plan was not to kill Dolon but to get him to

---

[9] See Bond, *Hyps.*, p. 98, for conjectures about who speaks these lines and when.

[10] Some form of ἐξαμαρτάνειν is conjectured to appear in Fr. 22 which Bond, *Hyps.*, places just before Fr. 60, in which ἑκουσίως appears. However, the passage is so fragmentary it can not be determined who is speaking and how the passage might fit in with what Hypsipyle says in Fr. 60.

[11] J.M. Bremer, *Hamartia: Tragic Error in the 'Poetics' of Aristotle and in Greek Tragedy*, (Amsterdam, 1969), 30. See his n. 23 for a list of the instances in Homer where this meaning obtains.

stop running away. To bring this about, however, Diomedes used his spear in a fashion that was not in accord with the usual, expected practice of spear throwing, viz., to strike one's intended target. Thus, although Diomedes did not make a mistake by failing to hit Dolon, he did nonetheless do something that ordinarily is a mistake. The FOV then, could interpret the expression, "ἑκών he missed the man" (ἑκὼν ἡμάρτανε φωτός), as an oxymoron: there was no error, i.e., Diomedes acted ἑκών, but what he did is the sort of thing that ordinarily is an error (ἡμάρτανε). It may be that the Diomedes' unusual use of his spear, which constitutes a breach of expected behavior, prompts the use of ἑκών beyond any poetic interest in the oxymoron. Since something is happening that ordinarily happens only when ἀνάγκη or error compels, there seems to be a special interest in marking the event with ἑκών and thereby emphatically denying any ἀνάγκη or error.[12]

This interest in marking and emphatically denying that something which usually takes place under ἀνάγκη or error has occurred in this way, can also be seen in a passage from Herodotus (4.43.7). Herodotus tells us he knows the name of a eunuch who escaped with a great deal of money after the death of his master, but Herodotus "ἑκών forgets" the name.

> τούτου δὲ τοῦ Σατάσπεος εὐνοῦχος ἀπέδρη ἐς Σάμον, ἐπείτε ἐπύθετο τάχιστα τὸν δεσπότεα τετελευτηκότα, ἔχων χρήματα μεγάλα, τὰ Σάμιος ἀνὴρ κατέσχε, τοῦ ἐπιστάμενος τὸ οὔνομα ἑκὼν ἐπιλήθομαι.
>
> (Hdt. 4.43.7)

Ordinarily, "forgetting" is a kind of error, and this prompts Herodotus to mark his "lapse" with ἑκών and deny error. Herodotus knows another name which he declines to mention at 1.52; but there he uses the verb ἐπιμνήσομαι: τοῦ ἐπιστάμενος τὸ οὔνομα οὐκ ἐπιμνήσομαι. "Revealing" or "mentioning" is not ordinarily something that happens only by necessity or error. Thus, at 1.52 Herodotus is not prompted to mark his action by ἑκών.

A passage from the *Knights* (1119–30) in which Demos, defending itself against the charge of the Chorus that its mind (νοῦς) is "out of town," says, "ἑκών I played the fool in these matters" (ἐγὼ δ' ἑκὼν ταῦτ' ἠλιθιάζω), should be understood along the same lines as the passage from Herodotus (4.43.7) just discussed. Acting foolishly is, like forgetting, the sort of behavior that ordinarily is due to error or is the outcome of some form of ἀνάγκη, but not indulged in otherwise.

---

[12] A similar explanation may lurk beneath other uses of ἑκών in strong opposition to ἀνάγκη where there is a question of why someone bothers to deny ἀνάγκη.

Consider next the famous words of Prometheus in the following passage:

Χο. οὐδ' ἐστὶν ἄθλου τέρμα σοι προκείμενον;
Πρ. οὐκ ἄλλο γ' οὐδὲν πλὴν ὅταν κείνωι δοκῆι.
Χο. δόξει δὲ πῶς; τίς ἐλπίς; οὐχ ὁρᾶις ὅτι
ἥμαρτες; ὡς δ' ἥμαρτες, οὔτ' ἐμοὶ λέγειν
καθ' ἡδονὴν σοί τ' ἄλγος. ἀλλὰ ταῦτα μὲν
μεθῶμεν, ἄθλου δ' ἔκλυσιν ζήτει τινά.
Πρ. ἐλαφρόν, ὅστις πημάτων ἔξω πόδα
ἔχει, παραινεῖν νουθετεῖν τε τοὺς κακῶς
πράσσοντας· εὖ δὲ ταῦθ' ἅπαντ' ἠπιστάμην.
ἑκὼν ἑκὼν ἥμαρτον· οὐκ ἀρνήσομαι·
θνητοῖς ἀρήγων αὐτὸς ηὑρόμην πόνους.
οὐ μήν τι ποιναῖς γ' ᾠόμην τοίαισί με
κατισχνανεῖσθαι πρὸς πέτραις πεδαρσίοις
τυχόντ' ἐρήμου τοῦδ' ἀγείτονος πάγου.
(*PrB* 257-70)

When the Chorus addresses Prometheus (259-61) with the words, "Don't you see that you erred (ἥμαρτες)? How you erred (ἥμαρτες) is not pleasant for me to talk about and it is painful for you," it may well see Prometheus' act as an error, a miscalculation. For the extreme punishment Prometheus undergoes is not the sort of thing one would ordinarily accept in a situation where one calculates the effects of a prospective action. The Chorus may reasonably consider that Prometheus "made a mistake" in exchanging such pain and humiliation for a gift to mankind. Prometheus denies error, however, before he repeats the verb ἁμαρτάνειν. He says first (265), "I knew well all these things," and continues (266-67), "ἑκών ἑκών I erred. I do not deny it. Helping mortals I myself brought on my suffering." I understand his claim to be that he was aware of all the relevant circumstances; he did not, therefore, act mistakenly. But since Prometheus goes on to say at lines 268-70 that he did not think he would be punished by being wasted away high in the air on a desolate cliff, he may seem to be qualifying "everything" (ἅπαντ') he knew in a way that leaves open the possibility that he did miscalculate. However, in light of his strong statement in line 266 which follows immediately on his assertion that he knew all, we can understand Prometheus in lines 268-70 to express surprise only about the actual form of his punishment. And we can allow his claim that he knew all to include knowledge of the general consequences of his act, severe reprisal from Zeus.

Thus, when Prometheus says, "I erred" (ἥμαρτον), we can understand him to use the word because the Chorus has just used it, and he is replying to them. But now, without implying that his act was done mistakenly, we can understand him to be saying that he missed the mark of accepted and expected behavior insofar as he acted contrary to the wishes of Zeus or insofar as he acted in a way that brought harm to himself. Ordinarily, such an action occurs under circumstances of ἀνάγκη or through error; but these are not the explanations of this act. Here too then, the FOV reading of ἑκών provides a powerful oxymoron,[13] but the conjunction of ἑκών and ἥμαρτον provides no evidence against the FOV.

Finally, a line from Sophocles' *Tyro* (665 *TrGF*) should be read closely with the passage from the *Prometheus*: "No evil person errs ἄκων" (ἄκων δ' ἁμαρτὼν οὔτις ἀνθρώπων κακός). Although the line is only a fragment, it is unlikely the context would support ἁμαρτών as an actual mistake due to ignorance of detail or miscalculation. For there would be no reason to expect the κακός (bad man) to make mistakes of this sort in a way unlike any other person, even though the κακός surely does act in ways that are not in accord with ordinary accepted and expected behavior. Here too the error is that the bad man does not do what is normally accepted and expected. Since the gnomic remark implies the κακός does miss the mark ἑκών, there is also implied an oxymoron of the sort discussed in the passage from *Prometheus*. The FOV can accommodate this passage in the same way it accommodates Prometheus' declaration that he erred ἑκών.[14]

These five examples, then, do not add to those passages that count against the FOV. Where ἑκών conjoined with ἀνάγκη counts against the FOV it is because the ἑκών agent is nonetheless acting under ἀνάγκη; and therefore, due to the broadness of what the FOV counts as ἀνάγκη, should be acting ἄκων. The FOV accommodates the examples just considered, like examples of strong disjunction between ἑκών and ἀνάγκη, by understanding ἑκών to emphatically deny what is ordinarily the explanation of the sort of action at hand. Furthermore, the emphatic ἑκών may be prompted by the fact that the actions are ordinarily the sort that happen because of error or compelling circumstances.

It should be noted that all the passages discussed above in which ἑκών words are found in situations where there is error or failure to act in the accepted and expected way, can also be accommodated by the Occasions for Describing Attitude View once it too is supplemented: circumstances of ἀνάγκη and also related situations involving error prompt the use of ἑκών group words, but are not interchangeable with them and do not exhaust their meaning.

---

[13]M. Griffith, *Com. PrB*, 137, makes a similar point about these lines.

[14]Cf. Epicharm. 78.1–2 Kaibel (ch. 2., n. 5 and discussion of *General statements* below) and discussion of Simon. 542.27–30 *PMG*, p. 61.

Agents who do harm or wrong

In many of the passages already discussed in the foregoing chapters some harm is done or suffered by the agent or victim described by the ἑκών group word. But such passages have been categorized under specific types of ἀνάγκη because some particular type of ἀνάγκη can be identified in them. In the passages now under discussion, those described by ἑκών group words do harm or wrong when there is no evidence of ἀνάγκη or that any ἀνάγκη is being denied.

The FOV readily accommodates passages where doing harm or some wrong is linked with ἑκών group words but there is no further evidence of compelling circumstances. Where the person or character is said to act ἄκων, this very word, ἄκων, tells us the agent acted under ἀνάγκη or in error, a relative of ἀνάγκη. There is no need of other information to substantiate this fact. Thus, for example, the following comic fragment (Ar. 602.1 *PCG*), ἄκων κτενῶ σε τέκνον (ἄκων I will kill you, son), and the provision of Dracon's homicide law which concerns the pardon of one who kills ἄκων (IG I³.104.16–18: ἐὰν δὲ τούτον μεδὲ hὲς ἓι κτ]ἐ/νει δὲ ἄκο[ν], γνῶσι δὲ hοι̣ [πε]ντ[έκοντα καὶ hὲς hοι ἐφέται ἄκοντ]α / κτῆναι, ἐσέσθ[ο]ν δὲ h̠[οι φ]ρ[άτορες ἐὰν ἐθέλοσι δέκα), can be understood to speak of killings committed under compulsion or in error without any other further specificity, solely on the basis of the occurrence of forms of ἄκων. Likewise, where an agent does some harm or wrong ἑκών, we are advised by the FOV that he did so under no compulsion and without error.[14] Passages which offer no hint of any specific type of ἀνάγκη that is being denied can be taken as excluding all ἀνάγκη and error.

A number of actions are represented in these passages, for example: killing (Aesch. *Ag.* 1607–16: the Chorus says Aegisthus ἑκών killed Agamemnon); physically coercive acts that fall short of killing (Soph. *Tr.* 192–99/#2: because the Trachinians crowd around Heracles and prevent him from proceeding on his way, Heracles is said [οὐχ ἑκών] to be among them ἑκοῦσιν); the harm and wrong done by failure to perform one's duty (Thuc. 7.81.1: the Syracusans held

---

[14] What exactly φόνος ἑκούσιος and φόνος ἀκούσιος amount to has been largely a debate about the relationship between ἑκών, ἄκων and the terms ἐκ προνοίας and μὴ ἐκ προνοίας. There have been some dissenters who insist on three types of homicide even early on, φόνος ἑκούσιος or ἐκ προνοίας, φόνος ἀκούσιος, and φόνος μὴ ἐκ προνοίας. But generally, ἑκών and ἐκ προνοίας and ἄκων and μὴ ἐκ προνοίας are treated as equivalent or redoubled expressions. See M. Gagarin, Drakon and Early Athenian Homicide Law (New Haven, 1981), 31–37, for a summary of competing views of this controversy. In my view the current prevailing opinion is mistaken and rests on a misunderstanding of ἑκών group words (and what it means to kill μὴ ἐκ προνοίας, a matter too complex to be discussed here). The FOV interpretation would mesh well with the standard view of φόνος ἑκούσιος and φόνος ἀκούσιος as intentional and unintentional homicide, respectively.

Gyllippos to blame as ἑκών letting the Athenians escape); and what appears to be the impropriety of neglecting a certain type of dancing, something no one is said to do ἑκών (Aesch. *Theoroi* 78c.37–38 *TrGF*).

The FOV is able to accommodate these passages because it sees any occurrence of ἑκών as a denial of ἀνάγκη or error and any occurrence of ἄκων as predication of ἀνάγκη or error. Thus, even where there is insufficient evidence to determine the circumstances of the action connected with the ἑκών group word, the FOV can read the presence or absence of ἀνάγκη or error into the passage. But the alternative view also under consideration, the Occasions for Describing Attitude View—that circumstances of ἀνάγκη and error occasion or prompt the use of ἑκών group words without exhausting their significance— can accommodate these passages too. For this view can be revised again to include situations in which some harm or wrong is done, along with situations involving ἀνάγκη or error, as those which prompt the use of ἑκών group words.

Although both the FOV and the ODA View both can accommodate these passages without resorting to any desperate tactics, and although the circumstances of these passages may seem further removed from the influence of ἀνάγκη than the passages discussed in the previous section, those involving error, there is another way of handling these cases, compatible with both the FOV and the ODA View, which is worthy of some speculation. Because confirmation of such a view would require investigation beyond the scope of this study, I will mention it but not press it too far.

Since there has already been reason to find an association between acting in error and acting under ἀνάγκη, insofar as missing the mark is ordinarily the sort of thing that happens due to compelling circumstances, it is worth considering whether there is a similar association between doing harm or wrong and error. Some connection can be seen already in the fact that cases of error, even in a primarily comic context, are noteworthy when something harmful or wrongful results from the error. Moreover, the fact that ἁμαρτάνειν, "missing the mark," spans error as well as breach of social norm, what is ordinarily a harmful or wrongful matter, itself suggests the possibility that, like error, doing harm is out of keeping with the ordinary behavior of the community. As far as the choices of the ordinary person are concerned, that is excepting the total sociopath or evil person, doing harm or wrong, a breach of accepted and expected behavior, is considered somewhat irrational, but explainable as the result of error or some other form of compulsion.

This suggestion merits further investigation, even beyond the lure of tidiness that would ensue if all or even nearly all passages in which ἑκών group words appear involve or are related to circumstances of ἀνάγκη.¹⁶ However, since it is beyond the scope of this study to substantiate it, a more conservative view is appropriate at this time. The overlap of situations where ἀνάγκη and harm occur should be noted. But one need infer only that actions of harm or wrong along with circumstances of ἀνάγκη and situations involving error prompt the use of ἑκών group words.

Third-party passages

Positive and negative forms of ἑκών group words are also found describing not the direct agent or victim of an action, but some third party interested in the action. Since the FOV imports ἀνάγκη or error to any passage that contains ἑκών group words, so that even where these circumstances are not otherwise evident the FOV still accommodates them, it makes no real difference to the FOV whether a victim, agent, or third party is described by ἑκών group words. Moreover, at the very least, in respect to the matter in which the third party is interested, the third party too is subject to the necessity of confronting circumstances as they are (ἀνάγκη iii), and the broadness of what counts as ἀνάγκη in the FOV allows it to accommodate many passages where a more restricted sense of ἀνάγκη would be inadequate. Thus the FOV seems ready to accommodate all third-party passages, even those in which a god is the third party described by a ἑκών group word. In these the FOV can press its account of the power of circumstances to affect even the gods.¹⁷ For example, the FOV has a ready, however unusual, explanation for the description of Zeus in Io's question to Prometheus, "Who will set you free while Zeus is ἄκων?" (τίς οὖν ὁ λύσων ἐστὶν ἄκοντος Διός; [*PrB* 771]). Io asks this question just after Prometheus tells her that Zeus' only hope to avoid being dethroned is to release Prometheus (767–70). David Grene's translation of line 771 is probably accept-

---

¹⁶In fact, although ἀνάγκη, because of the its pervasiveness in passages containing ἑκών group words, has been the organizing principle behind the interpretative views discussed in this study, nonetheless, I have begun to wonder whether doing or suffering harm might be the feature which better links all occurrences of ἑκών group words. I am, of course, mindful that such a view leads directly to the Socratic paradox that no one does wrong ἑκών and all of its attendant perplexities, a matter well beyond the scope of this study. This is reason enough to mention it now only in a footnote, but it is a possibility of great interest for anyone concerned to give an account of the tradition which includes Socrates and Socratic paradoxes.

¹⁷All but one of the third-party passages which concern the gods contain the epic formula ἕκητι or ἀέκητι with the genitive case. Another typical pattern is for the third-party described by an ἑκών group word to be described in a genitive absolute, a construction which itself shows the third-party status of the person or character so described.

able to most readers, "But who will free you, against Zeus' will?"[18] But according to the FOV, Io's question amounts to asking who will set Prometheus free while Zeus is constrained by the current circumstances (this could be understood to refer to the bind in which Zeus finds himself: to keep his throne he must let Prometheus go, but he also wants to punish Prometheus) or ignorant of them.

Even if the FOV's treatment of the above example is acceptable, there are passages the FOV does not satisfactorily accommodate, even if formally it does since the presence of ἑκών group words imports ἀνάγκη or error even where there is no other evidence. Consider for example, the passage in the *Iliad* (12.2–9) which concerns the wall built by the Greeks at Troy to protect their ships and booty. The passage implies that the Greeks' failure to offer proper sacrifice to the gods has something to do with the wall being built θεῶν ἀέκητι (with the gods ἄκοντες); and we are told it will not be standing very long: τὸ καὶ οὔ τι πολὺν χρόνον ἔμπεδον ἦεν. Apart from the FOV's reading of ἀέκητι, this information does not support the impression that the gods were constrained to accept the wall being built, and that they could not have prevented it. It is possible that, for example, the poet conflates "*did not* prevent the wall from being built" with "*could not* prevent the wall from being built" through some interaction of hindsight and the fact that the wall was built. But apart from what the FOV understands by the use of ἀέκητι, our picture is of gods who are interested in the matter and have power over it but do not exercise their power at the time in question. But we can construe the gods to be wronged by the action of the Greeks who built the wall without properly sacrificing to them. Thus, the ODA View can begin to account for the ἑκών group word in this passage since it also recognizes situations of harm or wrong as prompting the use of these words. Third-party passages will be taken up again in Chapter 5 where the full Occasions for Describing Attitude View will provide a more complete account of the use of ἑκών group words in third-party passages.[19]

General statements

Finally, there are a few passages which contain general statements about τὸ ἑκούσιον and τὸ ἀκούσιον. Cleon, in his speech about the Mytilenians (Thuc. 3.40.1/#2), considers whether or not they should be forgiven on the basis of the general principle that τὸ ἀκούσιον is forgivable. In a fragment from Sophocles

---

[18]*Prometheus Bound*, trans. D. Grene, *The Complete Greek Tragedies, Aeschylus II*, ed. D. Grene and R. Lattimore (Chicage, 1956).

[19]Although it is my inclination to reject the view I discussed in ch. 2, the meaning list approach, these last examples which do not fit the basic meanings "by force" or "through ignorance" can still be accommodated by that view: one merely adds, e.g., "willing" and "unwilling" to the list of the meanings of ἑκών group words, perhaps even with a note about the frequency with which this meaning is found when gods are being described.

(*TrGF* 746), the speaker claims to "make an exception" of τὴν ἀκουσίαν: ἐξαίρετον τίθημι τὴν ἀκουσίαν. Whether one supplies "judgment" (Lobeck γνώμην) or "error" (Campbell: ἁμαρτίαν) to fill the ellipse, τὴν ἀκουσίαν, the remark probably has to do with treating the ἀκούσιος act differently than the ἑκούσιος act. A similar thought, which also contains an ellipse, is found in the remark of the Chorus to Deianira in Sophocles' *Trachiniae*. The Chorus considers Deianira to be among those for whom softened anger is appropriate because they trip up "not from an ἑκούσιος judgment" (μὴ 'ξ ἑκουσίας; Kamerbeek: γνώμην):[20]

> Xo. ἀλλ' ἀμφὶ τοῖς σφαλεῖσι μὴ 'ξ ἑκουσίας
> ὀργὴ πέπειρα, τῆς σε τυγχάνειν πρέπει.
>   (Soph. *Tr*. 727–28)

Since these passages are comments about the concept of τὸ ἑκούσιον and τὸ ἀκούσιον rather than simple uses of ἑκών group words, the views under consideration cannot explain these occurrences, although whether the comments make sense or are appropriate given the particular interpretative views under consideration is important. From the discussions in the next chapters it will be clear that what these passages imply about society's response to τὸ ἑκούσιον and τὸ ἀκούσιον is in accord with what Aristotle says about the appropriate response and does not conflict with anything the FOV or the ODA View hold.[21]

---

[20] For other general statements cf. *TrGF* 80.1–4, Epicharm., 78.1–2 Kaibel, (see ch. 2, n. 5), *TrGF* 75a, and Phocylides 13 Gentili–Prato.

[21] It was consideration of passages containing general statements that led me to exclude Antiphon (where I count six general statements: *Or*. 1.27 [two], and 5.92; *Tetral*. 2.2.6 [two], and 3.1.6) from this study of occurrences of ἑκών group words through the fifth century B.C.E., and to conclude that all the orators ought to be examined together. If pity or forgiveness is due the one who acts ἄκων, in the courtroom where punishment is imminent, there is considerable incentive to argue the defendant is or is not ἄκων. Thus it seems to me the courtroom may provide an especially unique context for treating external circumstances (for which there is evidence apart from that supplied by the person on trial) as interchangeable with what is internal, a person's attitude. Indeed, one does not have to be in a courtroom to lie or misrepresent one's attitude, and the principle of forgiving one who acts ἄκων can reasonably be argued to underlie other claims to be ἄκων in other settings. But the special need to press the case for or against acting ἄκων in the courtroom may mean that such interchanging is more likely to be deliberately attempted in the forensic speeches of the orators, whether or not the FOV is an accurate general account of ἑκών group words, thereby making the use of these words in such cases of special interest. Whether or not this phenomenon can actually be substantiated in legal contexts, and if so, whether or not it is best understood as constituting a special usage vis a vis the ODA View, or simply as supplying more support for the FOV, or perhaps as constituting the source of the FOV, requires a full study of the orators, a task beyond the scope of the present inquiry. Of course, since there are exceptions to the FOV's ability to

Preliminary conclusions

The main conclusions to be drawn from the foregoing chapters are:

1. Ἑκών group words are found describing agents or their actions primarily under circumstances of constraint, ἀνάγκη. What counts as circumstances of ἀνάγκη includes hands-on force, social practices, and more generally, the circumstances in which an agent finds himself and with which he must contend at some crucial moment; and ranges from situations where persons or characters are totally passive victims to situations where they are agent victims. Although most frequently passive victims of actual hands-on force are found to be ἄκοντες, there are exceptions to this pattern; and victims of other sorts of ἀνάγκη may be ἑκόντες or ἄκοντες.

2. Other circumstances which may be related to circumstances of ἀνάγκη and under which ἑκών group words occur are cases of error, including cases of ignorance: agents who act in error are regularly ἄκοντες; situations where harm or wrong is committed: since there need be no evidence (apart from the presence of ἑκών group words) that the agent who may be ἑκών or ἄκων, does or does not labor under ἀνάγκη as he acts, it may be the case that the acts performed in these passages are regularly associated with circumstances of ἀνάγκη or error and that this regularity prompts the use of the ἑκών group words; and passages where ἑκών group words describe someone other than those directly involved with the action under consideration: those so described may be ἑκόντες or ἄκοντες.

3. The Functional Opposite View (which defines acting ἑκών and ἄκων in terms of ἀνάγκη and error such that one acts either under ἀνάγκη or in error and is ἄκων or one acts ἑκών) accommodates those passages in which acting ἄκων is conjoined with circumstances of ἀνάγκη and error; acting ἑκών is in strong opposition to acting under ἀνάγκη or error; and acting ἑκών or ἄκων with acts of harm or wrong or a third party. However, the FOV does not accommodate those passages in which acting ἑκών is conjoined with circumstances of ἀνάγκη

4. The Occasions for Describing Attitude View which holds that the particular circumstances under which ἑκών group words occur, prompt or trigger the use of these words without exhausting their significance, can accommodate even those passages the FOV cannot. How this view can accommodate third-party passages will be discussed in Chapter 5.)

---

accommodate passages, a special legal usage of this sort, however well it fits the FOV, would not be reason to reject the ODA View.

4. Aristotle on τὸ ἑκούσιον and τὸ ἀκούσιον

Although the Functional Opposite View seems to accommodate many occurrences of ἑκών group words, on the basis of the exceptions to this view, I have argued it is unsatisfactory to account for these words as meaning the presence or absence of the circumstances under which they are used, and sometimes only as a pleonastic emphasis. The usefulness of that view, however unsatisfactory it is ultimately, has been that it focused attention on regularities as well as exceptions to those regularities in the usage of ἑκών group words. In this chapter I will set out some of Aristotle's views on τὸ ἑκούσιον and τὸ ἀκούσιον and compare these views to the FOV.

The FOV's focus on ἀνάγκη, in particular βία and the relative of ἀνάγκη, error, generates a characteristically negative account because of the priority given to defining when an agent acts ἄκων. Thus, the FOV cannot but recall discussions of τὸ ἑκούσιον and τὸ ἀκούσιον in the ethical works of Aristotle. It will be seen that even the negative account found there is richer than the FOV; but nonetheless, like the FOV, there are certain limitations in what types of passages it accommodates. Moreover, even when the negative account is supplemented by the more positive account of τὸ ἑκούσιον and τὸ ἀκούσιον found elsewhere in Aristotle, there are still passages that are not satisfactorily accommodated. In this chapter then, I will identify two strands in Aristotle's discussion of τὸ ἑκούσιον and τὸ ἀκούσιον and clarify the differences and similarities between the negative strand and the FOV.

Aristotle's discussion is much richer than the FOV. But I am eager to make it clear that I am not proposing to settle in any comprehensive way what Aristotle has to say on the subject of τὸ ἑκούσιον and τὸ ἀκούσιον. There is much that Aristotle says that I will not discuss.[1] However, there are some things about τὸ ἑκούσιον and τὸ ἀκούσιον that Aristotle neglects to say and some things he does say which are subordinated to the particular interests of his discussions but germane to understanding τὸ ἑκούσιον and τὸ ἀκούσιον.

In this chapter I want to exploit the richness of Aristotle's discussion to once again push to the surface features of ἑκών group words that need to be ac-

---

[1]In particular, Aristotle's discussion of the *enkrates* and the *akrates* would have to be incorporated into a more thorough study of Aristotle's views. In those discussions we meet many features, characteristics, and concerns about the meaning of ἑκών group words which are not subsumed or accounted for by Aristotle's definitions which rely primarily on force and ignorance.

counted for. In the course of my discussion, particular differences between Aristotle and the FOV will emerge. But here I want to touch on the difference I perceive in Aristotle's perspective and aims, especially in his negative view, and explain why I think it appropriate to rely on Aristotle at all in my efforts to elucidate the meaning of ἑκών group words in literature which predates even Plato.

I will begin with the latter issue, why rely on Aristotle to explain usage which predates his discussion. First, it should be said that even as there would be no hesitation about testing the accuracy of modern discussions of ἑκών group words against actual usage, so too there ought to be no hesitation about considering Aristotle's discussion. Indeed, it seems odd to even consider passing over Aristotle's treatment, the earliest, most detailed, and direct discussion of these words that we have. Of course, there is always the possibility that development in their usage is such that Aristotle's treatment may not fit earlier usage in important ways. The point of examining Aristotle's discussion is not to be surprised or disappointed if his views do not satisfactorily elucidate earlier usage of these words, but to gather some useful perspective from his discussion for determining the meaning of the words. Unless it is proven that Aristotle essentially created a technical usage of these terms without any regard for their ordinary usage, there is reason to seek in Aristotle information about their usage at large. But even the discovery of special usage in Aristotle or development which comes to be especially evident in Aristotle will be profitable for the overall project. The aim is not to refute Aristotle, that is to argue that he is wrong in what he says because of the evidence of some passages of earlier literature, but rather to determine whether or not at least the core of Aristotle's views can satisfactorily accommodate the earlier usage of these words such that we can be confident we understand their meaning.

Moreover, in the *Nicomachean Ethics*, Aristotle's own stated methodology raises the possibility that his discussion may be of use in determining the meaning of these words even in earlier usage. He speaks of gathering information and reconciling disagreements.[2] We might consider this a matter of him determining what it means for an act to be ἑκούσιος or ἀκούσιος. Is Aristotle doing, in effect, something akin to what I am trying to do in this study? There is no simple answer to this question, and any answer is going to be

---

[2]See M. Nussbaum, "Saving Aristotle's Appearances," in *Language and Logos*, eds. M. Schofield and M. Nussbaum (Cambridge, 1982), for a comprehensive exposition of Aristotle's methodology beginning from his comments in *NE* 1145b1ff. As Nussbaum emphasizes, it is essential to understand that τὰ φαινόμενα are not the data of Baconian science but the world of human experience as humans perceive it, including what experts and ordinary people believe and say. In the *NE* passage Aristotle explains that having gathered all these φαινόμενα, we must work through the inevitable puzzles that emerge from conflicting views, and show the truth of the greatest number of these if not all.

controversial. Much depends on one's grasp of Aristotle's stated methodology, as well as one's determination of whether he is applying it in this particular matter, and if he is, how well he is applying it. Furthermore, what to make of Aristotle's discussion is also dependent on what one understands his question(s) to be and why he is pursuing it (them) when he collects and reconciles the relevant phainomena.

In general, it is my view that Aristotle is not pursuing my question. But what he says may well be of help and bring to the surface features of ἑκών group words that must be taken into account if ever we are to get at their meaning. My impression of Aristotle's discussions in the ethical works is that they aim to determine which actions are predictably or regularly ἀκούσιοι and ἑκούσιοι, and to ascertain reliable characteristics, both external and internal, of such actions. Admittedly, it is not easy to distinguish these aims from the aim to establish meaning, but I think there is a difference. In the *NE*, for example, Aristotle isolates actions which are regularly ἀκούσιοι, determines some characteristics true of such actions, and builds a definition of ἑκούσιοι actions from this basis. But it need not be the case that the actions identified or their identifying characteristics are interchangeable with ἑκών group words. We may infer, even with some confidence, that an action is ἀκούσιος or ἑκούσιος on the basis of the reliable characteristics of such actions. But these characteristics are not the same thing as ἀκούσιοι and ἑκούσιοι actions.

We will find, for example, that Aristotle's discussion does focus on cases which my analysis of the literature collected for this study has shown are regularly cases of ἀκούσιοι actions. To some extent then, my discussion bears out what I have suggested is at least one of Aristotle's goals, to discover actions regularly ἀκούσιοι. As an added bonus, this correspondence shows there is significant continuity between Aristotle's 4th century B.C.E. analysis and the tradition of usage before this period. But we will also find that Aristotle's discussion is not limited to identifying typical cases of ἀκούσιοι and ἑκούσιοι actions. He also discusses characteristics of such actions distinct from the characteristics of the regular cases on which he focuses but apparently relevant to designating an action ἑκούσιος or ἀκούσιος. It is not the purpose of this chapter to unravel this more complicated discussion. But, as I have said, a more thorough investigation of what Aristotle understands as the meaning of ἑκών group words must go beyond the core discussions investigated here.

THE ARISTOTELIAN NEGATIVE VIEW (ANV)

Actions which come about by force

In the *NE* Aristotle arrives at his definition of τὸ ἑκούσιον by first setting out what counts as τὸ ἀκούσιον.[3] Ἀκούσια are those actions which come about by force or through ignorance: δοκεῖ δὴ ἀκούσια εἶναι τὰ βίᾳ ἢ δι' ἄγνοιαν γινόμενα (*NE* 1109b35–1110a1).[4] Thus, τὸ ἑκούσιον is defined as that whose starting-point is in the one knowing the particular circumstances in which the action occurs: οὗ ἡ ἀρχὴ ἐν αὐτῷ εἰδότι τὰ καθ' ἕκαστα ἐν οἷς ἡ πρᾶξις (*NE* 1111a23–24). What counts as βία (by force) and δι' ἄγνοιαν (through ignorance) is spelled out very clearly by Aristotle. Βία is restricted to actual, superior force; but this force is not limited to that applied by human agents. Aristotle's examples include both a natural phenomenon that exerts superior force and the superior force of human agents. In Book 3 the examples are of a person being carried off by a wind or by persons stronger than himself (*NE* 1110a3–4); and in Book 5 there is a case of person A striking person C with

---

[3] Aristotle's discussion in Book 2 of the *EE* develops differently. Because of my limited purposes in this chapter there is much of interest in the *EE* and the *NE* as well as in the scholarship on these works that I will not discuss. For a more recent discussion, see A. Kenny, *Aristotle's Theory of the Will* (New Haven, 1979), pt. 1, 3–66. Kenny has many acute observations, but must be read with caution.

[4] With all due respect for the renewed interest in the *EE*, which I too share, I will continue to refer to the common books of the *NE* and the *EE* by their place in the *NE*. A passage in *NE* 1135a31–b2 is held by some commentators to support three types of τὸ ἀκούσιον: what is done through ignorance, what is done neither through ignorance nor is in our power, and what is done by force (τὸ δὴ ἀγνοούμενον, ἢ μὴ ἀγνοούμενον μὲν μὴ ἐπ' αὐτῷ δ' ὄν, ἢ βίᾳ, ἀκούσιον). The next sentence, πολλὰ γὰρ καὶ τῶν φύσει ὑπαρχόντων εἰδότες καὶ πράττομεν καὶ πάσχομεν, ὧν οὐδὲν οὔθ' ἑκούσιον οὔτ' ἀκούσιόν ἐστιν, οἷον τὸ γηρᾶν ἢ ἀποθνήσκειν, is then taken to further explicate the second type of τὸ ἀκούσιον in the preceding sentence. This, however, requires somehow emending the so-called explanatory sentence since οὔτ' ἀκούσιον contradicts the view. (See for example, ad loc., J.A. Stewart, *Notes on the Nicomachean Ethics of Aristotle* [Oxford, 1892], following the interpretaion of H. Rassow, *Forschungen über die nikomachische Ethik des Aristoteles* [Weimar, 1874], and L. Spengel, *Aristotelische Studien* [Munich, 1864]). I agree with Jolif (R.A. Gauthier and J.Y. Jolif, eds., *L' Éthique é Nicomaque*, 2nd ed., vol. 2, pt. 1 [Paris, 1970], 398–99), following Michael of Ephesus (*In Librum Quintum Ethicorum Nicomacheorum Commentarium*, ed. M. Hayduck, CAG XXII.iii [Berlin, 1901], 52.9–10) that ἢ βίᾳ should not be taken as disjunctive but explanatory of what is said in the μέν...δέ... clause. As Jolif notes, in his discussion of acting through ignorance in Bk. 3.2, Aristotle has already introduced οὐχ ἑκούσιον for what is neither ἀκούσιον nor ἑκούσιον. Cf. Aristotle's examples in Bk. 3.5 of what is neither "ἐφ' ἡμῖν" nor "ἑκούσια": being hot, in pain, hungry, etc. We also need not conclude with Stewart that these are ἀκούσια. The *DeM* also has a class of motions that are οὐχ ἑκούσια, see 703b8ff.

person B's hand in such a way that we can assume B was overpowered by A so that he was a mere instrument of A's action (*NE* 1135a26–28). The force exhibited in these examples fits Aristotle's general characterization of action that is βίαιον as that action whose starting-point is from outside such that the one acting or being acted on contributes nothing: βίαιον δὲ οὗ ἡ ἀρχὴ ἔξωθεν, τοιαύτη οὖσα ἐν ᾗ μηδὲν συμβάλλεται ὁ πράττων ἢ ὁ πάσχων (*NE* 1110a1–3).[5]

In the *EE*, Aristotle gives a broader discussion of βία in phenomena, including what it is for inanimate things to act under βία (*EE* 1224a10ff.). But his discussion of βία and τὸ ἀκούσιον comes to the same conclusions as the *NE* discussion: "likewise, both among living things and animals, we see many things suffering and doing by force whenever something from outside moves them contrary to the inclination within them" (ὁμοίως δὲ καὶ ἐπὶ ἐμψύχων καὶ ἐπὶ τῶν ζῴων ὁρῶμεν βίᾳ πολλὰ καὶ πάσχοντα καὶ ποιοῦντα, ὅταν παρὰ τὴν ἐν αὐτῷ ὁρμὴν ἔξωθέν τι κινῇ [*EE* 1224a20ff.]). The use of ὁρμή rather than ἀρχή articulates more clearly than the *NE* that the interest is in the starting-point of motion.[6] Evidence from several of his works support this view.

Aristotle uses ὁρμή for the natural internal inclination to change, move, or act. In the *Physics* (2.192b8ff.), for example, he contrasts those things that are due to nature with those things due to other causes. The former include animals and their parts, plants, and natural kinds like earth, fire, air, and water. He says: "Each of these has within itself the starting-point of motion and standing still, some in regard to place, others in regard to increase and decrease, and others in regard to alteration" (τούτων μὲν γὰρ ἕκαστον ἐν ἑαυτῷ ἀρχὴν ἔχει κινήσεως καὶ στάσεως, τὰ μὲν κατὰ τόπον, τὰ δὲ κατ' αὔξησιν καὶ φθίσιν, τὰ δὲ κατ' ἀλλοίωσιν [*Ph.* 192b13–15]). But of a bed or a cloak, insofar as they are manufactured items (ἀπὸ τέχνης), he says they have "no natural inclination of change" (οὐδεμίαν ὁρμὴν ἔχει μεταβολῆς ἔμφυτον" [*Ph.* 192b18–19]). In *Metaphysics* Book 4 (1023a17ff.), one of the senses of τὸ ἔχειν Aristotle distinguishes is what hinders something from moving (κινεῖσθαι) or acting (πράττειν) according to its own ὁρμήν (κατὰ τὴν αὐτοῦ ὁρμήν). Thus, according to some poets and even physicists, Aristotle explains, Atlas is said "to hold the sky" (τὸν οὐρανὸν ἔχειν) "as if the sky would collapse against the earth" if Atlas did not "hold" it (1023a19ff.). In this sense, if what "holds together" (τὸ συνέχον) did not "hold" (ἔχειν) what it holds together, that held together would separate according to its own ὁρμήν (1023a22ff.). Finally, in a passage from the *Posterior Analytics* that is reminiscent of *EE* 1224a10ff., Aristotle distinguishes ἀνάγκη that is "according to nature and inclination"

---

[5]Cf. *NE* 1110b1–3 and 15–17.

[6]Cf. *EE* 1224b7ff. The actions of the *enkrates* and the *akrates* do not occur under βία because for each ἡ ὁρμή is ἐνοῦσα and not ἔξωθεν.

(κατὰ φύσιν καὶ τὴν ὁρμήν) and ἀνάγκη that is "by force and contrary to the ὁρμή" (ἡ δὲ βία ἡ παρὰ τὴν ὁρμήν [94b37ff.]). Thus, a stone travels upwards and downwards by necessity, but not the same necessity (95a1-3). The necessary downward motion of the stone is caused by its own natural internal inclination, as contrasted with the external source of motion that forces the stone to move upwards.

In the *NE*, actions in which the ἀρχή, the starting-point of motion, is totally outside the individual concerned such that he contributes nothing, are also characterizable as actions that are not "in his own power," ἐφ' αὐτῷ. Aristotle makes the general statement in *NE*, Book 3, that where the ἀρχή is in the person, the power to act or not to act is also in the person: ὧν δ' ἐν αὐτῷ ἡ ἀρχή, ἐπ' αὐτῷ καὶ τὸ πράττειν καὶ μή (*NE* 1110a17-18). Thus, for example, in Book 5 where A strikes C with B's hand, Aristotle says this act was not in B's power: οὐ γὰρ ἐπ' αὐτῷ (1135a26-28). The ἀρχή of this action was totally outside B; B did not himself move his body parts. Thus, it was not in B's power to act or not act.[7]

Book 2 (ch.6) of the *EE* also makes a strong connection between the starting-point of motion and what is ἐφ' αὐτῷ.[8] A human being is a starting-point (ἀρχή) of motion (κίνησις) because he is a starting-point of action (πρᾶξις). Insofar as starting-points (ἀρχαί) of motions are called "supreme" or "authoritative" (κύριαι), the human is also a κυρία ἀρχή. Since the ἀρχή is an αἰτία (explanation or cause) of what is or comes about through it, the human is also the explanation of what comes about through him. One is αἴτιος of what is in one's power (ἐφ' αὐτῷ) to do or not do, and if something is ἐφ' αὐτῷ, one is αἴτιος of it. Actions that are ἐφ' αὐτῷ are those that are not ἐξ ἀνάγκης (*EE* 1222b15ff.).[9]

It is important to note that Aristotle is rather strict in the *Nicomachean Ethics* in delimiting the starting-point of an agent's action and whether the act is in the agent's power. For he focuses on the actual movement of body parts at the time of the action. Whether the ἀρχή is ἐν αὐτῷ or ἔξωθεν depends on who or what moved the agent's body parts. It is not a fact about larger circum-

---

[7]Cf. *EE* 1224b12 where Aristotle uses this case as an example of who is ἀναγκαζόμενος and argues that the *enkrates* and *akrates* are not ἀναγκαζόμενοι.

[8]Kenny, *Theory of the Will* (8ff.), uses *NE* 1135a31-b2 (*NE* 5.8 = *EE* 4.8), discussed above in n. 4, to argue for a sense of ἐφ' ἡμῖν in the *EE* that is broader than the *NE*'s use. However, since he ignores ἢ βίᾳ in his exposition, his argument for a broader sense of ἐφ' ἡμῖν based on this passage is dubious.

[9]Aristotle concludes: ὥστε ὅσων πράξεων ὁ ἄνθρωπός ἐστιν ἀρχὴ καὶ κύριος, φανερὸν ὅτι ἐνδέχεται καὶ γίνεσθαι καὶ μή, καὶ ὅτι ἐφ' αὐτῷ ταῦτ' ἐστὶ γίνεσθαι καὶ μή, ὧν γε κύριός ἐστι τοῦ εἶναι καὶ τοῦ μὴ εἶναι. ὅσα δ' ἐφ' αὐτῷ ἐστὶ ποιεῖν ἢ μὴ ποιεῖν, αἴτιος τούτων αὐτός ἐστιν· καὶ ὅσων αἴτιος, ἐφ' αὐτῷ (1223a4-9).

stances that influence human actions that Aristotle looks to, that is, any broader sense of the starting-point of explanation for the action; rather Aristotle looks to the starting-point of the actual motion that is the action. Even in his discussion of "mixed actions" in the *NE*, Aristotle concludes that in situations like that of the pilot who threw his cargo overboard in a storm, the agent acted ἑκών since the agent himself moved his own body parts, and where the agent is himself the starting-point of moving his body parts, to act or not act is in his power (*NE* 1110a15–18). Thus, it will be useful to take up "mixed acts" next, before discussing Aristotle's other group of ἀκούσιοι actions, those that come about through ignorance.

Μικταὶ πράξεις *(mixed acts) and the Aristotelian Negative View*

Many passages whose circumstances are categorized under the FOV's liberal view of actions that take place under ἀνάγκη, but which do not meet Aristotle's criteria for τὸ ἀκούσιον because of τὸ βίαιον, can be considered under what Aristotle in the *NE* calls "mixed" acts. In discussing these mixed acts, it will be necessary to draw a distinction between the treatments of the *NE* and the *EE*. The discussion in Book 2 of the *EE* comes closer to the FOV than does the discussion in Book 3 of the *NE*. In fact, Aristotle's account of mixed acts in the *NE* distinguishes this account from the FOV even further. The FOV, it will be recalled, can accommodate all those passages where ἀνάγκη is conjoined with ἄκων but can not accommodate passages where the agent acts ἑκών under ἀνάγκη. It will be seen, however, that Aristotle's account of mixed actions will accommodate those passages the FOV can not. The problem passages for Aristotle will be those cases where the agent is said to be ἄκων when the action is mixed.

Μικταὶ πράξεις (mixed acts) are actions about which Aristotle says there is disagreement concerning whether they are ἀκούσιοι or ἑκούσιοι (*NE* 1110a7–8). They are the sort of things people do either because of fear of greater evils or because of some good: διὰ φόβον μειζόνων κακῶν...ἢ διὰ καλόν τι (4–5). For example, when a tyrant has power over someone's family and threatens to kill them unless this person performs the shameful act the tyrant orders (5–7); or the sort of thing the ship's pilot does when he throws his cargo overboard during a storm. Aristotle says that without some qualification (ἁπλῶς), this is something no one would do ἑκών, but every sensible person would do for the sake of safety (8–11).

Since Aristotle tells us there is disagreement about mixed cases, we can infer that he is not only telling us what he thinks about them but is reporting what others say about them. In fact, even his use of ἑκών at 1110a8–11 paraphrased just above, does not unproblematically fit with his definitions of τὸ ἑκούσιον and τὸ ἀκούσιον. This is a passage in which Aristotle seems to be at work reconciling τὰ λεγόμενα.[10] He tells us it is understandable why such actions are said without qualification (ἁπλῶς) to be ἀκούσιοι: no one would choose for itself anything of the sort the pilot or victim of the tyrant chooses (οὐδεὶς γὰρ ἂν ἕλοιτο καθ' αὑτὸ τῶν τοιούτων οὐδέν [19]). However, Aristotle says twice that mixed actions are more like ἑκούσιοι actions (1110a12 and 1110b6), because such actions are chosen or choiceworthy (αἱρεταί) at the time they are done, and whether an action is ἑκούσιος or ἀκούσιος must be determined from what pertained at the time of the action (1110a12–15).[11] But Aristotle goes on to explain that in these cases, at the time of the action, the agent acts ἑκών because the agent is himself the starting-point of the movement of his body parts: πράττει δὲ ἑκών· καὶ γὰρ ἡ ἀρχὴ τοῦ κινεῖν τὰ ὀργανικὰ μέρη ἐν ταῖς τοιαύταις πράξεσιν ἐν αὐτῷ ἐστίν (15–17).

Since πράξεις are in the class of particulars, ἐν τοῖς καθ' ἕκαστα, and these particulars are ἑκούσια (1110b6–7), Aristotle puts less weight on the unqualified (ἁπλῶς or καθ' αὑτά) choiceworthiness of mixed acts than he does on choiceworthiness at the time of action. For actions are particulars and the designation ἑκούσιος or ἀκούσιος must be based on the particular token not the type of action. It is not the case that mixed actions at the time of action become choiceworthy in themselves without qualification. Their choiceworthiness is still limited to their preferability only at the time of action. Thus, although being αἱρετός is relevant to the discussion of whether an action is ἑκούσιος or ἀκούσιος, for Aristotle the unqualified choiceworthiness of an action is subordinated to the actual choice and the actual source of motion that produces or is the action. The fact that the mixed actions are not in themselves choiceworthy, even though the agent is not a victim of βία or acting δι' ἄγνοιαν, may be the grounds (at least in part) on which others call such actions ἀκούσιοι. But for Aristotle the designation ἑκούσιος rests on the fact that the agent, knowing the particular circumstances in which he acts, moves his own body to perform the act. Ultimately, such actions are ἑκούσιοι because there is no question of ignorance, and they do not qualify as βίαια[12] (1110b1–5) which are strictly

---

[10] See above, n. 2.

[11] αἱρεταί may mean "chosen" or "choiceworthy" or perhaps both. For at the time of the action, the agent finds the act choiceworthy, and he chooses it. Or better, the choiceworthiness of the act is evidenced by its being chosen. This is a weaker sense of choiceworthy than being choiceworthy ἁπλῶς. Cf. Kenny's discussion of the ambiguity (*Theory of the Will*, 31ff.).

[12] Ordinarily, I use the masculine and nominative forms –ος and –οι for adjectival forms of Greek words describing actions. However, especially in this discussion of Aristotle, the neuter forms –ον and –α will also occur. These forms reflect Aristotle's persistent use of the neuter which recalls the general category under discussion even where a masculine or feminine antecedent is clear.

limited: the ἀρχή[13] must be ἔξωθεν and the person acting or being acted on contribute nothing (1110a1-3).[14] Thus, although Aristotle is extremely sympathetic in Book 3 ch. 1 in describing how difficult it is to make choices in such cases, to decide what should be endured and what things should be chosen, even where someone does something wrong under pressure that no human could have withstood, Aristotle does not say such a person acted ἄκων, only that he receives pardon for his act (1110a23-26). Even this extreme pressure does not count as βίαιον. Aristotle focuses on the time of action and rejects unqualified choiceworthiness, a wider explanation which would include details about the agent's attitudes or values, as a criterion for judging an action ἑκούσιος or ἀκούσιος. But even though he notes the choiceworthiness of the action at the time of the action, Aristotle does not build this characteristic into his definitions. He locates the starting-point of motion and designates the act ἑκούσιος or ἀκούσιος on the basis of whether this ἀρχή is within or without.

I do not seek to minimize Aristotle's comment that mixed actions are more like actions that are ἑκούσιοι because they are choiceworthy, αἱρεταί, when they are done, and the end of an action is relevant to the time of the action, the time for which one judges whether the action is ἀκούσιος or ἑκούσιος (NE 1110a12-15). This comment does involve the agent's desires and cognitions as well as the broader external circumstances of the situation. However, although we may expect there is a serious relationship between choiceworthiness and movement, in this passage Aristotle relies heavily on the actual movement of one's own body parts, a fact which excludes the action from being βίαιος, in his determination that the agent acts ἑκών. (There is no question of ignorance in this case, which could exclude the agent from acting ἑκών even though he does move his own body.) Thus, the mixed action is unlike action that is βίαιος because in the mixed action the agent does himself move his own body parts. Whatever else may be true of those who are the victims of βία, in

---

[13]At 1110a1 Aristotle speaks of ἡ ἀρχή of what is βίαιον as being from the outside; but at 1110b2 he speaks of ἡ αἰτία as being from the outside. I understand the use of αἰτία to be restricted to the explanation of the source of motion the way ἡ ἀρχή is used at 1110a15-16: τοῦ κινεῖν τὰ ὀργανικὰ μέρη. ἡ ἀρχή clearly substitutes for ἡ αἰτία in Aristotle's summary at 1110b1-5: τὰ δὴ ποῖα φατέον βίαια; ἢ ἁπλῶς μέν, ὁπότ' ἂν ἡ αἰτία ἐν τοῖς ἐκτὸς ᾖ καὶ ὁ πράττων μηδὲν συμβάλλεται; ἃ δὲ καθ' αὑτὰ μὲν ἀκούσιά ἐστι, νῦν δὲ καὶ ἀντὶ τῶνδε αἱρετά, καὶ ἡ ἀρχὴ ἐν τῷ πράττοντι, καθ' αὑτὰ μὲν ἀκούσιά ἐστι, νῦν δὲ καὶ ἀντὶ τῶνδε ἑκούσια.

[14]Kenny (Theory of the Will, 29-30) interprets "contributes nothing" to include whatever internal feelings the agent may have about what is happening. I am not so sure this is what Aristotle is saying here. It is not at all clear that Aristotle has in mind the rare occasion when a person might enjoy what he is used as an instrument to do. I understand Aristotle to mean the agent contributes nothing to the movement which the act requires. See discussion below, pp. 106-108 and n. 22.

Aristotle's examples of action that is βίαιος in Book 3 and the example mentioned from Book 5, it is clear that they themselves do not move their own body parts. The action of the pilot who saves his ship and crew is not of this sort.

Being choiceworthy may well be a characteristic of many actions considered ἑκούσιοι, but Aristotle himself in the *EE* rejects the hypothesis that all ἑκούσιοι actions are in accord with choice (*EE* 2.7–8). It is a characteristic Aristotle seems to appreciate as relevant to the whole discussion of whether an action is ἑκούσιος or ἀκούσιος, but it is not a characteristic Aristotle built into his definitions. For our purposes here it is important that we do not begin to treat choiceworthiness as the characterizing feature with which some special group of ἑκούσιοι actions are to be identified. That is, in addition to those actions which are ἑκούσιοι because they are not excluded as being cases of τὸ βίαιον, we ought not to add another sense of τὸ ἑκούσιον, what is choiceworthy. This is not the route Aristotle takes, and it is a route I have criticized already as producing a list of meanings or senses too diverse to be satisfying as an account of the use of ἑκών group words. What we can appreciate from Aristotle's remark about choiceworthiness is that, although his use of the forced (τὸ βίαιον) as a criterion for determining τὸ ἀκούσιον, like the FOV, focuses our attention more on what is outside of the agent, choiceworthiness is a characteristic that begins to turn our attention to something inside the agent and relevant to understanding the meaning of ἑκών group words, even if it is not a characteristic of the typical cases on which Aristotle focuses and from which he develops his definitions.

As he reconciles what people say about these matters, Aristotle accounts for mixed cases called ἀκούσιοι. However, his conclusions that mixed actions are more like ἑκούσιοι actions suggests that according to his account of τὸ ἑκούσιον (as opposed to what he can account for in τὰ λεγόμενα) mixed actions are ἑκούσιοι because they do not meet the criteria of βίαια. (Ignorance is not even an issue in these cases.) Thus, in discussing actions which Aristotle would call mixed actions, it is Aristotle's account of τὸ ἑκούσιον and τὸ ἀκούσιον including his preference for mixed acts, that will be tested to see if it can accommodate the use of ἑκών group words. What we will find is that there are many passages that fall under μικταὶ πράξεις where we find the agent is not called ἑκών, Aristotle's preference or perhaps prescription, but ἄκων. This finding is not surprising, if, as I believe, Aristotle's discussion only isolates typical cases, but does not offer an integrated account based on these discoveries that adequately captures what ἑκών group words express. There is a large difference between ἄκων signifying an agent who does not move his own body parts and one who does something that is ordinarily not choiceworthy, not to mention the agent who acts δι' ἄγνοιαν.[15] In the next chapter I will pursue whether there is a more comprehensive way to describe the function of ἑκών group words without resorting to a disparate list of species of τὸ ἀκούσιον.[16]

Mixed acts in the Eudemian Ethics

In the *EE* too Aristotle is interested in reconciling what people say, τὰ λεγόμενα.[17] But here I think Aristotle goes beyond accounting for and sympathizing with what some people say. In the *EE*, Aristotle comes much closer to the conclusions of the FOV in dealing with these so-called mixed acts. The FOV counts as acting under ἀνάγκη cases where there is a threat of force or when circumstances compel a choice to be made. Aristotle takes the trouble to exclude cases where the good or avoidance of something bad for the sake of which the agent performs some shameful act, is of no great consequence. His example is a case of blind man's bluff where someone kills in order not to be tagged (*EE* 1225a14ff.). But, since the passages on which the FOV is based contain no such "laughable" cases, I take it that both views are concerned with similar circumstances.

Aristotle does counter the view that those who perform something painful and shameful under threat of torture or death are compelled (ἀναγκασθέντες) by saying the agent is ἑκών since it is in his power, ἐφ' αὑτῷ, not to perform the act but suffer the penalty (1225a7–8). He says explicitly that if the agent does something he does not wish to do (ἃ μὴ βούλεται), he acts ἑκών if the act is ἐφ' αὑτῷ (9ff.). However, in the course of his discussion, it becomes clear that there are cases Aristotle would agree are not in the agent's power to do or not do, which are also not cases of the ἀρχή or ὁρμή of the act being from outside (ἔξωθεν). These cases include those where someone does something evil for the sake of good or for deliverance from another greater evil (18–19). In these cases he says the agent would seem all the more to act under force (βίᾳ)

---

[15] I am not the only commentator to be jarred by the diversity of what counts as ἀκούσιον: cf. Aspasius, *Commentaria*, 59. 1–11 (*Aspasii In Ethica Nicomachea Quae Supersunt Commentaria*, ed. G. Heylbut, *CAG* XIX.i [Berlin, 1889]).

[16] It may be that there are reasons peculiar to Aristotle that led him to emphasize or prefer certain features of ἑκών group words rather than others. For example, Aristotle has a larger interest in explaining all animal motion, and he is especially interested in what lawgivers need to know about these matters. Since lawgivers are faced with the problem of adjudicating difficult cases, it should be emphasized that dependable definitions, even if they do not encompass every case, might be especially useful for them in their efforts to maintain fairness. This would be particularly important when special pleading may be involved or where only the accused who is always under suspicion of lying to protect himself, can give the true account.

[17] Cf. expressions like λέγονται δὲ κατ' ἄλλον τρόπον (*EE* 1225a2), and ἔτι ἴσως τούτων τὰ μὲν φαίη τις ἂν τὰ δ' οὔ (*EE* 1225a9).

and ἄκων when he acts to avoid severe pain rather than slight pain, and when he acts to avoid pain rather than gain enjoyment (23–25).[18] Aristotle does not completely break with the *NE* in this matter since he says agents in these cases act "under force in a sense" (βίᾳ πῶς) and not "absolutely" (ἁπλῶς). For they do at least have preference for that for the sake of which they act even if it is not in their power not to act (1225a12ff.).

The reason Aristotle gives for allowing that an agent in these cases is ἄκων is that it is beyond his nature (φύσις) to act otherwise. At 1225a25–27 Aristotle explains what counts as ἐφ' αὐτῷ. "For the 'ἐφ' αὐτῷ,' on which the whole matter turns, is what one's nature is able to bear; what one's nature is not able to bear and does not arise from his natural desire or reasoning, is not ἐφ' αὐτῷ" (τὸ γὰρ ἐφ' αὐτῷ, εἰς ὃ ἀνάγεται ὅλον, τοῦτ' ἐστιν ὃ ἡ αὐτοῦ φύσις οἵα τε φέρειν· ὃ δὲ μὴ οἵα τε μηδ' ἐστὶ τῆς ἐκείνου φύσει ὀρέξεως ἢ λογισμοῦ, οὐκ ἐφ' αὐτῷ). I understand Aristotle to be speaking here of what is beyond human nature to endure, rather than some individual's nature. In the *NE* Aristotle clearly means human nature when he speaks of pardon for certain people who do shameful acts under pressure: συγγνώμη δ', ὅταν διὰ τοιαῦτα πράξῃ τις ἃ μὴ δεῖ, ἃ τὴν ἀνθρωπίνην φύσιν ὑπερτείνει καὶ μηδεὶς ἂν ὑπομείναι (*NE* 1110a24–26). Moreover, Aristotle's objection to the blind man's bluff case and the preference shown for cases where one's object is to avoid severe pain (rather than mild pain) or avoid pain rather than gain pleasure, suggests that the kind of circumstances he has in mind would be granted by all to be beyond nature. Thus, while some count passion, some cases involving *thumos*, and natural conditions (ἔρως, θυμοὶ ἐνίοι, and τὰ φυσικά, respectively) as strong beyond nature to endure and therefore pardonable as forcing (βιάζεσθαι) nature (*EE* 1225a20ff.), Aristotle himself is not likely automatically to count all such cases. There may be cases of these sorts, however, which all would agree to involve force beyond nature to endure. Which of the passages collected in this study definitely represent the sort Aristotle would count as not ἐφ' αὐτῷ would be difficult to say, although there are some guidelines.

In Book 3 of the *NE* Aristotle is critical of the circumstances held to have "forced" Euripides' Alcmeon to kill his mother, and he asserts that perhaps it is impossible to be forced to perform some acts (1110a26–29). Alcmeon was ordered by his father to kill Eriphyle.[19] The FOV would count this order as a compelling circumstance, ἀνάγκη (ii), but apparently Aristotle would not. When speaking of the captain who throws his cargo overboard, he says "everyone having sense" (ἅπαντες οἱ νοῦν ἔχοντες) would do the same thing

---

[18]Cf. *NE* 1110a19ff.

[19]In Ps.-Apollodorus, 3.6.2, Amphiarius is said to have commanded his sons to kill their mother; in 3.7.5 Alcmeon (with or without his brother's help) is said to have killed Eriphyle in compliance with an oracle from Apollo.

in the same circumstances (1110a9-11). The *NE* of course, insists this act is ἑκούσιος; but following the *EE*, if the fear is strong enough, the act could be ἀκούσιος. The FOV would also count the act as ἀκούσιος under compelling circumstances, ἀνάγκη (iii). This last example is comparable to at least one of two examples discussed in the first common book of the *Ethics* (1135b4-8). There Aristotle explains that a person can commit an act of justice or an injustice only incidentally. He gives an example of each: a person who ἄκων returns a deposit from fear; and a person who compelled (ἀναγκαζόμενος) and ἄκων fails to return a deposit. In the second case the ἄκων agent who fails to return the deposit may have been a victim of βία whereby this case would conform with the criteria for ἀκούσιοι actions in *NE* 3; or he could be another example of the *EE*'s special cases of τὸ ἀκούσιον. There is not enough detail to decide one way or the other. The first ἄκων agent however, like the ship's pilot, does not meet the *NE*'s criteria. *NE* 3 would find him ἑκών; but *EE* 2 could allow him to be ἄκων. Finally, despite the dubious status of the *Magna Moralia*, I would like to mention its example of someone who is counted as ἀναγκαζόμενος (compelled) and presumably therefore also ἄκων (*MM* 1.15). The passsage explains that τὸ ἀναγκαῖον (the compelling) is not in everything but in things outside (ἐν τοῖς ἐκτός). Thus, acting for the sake of pleasure, e.g., does not count as a case of being compelled (ἀναγκαῖον).[20] Τὸ ἀναγκαῖον can be found in the case of the person who is compelled to forego one thing for the sake of something of greater importance. The specific example given is the case of a person who says he was compelled to visit his estate very frequently because if he did not do so, he would find his crops ruined (οἷον ἠναγκάσθην συντονώτερον βαδίσαι εἰς ἀγρόν· εἰ γὰρ μή, ἀπολωλότ' ἂν εὗρον τὰ ἐν ἀγρῷ). Here the *MM* comes closer to the FOV which would also count these circumstances as compelling, ἀνάγκη (iii); *NE* 3 would not; and *EE* 2 might.

These examples should be kept in mind when particular passages are discussed. For now it will be enough to conclude that insofar as Aristotle goes beyond what is narrowly construed as βίαιον, he comes closer to the FOV in the *EE* account of mixed acts. It may still be the case, though, that the FOV is much more liberal about what happens under ἀνάγκη than Aristotle.

In the next chapter I will discuss in relation to the views of both the *NE* and the *EE* a range of cases considered by the FOV to occur under ἀνάγκη. Of particular interest will be mixed actions, which will be examined to see whether those that are ἀκούσιοι meet Aristotle's criteria in the *NE*; and cases where, under the same sort and degree of compelling circumstances, an agent can be ἑκών or ἄκων. These passages will bring to the surface the fact that it is not simply because Aristotle would not count the passage as the requisite sort of not being

---

[20]Cf. *EE* 1188b8-14 where acting under desire does not count as a case of τὸ βίαιον.

ἐφ' αὑτῷ that even the *EE* view does not accommodate all mixed actions. Rather, something else which Aristotle does not capture is being expressed by the use of ἑκών group words.

Μηδὲν συμβάλλεται *(contributes nothing) in the Aristotelian Negative View*

Interpretation of what is meant by "contributes nothing" in Aristotle's definition of βίαιον also brings to our attention certain internal features of agents important for understanding ἑκών group words. Once again, for the purposes of this study, care must be taken in order not to treat these features in a way that generates special cases which only further lengthen a diverse list of meanings.

I understand "contributes nothing" to refer to the victim of βία who does not at all move his body parts in a way that contributes to the action. However, from Aristotle's discussion in *EE* 8.7–16 of the *enkrates* and the *akrates* (who do not act by βία or ἀνάγκη since the starting-point of their actions is within) one might suppose that more than this is involved. At 1224b13–14 Aristotle gives a counterexample to the situation of the *enkrates* and *akrates*.[21] The case is that of the man whose hand was taken by another and used to strike a third person: ὥσπερ εἴ τις λαβὼν τὴν χεῖρα τύπτοι τινὰ ἀντιτείνοντος καὶ τῷ βούλεσθαι καὶ τῷ ἐπιθυμεῖν (1224b13–15). The person who is used as an instrument seems to resist not physically, but psychologically, "with what he wishes and desires" (τῷ βούλεσθαι καὶ τῷ ἐπιθυμεῖν). We are not told that he strives with his might to move his hand in some other direction. Likewise, we are not told in the *NE* that the person lifted by the wind or stronger persons must physically resist to be counted as acting under βία. The person in the *EE*, however, does resist both in wish and desire. Kenny, although he does not cite the *EE* passage, seems to understand the *NE* criterion "contributes nothing" to be similar in its implications to the resistance in wish and desire described in the *EE* passage. For he would exclude from ἀκούσιοι actions on the basis of the "contributes nothing" criterion both a case where even though overpowered and

---

[21] Using this passage to elucidate the "contributes nothing" criterion for τὸ βίαιον is problematic because strictly speaking, the example is given as an explanation of ἀνάγκη and not βία. At 1224b10–14 Aristotle explains the *enkrates* and *ankrates* act neither under βία nor ἀνάγκη but explains why they do not act under ἀνάγκη with the example of the person whose hand is used to strike another. It is true that before giving this example he describes what is called ἀνάγκη very much the same way he has described what is said to be done by βία a few lines above at 1224b7–8: for both designations an external ἀρχή moves or hinders something contrary to that thing's ὁρμή. Moreover, this example but without the description of the victim resisting in wish and desire, is used at *NE* 1135a26–28 as an example of someone acting under βία. However, if there is a difference between βία and ἀνάγκη in this passage, although a clear distinction between βία and ἀνάγκη is not sustained in chapter 8 of the *EE*, the difference seems to be the added description that the person who acts under ἀνάγκη resists in wish and desire.

used instrumentally the victim approves the action in some sense, and a case where one plans ahead to be used instrumentally by another.[22] Aspasius also counts this second case as one in which the ἀρχή is within the person so used.[23]

It is not clear to me, however, that Aristotle has in mind to exclude from ἀκούσιοι actions both cases by the criterion "contributes nothing." In the *NE* the concern is to pinpoint the starting-point of motion and exclude from τὸ ἀκούσιον based on τὸ βίαιον, those cases in which the person does himself move his own body parts even when subject to threats of force or other external coercion. Thus, the second case, where person B is ordered by person A to move person A, is excluded by the *NE* definition. A is the source of A's motion although A does not move himself in the ordinary way but uses B instrumentally to bring about the motion. A is not the victim of βία. But in the first case, although A happens not to mind or even approves, A is not the starting-point of A's motion. Since B uses A instrumentally, it seems to be a legitimate case of τὸ βίαιον. The problem is A's attitude and whether or not his positive attitude can be a reason to reject this as a case of τὸ βίαιον because of the criterion that the agent "contribute nothing."

The discomfort induced by this exceptional case cannot be resolved simply by assuming Aristotle means to include an attitudinal criterion for cases of τὸ βίαιον. Establishing such a criterion would prove to be a complex matter since having a particular attitude about what one suffers could be described as actually contributing to an action which meets the outside ἀρχή criterion only under certain conditions. For example, one could argue that the victim's positive attitude contributed to the action if some effort on the victim's part to counteract the force exerted on him could significantly alter what happens to him, but the victim makes no such effort because of his positive attitude toward that which he is suffering. On the whole, I think it unwise to complicate Aristotle's position with an attitudinal criterion since Aristotle does not discuss the role even of physical resistance in describing what counts as τὸ βίαιον, and since he states no condition that there must be evidence of attitudinal resistance in order to count a case as one of τὸ βίαιον.

Can a victim of βία, βία narrowly construed to meet Aristotle's criteria, be ἑκών? I think such a case is a problem for Aristotle because by his criteria, we would expect such a person to be ἄκων. For the reasons I have just outlined, a resolution of this problem based on the "contributes nothing" criterion (that is, counting the case of the person used instrumentally while subject to βία as

---

[22]See Kenny, *Theory of the Will*, 29–30. According to Kenney, another way "something forced may fail to be involuntary" by the contributes nothing criterion, is a case where the agent "fails to resist when he could." I find Aristotle's silence on this detail curious. But since he is silent, I do not suppose one must physically resist in order to legitimately claim βία.

[23]Aspasius, *Com.* 59.16–17 (see above, n. 15).

nonetheless ἑκών because this person's attitude toward this event was somehow positive) is unsatisfactory. But consider what kind of a solution it would be: it is the sort of special case solution I have already rejected, the sort which leads to multiple and diverse meanings quite distinct from the definitional core of τὸ ἀκούσιον based on whether the ἀρχή of motion is internal or external. This time it is wishing and desiring that are treated as underlying special senses of ἑκούσιος.[24]

Some examples and exceptions

What clearly counts as βίαιον in the ANV for animate creatures, viz., action whose starting-point of motion is outside the creature moved, action in which it is not in this creature's power to act or not act, is much narrower than what counts under the FOV. For the FOV counts even threats of βία as βία, and all βία as just one sort of ἀνάγκη. So far then, the *NE* negative account can readily be seen to accommodate passages where ἄκων is conjoined with actual superior force, e.g., Persephone carried off by robbers (*HDem.* 122–25), but not the many passages involving only threatened βία or other types of ἀνάγκη where the agent victim is ἄκων. These are not in accord with Aristotle's preference that the agent be considered ἑκών under such circumstances. Passages where βία, narrowly construed, is in strong opposition with being ἑκών, can also be accommodated by the *NE* negative account. However, the examples of strong opposition discussed in Chapter 2 that the FOV accommodates did not take account of a distinction between actual force and threatened force along with other sorts of ἀνάγκη since the FOV is generous in what it counts as βία and ἀνάγκη. Thus, those passages discussed in Chapter 2, which show strong opposition between acting ἑκών and acting under threatened βία or other types of ἀνάγκη, say too much for the *NE* negative account. A good example of strong opposition between ἑκών and βία narrowly construed to meet Aristotle's criteria, would be the passage from Sophocles' *Philoctetes* (981–88) where the contrast is between Philoctetes being carried off by the superior force of Odysseus' henchmen or going on his own. The implication from the exchange between the two characters is that Philoctetes would go ἑκών as long as he goes himself, i.e., moves his own limbs, rather than carried by Odysseus' men. This passage resembles Aristotle's mixed cases and is in accord with his preference for them. In contrast, this same passage has been identified as an exception to the FOV

---

[24]The *EE* ruled out wish and desire as sole bases for determining whether an action is ἑκούσιος or ἀκούσιος (*EE* 2.7). It is also fair to mention that since attitude is the essence of ἑκών group words in my own view, I am inclined to resist burying this feature without sufficient recognition in the contributes nothing criterion of τὸ βίαιον.

since a real threat of force would persist even as Philoctetes moved his own limbs.[25]

The *NE* negative account also does not accommodate passages where βία, narrowly construed as superior actual force, is conjoined with being ἑκών. The passage from Gorgias' *Defense of Palamedes* (B.11a.11DK) which I singled out in Chapter 2 as an example of ἑκών conjoined even with actual force, falls short of meeting Aristotle's criteria for the βίαιον since the slaves involved do themselves move their own body parts as they accuse their master. Thus, this passage speaks only against the FOV with its broader definition of βία, since the force involved in this passage is more akin to the severe actual force suffered by victims who are regularly ἄκοντες under the FOV. But, because Aristotle's criteria for βίαιον are stricter than the FOV, this example does not speak against the *NE* negative account. Moreover, those passages in which victims of what counts as βία for the FOV are ἑκόντες, discussed in Chapter 2 as counting against the FOV, also do not count against the *NE* negative account, since the βία would not meet Aristotle's criteria. In fact, as in mixed cases, the *NE* negative account accommodates them quite well, since Aristotle's preference is that the agent victims under such circumstances are ἑκόντες. However, of the passages discussed in Chapter 2 as exceptions to the FOV, there are two cases in which characters are subject to force which can be construed to meet Aristotle's criteria, although the victims are ἑκοῦσαι.

In Euripides' *Electra* (1065–68), Electra, speaking of Helen to Clytemnestra, says she was seized and destroyed ἑκοῦσα (ἡ μὲν γὰρ ἁρπασθεῖσ' ἑκοῦσ' ἀπώλετο); in Euripides' *Alcmeon* (68.1–2*TGF*), Alcmeon is asked whether or not he killed his mother ἑκοῦσαν (⟨Α⟩ μητέρα κατέκταν τὴν ἐμήν, βραχὺς λόγος. ⟨Φ⟩ ἑκὼν ἑκοῦσαν ἢ ⟨οὐ⟩ θέλουσαν οὐχ ἑκών;). The actions in both passages are of the sort discussed in Chapters 1 and 2 and found to typify βία. There may be disagreement nonetheless about whether these passages do actually meet Aristotle's criteria. But ultimately, I suspect the hesitation to agree that the force involved does meet Aristotle's criteria is due more to the as-

---

[25] Recall that in ch. 2, when setting out the developing or technical senses approach to reconciling what appear to be exceptions to the FOV, this passage was discussed as a possible indication of a special technical or legal usage. It might be thought that Aristotle's focus on so strong and narrow a view of βία is yet another indication that there was such a technical sense developing in the 5th century and full-blown in Aristotle. In addition to my criticism of this way of dealing with apparent exceptions, it should again be emphasized that Aristotle's project may be less to establish the meaning of ἑκών group words, than to determine reliable and basic cases of τὸ ἀκούσιον and τὸ ἑκούσιον. In contrast, the FOV and my own view are meant to establish the meaning of these words. From the evidence examined, it is quite true that ordinarily a person is ἄκων when subject to actual, overwhelming force (or when the person has erred because of ignorance). But identifying cases in which a person is regularly ἄκων is not the same thing as saying what it means to be ἄκων.

sumption that someone subject to such force could not be ἑκών than to some doubt about the kind of force ordinarily implied by the actions described. Being ἑκοῦσα and being a victim of superior force are assumed to be mutually exclusive. But if we do not take the fact that the victims are ἑκοῦσαι as reason to exclude superior force, then in these cases the victims can be understood to be ἑκοῦσαι and subjected to βία construed narrowly. For example, it is not unreasonable, indeed it is quite plausible, to imagine Helen literally carried off by Paris or his comrades. Nor is it necessary to ignore the passive participle ἁρπασθεῖσ' and imagine Helen walking under guard—an action that would not meet Aristotle's criteria for βίαιον.

It is true that the ANV, relying on its criterion of "contributes nothing," could accommodate the passages while granting the βία is strong, if the victims are understood as being the starting-points (ἀρχαί) of their sufferings. The victims would have to be construed as having initiated the actions performed on them. This is the sort of scenario Aspasius imagines when he writes, "In fact, if someone having taken hold of me should carry me lifted off the ground, when I gave the command and wished it, the starting-point is in me."[26] But there is no reason to think Eriphyle ordered her son to kill her; and one would have to assume an unusual version of the Helen story to suppose it was Helen's idea that she be carried off to Troy.[27] In the case of Eriphyle, however, since it is a stranger uninformed about the details of the story who asks whether she was killed ἑκοῦσα, this reading cannot be dismissed as a possible explanation of his question. Thus, if the stranger had in mind that Alcmeon's mother may have initiated her own death, the ANV could account for the use of ἑκοῦσα here. If not, then both women can be pictured as victims of force, but their attitudes are not the usual attitudes of victims of force. Furthermore, it should be noted that the version of the "contributes nothing" criterion in Aristotle's definition of τὸ ἀκούσιον which I rejected above, would allow these examples to fit the ANV. The grounds would be that the victims' positive attitudes alone prevent them from meeting the "contributes nothing" criterion. But I have argued that criterion has to do with a contribution to the motion of the action, so that merely having a positive attitude toward the action would not be enough to breach the criterion and disallow each of the victims from being ἀκοῦσα. Thus, the ANV cannot accommodate these passages if the characters are taken to be victims of βία narrowly construed. Their being victims of such force ought to exclude them from being ἑκοῦσαι.

---

[26]Aspasius, *Com.* 59.16–17.

[27]See E. Beta in *RE* 61.461–62 and 72.2831–35 or H.J. Rose, *A Handbook of Greek Mythology Including Its Extension to Rome*, 6th ed. (London, 1958), 221, n. 30 and 249, n. 7, for sources on Eriphyle and Helen, respectively.

Actions which come about through ignorance

Like his account of actions that are ἀκούσιοι because of βία, Aristotle is specific in his account of actions that are ἀκούσιοι because of ignorance (δι' ἄγνοιαν).[28] First (NE 1110b18–20), one who acts δι' ἄγνοιαν must also be "pained" or "regret" his act in order for the act to count as ἀκούσιος. But merely acting δι' ἄγνοιαν is enough to exclude the act from τὸ ἑκούσιον: τὸ δὲ δι' ἄγνοιαν οὐχ ἑκούσιον μὲν ἅπαν ἐστίν; and ἑκὼν μὲν οὐ πέπραχεν, ὅ γε μὴ ᾔδει. Likewise, an agent's not being pained (μὴ λυπούμενος) at his act is enough to exclude the act from τὸ ἀκούσιον: οὐδ' αὖ ἄκων, μὴ λυπούμενός γε (1110b21–22).[29] Thus, granting a strong connection between being pained and feeling regret, of those who act δι' ἄγνοιαν, the agent who feels regret is ἄκων, while the agent who does not is designated οὐχ ἑκών to distinguish him from both the ἑκών agent and the ἄκων agent: τοῦ δὴ δι' ἄγνοιαν ὁ μὲν ἐν μεταμελείᾳ ἄκων δοκεῖ, ὁ δὲ μὴ μεταμελόμενος, ἐπεὶ ἕτερος, ἔστω οὐχ ἑκών· ἐπεὶ γὰρ διαφέρει, βέλτιον ὄνομα ἔχειν ἴδιον. (NE 1110b22–24).

When Aristotle sets this condition, it should be noted that he makes pain and regret characteristics of τὸ ἀκούσιον generally and not only of τὸ ἀκούσιον that is δι' ἄγνοιαν: ἀκούσιον δὲ τὸ ἐπίλυπον καὶ ἐν μεταμελείᾳ (NE 1110b18–19). In the NE this characteristic of τὸ ἀκούσιον is not all that prominent in the discussion of what counts as ἀκούσιον because of βία, but it is not entirely lacking there either. In the EE, although Aristotle is silent about the connection between pain and regret and being ἄκων in cases of ignorance, he relies on a strong relationship between βίαιον and λυπηρόν in his discussion of whether all τὸ ἑκούσιον is according to desire (κατ' ἐπιθυμίαν): τὸ γὰρ ἀκούσιον πᾶν δοκεῖ εἶναι βίαιον, τὸ δὲ βίαιον λυπηρόν...ὥστ' εἴ τι λυπηρὸν βίαιον καὶ εἴ τι βίαιον λυπηρόν (EE 1223a29ff.). In both the NE and the EE Aristotle's arguments about the enkrates and the akrates, that what is pleasant (τὰ ἡδέα) and beautiful (τὰ καλά), viewed as things that coerce from without, do not count as βίαια, implies that pain is a necessary characteristic of what happens by force and is ἀκούσιον.[30]

---

[28]I will rely primarily on the NE's discussion of action that is ἀκούσιος because of ignorance, since it is more detailed than the parallel discussion in EE 2.9.

[29]See also Aristotle's summary about ἀκούσιον that is δι' ἄγνοιαν, NE 1111a19–21.

[30]See also NE 1110b11–13, EE 1224a30ff. Kenny, *Theory of the Will*, 53–54, is particularly unappreciative of this characteristic of τὸ ἀκούσιον. He says, "Aristotle makes a slightly puzzling connection between involuntariness and repentance or remorse" (53). His criticism of Aristotle begins from what we would say about "voluntary" and "involuntary" without any hesitation as to whether or not the inference is legitimate for τὸ ἑκούσιον and τὸ ἀκούσιον. Without apparent concern about how the concepts he uses correspond with the Greek ones em-

Next, Aristotle distinguishes acting δι' ἄγνοιαν from acting ἀγνοῶν, thereby excluding from τὰ ἀκούσια the actions of someone who is drunk or enraged (ὀργιζόμενος: *NE* 1110b24–27). Our idiom too would say of such an agent that he "does not know what he is doing." But this is not a sense of ignorance involved in an ἀκούσιος act. Also, ignorance of what sorts of things should be chosen and avoided generally is not the sort of ignorance involved in the ἀκούσιος act (*NE* 1110b28ff.). What does render an action ἀκούσιος in conjunction with pain or regret, is ignorance of particulars, those circumstances in which the action occurs and which the action concerns. For pity and forgiveness, the appropriate responses to what is ἀκούσιον,[31] are appropriate to those ignorant of the particular details of an action; but only blame is due to those ignorant of what sorts of things ought to be chosen:

> οὐ γὰρ ἡ ἐν τῇ προαιρέσει ἄγνοια αἰτία τοῦ ἀκουσίου ἀλλὰ τῆς μοχθηρίας, οὐδ' ἡ καθόλου (ψέγονται γὰρ διά γε ταύτην) ἀλλ' ἡ καθ' ἕκαστα, ἐν οἷς καὶ περὶ ἃ ἡ πρᾶξις· ἐν τούτοις γὰρ καὶ ἔλεος καὶ συγγνώμη· ὁ γὰρ τούτων τι ἀγνοῶν ἀκουσίως πράττει
>
> (*NE* 1110b31–1111a2).

From what Aristotle says especially of the drunk (*NE* 1113b30ff.), it would seem that even if he acts while ignorant of the sort of details that are ordinarily part of the ἀκούσιος act, the special circumstances of his condition takes precedence, and his ignorance of detail is not relevant. We can infer that ordinarily, the acts of someone who is drunk are to be counted as ἑκούσιοι (unless perhaps because of unusual circumstances of force or ignorance, the agent can be counted as ἄκων when he became drunk, or perhaps because he acts under βία which would have moved him even if he had not been drunk). Likewise from Aristotle's remarks at the conclusion of *NE* 3.1, we should also count acts done from *thumos* (ἀπὸ θυμοῦ) and from desire (ἀπὸ ἐπιθυμίας) as ἑκούσιοι. Aristotle concludes it would be absurd to think such acts ἀκούσια: ἄτοπον δὴ τὸ τιθέναι ἀκούσια ταῦτα (*NE* 1111b3). But it should be noted that in this passage Aristotle is offering arguments against what some actually say about such acts. Aristotle concludes that the drunk or someone whose acts are due to *thumos* or appetite should not be counted as ἄκων, but we can infer that others would count such persons as ἄκοντες. Thus, we can expect that what we find in the passages collected for this study may differ from Aristotle's conclusions. It happens, for example, that in the examples of a victim subject to internal

---

ployed in Aristotle, he concludes his remark on *NE* 3.1, saying, "Probably, Aristotle is here influenced by the use of ἄκων to mean 'unwillingly' 'reluctantly'..." (53).

[31] See *NE* 1109b31–32. Cf. the passages discussed at the end of ch. 3, which mention forgiveness and pity as the appropriate responses to τὸ ἀκούσιον.

force (βία [ia]) discussed in Chapter 2, each of the victims is ἄκων.³² Consider too the following passages in which agents who are intoxicated are described by ἑκών group words. In a fragment from a Sophoclean drama, the speaker tells of the consequences of being intoxicated:

> τί ταῦτ' ἐπαινεῖς; πᾶς γὰρ οἰνωθεὶς ἀνὴρ
> ἥσσων μὲν ὀργῆς ἐστι, τοῦ δὲ νοῦ κενός·
> φιλεῖ δὲ πολλὴν γλῶσσαν ἐκχέας μάτην
> ἄκων ἀκούειν οὓς ἑκὼν εἴπῃ λόγους.
> (Soph. *TrGF* 929.1–4)

Yielding to his temper and witless, the intoxicated man has a loose tongue. We can infer that ἑκών describes the agent when he speaks while intoxicated; he may be drunk or recovered when he ἄκων hears the sort of words he himself spoke while intoxicated. In a fragment from Euripides' *Auge* (265.1–2*TGF*), the speaker admits to having committed an act of injustice while drunk, but he says it was not ἑκούσιον: τὸ δ' ἀδίκημ' ἐγένετ' οὐχ ἑκούσιον. It is true that a defendant can be expected to say almost anything in his own defense. Nevertheless, to be effective the plea must be plausible. Aristotle's negative view seems to fit the use of ἑκών in the first passage but not the second. We will see later that his Positive View can accommodate both.

Aristotle lists the particulars that do render an action ἀκούσιος if the action is also painful and the agent has regret: τίς τε δὴ καὶ τί καὶ περὶ τί ἢ ἐν τίνι πράττει, ἐνίοτε δὲ καὶ τίνι, οἷον ὀργάνῳ, καὶ ἕνεκα τίνος, οἷον σωτηρίας, καὶ πῶς, οἷον ἠρέμα ἢ σφόδρα (*NE* 1111a3–6), and τοῦ δὴ κατὰ τὴν τοιαύτην ἄγνοιαν ἀκουσίου λεγομένου ἔτι δεῖ τὴν πρᾶξιν λυπηρὰν εἶναι καὶ ἐν μεταμελείᾳ (*NE* 1111a19–21)³³ He eliminates the possibility that one could be ignorant in all these ways without being mad *NE* 1111a6–7), in which case the action probably would be neither ἑκούσιον, nor οὐχ ἑκούσιον, nor ἀκούσιον.³⁴ He also seems to eliminate being ignorant of who is acting, τίς, since it appears to Aristotle it is not possible to be ignorant of oneself: πῶς γὰρ ἑαυτόν γε; (*NE* 1111a7). Perhaps we should infer that to be so ignorant

---

³²See discussion in ch. 2 pp. 40–41 on Theog. 371–72 and Simon. Fr. 541.7–11 *PMG*.

³³See Gauthier and Jolif, vol. 2, pt. 1, ad loc for various views on περὶ τί ἢ ἐν τίνι πράττει. Also, compare the list of particulars in *NE* 1135a23ff.; see remarks below in n. 37.

³⁴The madman would have to count as acting δι' ἄγνοιαν in order for his act to be either οὐχ ἑκούσιος or ἀκούσιος (*NE* 1110b18–19). But I take the implication of Aristotle's remark that someone who is ignorant in all the ways he lists is mad, to be that the madman's extreme ignorance is not what he has in mind as what counts as acting δι' ἄγνοιαν. The madman could fit well, however, with those who act ἀγνοοῦντες, the drunk or enraged man. Because the madman does not act knowingly, his act cannot be ἑκούσιος (*NE* 1110b24–27).

would also be characteristic of a madman whose actions are not included in the discussion.³⁵ This leaves τί; περὶ τί ἢ ἐν τίνι πράττει; τίνι, οἷον ὀργάνῳ; ἕνεκα τίνος, οἷον σωτηρίας; and πῶς, οἷον ἠρέμα ἢ σφόδρα. Aristotle continues with a series of examples which match-up in order with these generalized expressions of the ways people can act through ignorance; and do so ἄκοντες.

His examples of what one is doing, τί, include letting something slip out while speaking or not knowing what one says is a secret or setting off a catapult when only intending to explain how it works. Aristotle's example of what or whom one acts on, περὶ τί ἢ ἐν τίνι πράττει, is the case of Merope who supposed someone to be an enemy who was actually her own son.³⁶ Thinking one's spear was tipped with a button or that a stone was only pumice are examples of mistakes about instruments, τίνι, οἷον ὀργάνῳ. Giving a man a draught to save him that actually kills him, corresponds to that for the sake of which one acts, ἕνεκα τίνος, οἷον σωτηρίας. Finally, the example of one who intends only to touch his partner while sparring but actually wounds him, fits how one acts, πῶς.³⁷

Using Aristotle's list of particulars and examples, several of the passages discussed in Chapter 3 under error can be accommodated easily. There is, for example, Philocleon (Ar. *Wasps* 990–92, 999–1002/#1–2) who acquitted the canine defendant by misplacing his ballot, a case of instrumental error; and in Thucydides (4.30), although there is no detail about the fire set ἄκων, still it is likely that ignorance of one or the other of Aristotle's particulars could account for the error.³⁸ Some of the examples may correspond to more than one of Aristotle's particulars. For example, in Sophocles' *Trachiniae* (932–35 and 1122–23), Deianira's killing of Heracles involves ignorance of instrument, τίνι, and of end, ἕνεκα τίνος.

---

³⁵Although Oedipus, for example, can be described as being ignorant of τίς πράττει, as M. Ostwald has commented to me, Aristotle does not seem to take this view. See the discussion of περὶ τί ἢ ἐν τίνι πράττει, above.

³⁶See Gauthier and Jolif, vol. 2. pt. 1, 184–185 for a discussion of whether περὶ τί ἢ ἐν τίνι πράττει refers specifically to the thing or person that is the object of the action or more generally to the "domain" of the action.

³⁷In *NE* 5.8 where Aristotle distinguishes; ἀτύχημα, ἁμάρτημα, and ἀδίκημα, he more briefly states and gives examples of the sorts of ignorance that render an agent ἄκων (1135a23ff.). His summary, μήτε ὃν μήτε ᾧ μήτε οὗ ⟨ἕνεκα⟩, suggests the object or person acted on, the instrument, and the end of the action are the most important particulars. (Ignorance of the instrument is left out in Aristotle's statement of the most important details in *NE* 1111a15–19.) Since the first member of the list, ὅν clearly refers to a person acted on, I am inclined to read περὶ τί ἢ ἐν τίνι πράττει at 1111a3–6 as an expansion of the rather general τί.

³⁸The wind that fanned the small fire and caused large scale destruction arose after the small fire was started by the soldier. I take it that this natural and perhaps παραλόγως event was not part of the soldier's error.

In other passages where the ignorance under which the agents labored was supernaturally imposed, the ignorance is nonetheless of particulars. Thus, in Euripides' *Hippolytus* (1431-36), Theseus, ignorant of what really transpired between Hippolytus and Phaedra, is said ἄκων to have destroyed his son; and Oedipus, (Soph. *OC* 960-99/#1,2,4), ἄκων killed his father and ἄκων married his mother, ignorant in both cases of περὶ τί ἢ ἐν τίνι πράττει. Aristotle actually gives the example of someone striking a man he does not know is his own father in *NE* 5 where he recapitulates in a shorter fashion what he said earlier in Book 3 about ἀκούσια through ignorance. In the Book 5 passage, the example is more clearly stated as ignorance of whom one strikes, τίνα τύπτει (*NE* 1135a25).

A further distinction Aristotle makes in the *NE* (5.8) relevant to acts that happen through ignorance is that between ἁμάρτημα and ἀτύχημα.[39] He explains there are three sorts of harm (βλάβαι): ἁμαρτήματα, ἀτυχήματα, and ἀδικήματα. The first two are of concern here:

τριῶν δὴ οὐσῶν βλαβῶν τῶν ἐν ταῖς κοινωνίαις, τὰ μὲν μετ' ἀγνοίας ἁμαρτήματά ἐστιν, ὅταν μήτε ὃν μήτε ὃ μήτε ᾧ μήτε οὗ ἕνεκα ὑπέλαβε πράξῃ... ὅταν μὲν οὖν παραλόγως ἡ βλάβη γένηται, ἀτύχημα· ὅταν δὲ μὴ παραλόγως, ἄνευ δὲ κακίας, ἁμάρτημα (ἁμαρτάνει μὲν γὰρ ὅταν ἡ ἀρχὴ ἐν αὐτῷ ᾖ τῆς αἰτίας, ἀτυχεῖ δ' ὅταν ἔξωθεν)
(*NE* 1135b11-19)

What counts as παραλόγως (contrary to reason), the characteristic of ἀτυχήματα, is not clear from the passage, especially since Aristotle gives no example. From a passage in the *Physics*, however, in a discussion of τύχη (chance), we learn that something which occurs παραλόγως occurs contrary to what happens always or for the most part: καὶ τὸ φάναι εἶναί τι παράλογον τὴν τύχην ὀρθῶς· ὁ γὰρ λόγος ἢ τῶν ἀεὶ ὄντων ἢ τῶν ἐπὶ τὸ πολύ, ἡ δὲ τύχη ἐν τοῖς γιγνομένοις παρὰ ταῦτα (*Ph.* 197a18-20)[40] With this in mind, of the error examples just discussed, the action of the fellow in Thucydides who started a fire ἄκων is a more likely candidate for an ἀτύχημα than the actions of Deianira or Philocleon.[41]

The point to be made is that in those passages where according to Aristotle's criteria the agent acts δι' ἄγνοιαν, if the agent feels pain or regret, whether the acts are considered to be; ἁμαρτήματα or ἀτυχήματα, they can be accommodated by Aristotle's ἀκούσιον. Ἀτυχήματα as well as ἁμαρτήματα may in-

---

[39]The distinction is made elsewhere too. See *Rhetoric* 1374bff.

[40]Cf. *EE* 1247a31-33.

[41]It is interesting to note that the story of Oedipus provides much to recommend it as a case of ἀτύχημα, but in the *Poetics* (1453a7ff.), it is Aristotle's prime example of an ἁμάρτημα.

volve ignorance of the sort that Aristotle counts as relevant to what is ἀκούσιον because of ignorance, δι' ἄγνοιαν.[42] The difference between the two types of acts is that in cases of ἀτυχήματα which involve ignorance, the agent could not have expected the circumstances of which he was ignorant.[43] Generally then, Aristotle's negative view, like the FOV, can accommodate passages where the agent acting through ignorance is ἄκων. But one other passage which was discussed in Chapter 3 under error should be discussed here to see if Aristotle's account of τὸ ἀκούσιον can accommodate it.

---

[42] In my view this kind of τὸ ἀκούσιον is to be distinguised from that which occurs by force (βίᾳ) where the starting-point of motion is the important issue. In ἀτυχήματα (NE 1135b18–19), because of circumstances that are παραλόγως, the starting-point of the αἰτία (ἡ ἀρχὴ τῆς αἰτίας) is from without (ἔξωθεν); but in ἁμαρτήματα, the starting-point of the αἰτία is in the agent (ἐν αὐτῷ). I understand τῆς αἰτίας to refer more broadly to "explanation." Where circumstances relevant to an agent's act are παραλόγως, they must be referred to in an adequate account of that act. But in many cases (not those like Aristotle's example of the falling statue in the *Poetics*, [1452a4ff.]) the agent is nonetheless the starting-point of motion (ἡ ἀρχὴ τοῦ κινεῖν) according to the Book 3 ch. 1 understanding of ἀρχή, even if an adequate account of his act must include those external circumstances that occurred παραλόγως. In cases of both ἀτυχήματα and ἁμαρτήματα, the starting-point of motion (NE 1110a15) is within the agent. However, his act is not ἑκούσιος because he acts δι' ἄγνοιαν (rather than ἀγνοῶν) and if he feels pain or regret, his act is ἀκούσιος. Jackson (*Aristotle: Ethica Nicomachea Book V*, ed. H. Jackson [Cambridge, 1879]), argues that the "strange phrase" ἡ ἀρχὴ τῆς αἰτίας, is a corruption of ἡ ἀρχὴ τῆς ἀγνοίας. He cites as evidence NE 3.5.8 and MM 1195a27–b4 where the distinction is drawn between cases where the agent is αἴτιος of the ignorance under which he acts and those cases where he is not. Stewart argues that the phrase is odd and says it does not appear elsewhere in Aristotle; but on the basis of the Hippocratic περὶ ἀρχαίης ἰητρακῆς where he thinks the phrase does occur in the sense of *principium causae*, he does not emend the text nor does he read αἰτίας as *criminis*. Joachim (*Commentary*, ad loc) says of Jackson's emendation that if it is accepted, the distinction between ἀτύχημα and ἁμάρτημα will "perhaps" correspond to the Book 3 (1110b18–30) distinction between δι' ἄγνοιαν and ἀγνοῶν. But this distinction does not seem to me to be relevant to the distinction Aristotle makes about things happening παραλόγως. I see no reason to liken the agent involved in an ἀτύχημα to a drunk or madman. The agent's world may seem mad, but not the agent. Jolif (vol. 2, pt.1, 401) however, notes that some manuscripts (M^b H^a B^2) have κακίας instead of αἰτίας and that an ancient reading of αἰκίας could be conjectured. According to Liddell and Scott, *Greek-English Lexicon*, in prose, this word is a legal term for "assault." If one does prefer the reading κακίας or αἰκίας, the point still seems to be about a more general explanation of the act taken as κακία or αἰκία, and the agent is still the starting-point of motion.

[43] Cf. Joachim ad loc. He too takes ἀτυχήματα to fall under τὸ ἀκούσιον because of ignorance (Aristotle, *The Nicomachean Ethics: A Commentary by the Late H.H. Joachim*, ed. D.A. Rees [Oxford, 1951]).

In a passage of the Theognidean corpus (1377–80), the poet speaks of his failure to win the love of a παῖς: ἐγὼ δ' ἀέκων τῆς σῆς φιλότητος ἁμαρτών. This sense of ἁμαρτάνειν, missing the mark as failure to achieve one's goal, does not readily fit with the kinds of error Aristotle counts in designating τὸ ἀκούσιον. Although one could conjecture about all sorts of details about the beloved of which the failed lover is ignorant, this sort of ignorance does not seem to be the explanation of the lover's failure. It does not seem that the lover does not know what he is doing, τί, in a way that fits Aristotle's understanding and examples; nor will it help to introduce what happens παραλόγως. More to the point is that the success of the undertaking does not depend solely on the agent lover and his awareness of the particulars of what he is trying to accomplish. What the lover is attempting to establish is a relationship which depends not only on the lover but on the beloved too. The lover cannot be successful without the participation of the beloved. Getting the beloved to participate in a relationship is not the sort of thing that can be accomplished merely on the basis of the lover's action, however well-informed he might be of the relevant details of the situation. The action simply is not the sort of thing that is securely within the power of the agent lover to do.

The passage is accommodated by the FOV since the FOV does not have as narrow a view of error as does the ANV. But according to the *NE* account, it is not a case of acting; δι' ἄγνοιαν or under βία and therefore does not count as ἀκούσιος (or οὐχ ἑκούσιος). The passage will have to await the positive account of τὸ ἑκούσιον before it can be determined whether Aristotle can accommodate it at all.

Finally, it should be noted that the distinction Aristotle draws between ἄκων and οὐχ ἑκών is not born out in the passages. Deianira, for example, who surely suffered pain and regret for her act, is described by both ἄκουσα (Soph. *Tr.* 932–35) and οὐχ ἑκουσία (1122–23). Philocleon too is both ἄκων and οὐχ ἑκών (Ar. *Wasps* 990–92, 999–1002/#1–2), and no one could be more full of regret than he for ever having acquitted even a dog. This does not mean that Aristotle's account of τὸ ἀκούσιον does not accommodate these passages. Even where it is not clear that an agent felt regret (e.g., the fellow who started the fire in Thuc. 4.30), in all the passages involving error where the agent is described as ἄκων, there is no case where it is likely the agent did not feel regret, and the errors do involve ignorance of the particulars as Aristotle sets them out. Aristotle's account of τὸ ἀκούσιον fits the passages; it is the distinction between ἄκων and οὐχ ἑκών that is not evident.

THE ARISTOTELIAN POSITIVE VIEW (APV)

Description

In contrast to the views expressed in the ethical works, Aristotle presents a positive account of τὸ ἑκούσιον, one that does not rely on first defining what is ἀκούσιος, in the *De Anima* and the *De Motu Animalium*. For the basic description of this positive account, I will rely on M. Nussbaum's clear presentation.[44]

As Nussbaum describes Aristotle's view in her explication of *DeM*, ch.6, there are "(generically) two 'movers' of the animal, both of which will play a role in our explanation" (*CE* 137). Aristotle calls them νοῦς and ὄρεξις.[45] νοῦς includes διάνοια, φαντασία, and αἴσθησις; ὄρεξις includes βούλησις, θυμός, and ἐπιθυμία; and προαίρεσις shares in both divisions. Every explanation of an action must make reference to some form of each of these generic divisions. Nussbaum explains, "neither is, alone, sufficient to move the animal."[46] Her description of how some form of νοῦς and ὄρεξις are involved in each action is worth quoting:

> Many objects in the world are presented to the animal by its cognitive faculties. Among these, some will be objects of some sort of ὄρεξις and some will not. Among the objects of ὄρεξις, in turn, some will turn out to be available or 'possible': the animal will either see them or reason out some way to get them. The full answer to chapter 7's question, 'How does it happen that cognition is sometimes accompanied by action and sometimes not?' involves reference not only to the creature's ὀρέξεις but also to some cognitive activity that will supply the 'premise' 'of the possible'. The cognitive faculties perform, then, a double role. They present the goal to the animal's awareness initially, and they also perform work that gets the animal from ὄρεξις for the goal to action directed at a specific available object in the world. In many cases, these two operations will not be distinct: the animal's ὄρεξις may be aroused to activity just by seeing the very item for which it then goes... The final result is that ὄρεξις, as a 'mover', is absolutely central; but it does nothing alone, without the aid of perception or thought. Ani-

---

[44] See M. Nussbaum, "The 'Common Explanation' of Animal Motion," *Symposium Aristotelicum*, ed. P. Moraux and J. Wiesner (Berlin, 1983), 116–156 (hereafter Nussbaum, "Common Explanation," with citations appearing as *CE* with page numbers). Nussbaum's book, *Aristotle's De Motu Animalium*, (Princeton, 1978), especially the commentary on ch. 11 and essay 5 on φαντασία, provides more on issues touched upon in the article.

[45] As Nussbaum explains, νοῦς is used as a generic term here for the cognitive faculties. See her Commentary on 700b17. See Nussbaum, *CE*, for Aristotle's development of this technical term.

[46] Nussbaum, *Aristotle's DeM*, p. 333 on 700b17.

mals act in accordance with desire, but within limits imposed by the world of nature, as they see it. The 'good' and the 'possible' must come together in order for movement to result (*CE* 137–8).⁴⁷

In chapter 11 of *DeM*, these movements which come about through the creature's desires and cognitions are called ἑκούσιοι: Πῶς μὲν οὖν κινεῖται τὰς ἑκουσίους κινήσεις τὰ ζῷα, καὶ διὰ τίνας αἰτίας, εἴρηται (703b3–4).⁴⁸ In addition, Aristotle distinguishes two other sorts of movements: movements he calls ἀκούσιοι include the movement of the heart and penis; movements called οὐχ ἑκούσιοι include going to sleep, waking, and respiration:

κινεῖται δέ τινας καὶ ἀκουσίους ἔνια τῶν μερῶν, τὰς δὲ πλείστας οὐχ ἑκουσίους. λέγω δ' ἀκουσίους μὲν οἷον τὴν τῆς καρδίας τε καὶ τὴν τοῦ αἰδοίου (πολλάκις γὰρ φανέντος τινός, οὐ μέντοι κελεύσαντος τοῦ νοῦ κινοῦται), οὐχ ἑκουσίους δ' οἷον ὕπνον καὶ ἐγρήγορσιν καὶ ἀναπνοήν, καὶ ὅσαι ἄλλαι τοιαῦταί εἰσιν (οὐθενὸς γὰρ τούτων κυρία ἁπλῶς ἐστιν οὔθ' ἡ φαντασία οὔθ' ἡ ὄρεξις)   (703b4–11).

Nussbaum explains the ἀκούσιοι as "reflex responses of certain bodily parts: the leap of the heart from fright and the sudden (unwilled) erection of the penis"; and the οὐχ ἑκούσιοι as "systemic movements such as going to sleep, waking, and respiration" (*CE* 146).⁴⁹ The οὐχ ἑκούσιοι involve neither desire nor cognition; the ἀκούσιοι involve cognition of some sort but not desire.⁵⁰

---

⁴⁷Nussbaum refers us to her commentary and Essay 4 for a fuller account, background, and discussion of specific interpretive problems.

⁴⁸Nussbaum notes in *CE* 135–136, that in the *De Anima* Aristotle leaves unanswered, among other questions, this question which he does answer in the *DeM*: "Which movements of animals are explained by reference to desire and cognition?"

⁴⁹See *Aristotle's De M* ad loc for parallel passages.

⁵⁰Nussbaum, *CE* 146–147, explains: "In the *De Anima* it was left unclear whether all animal movement was to be viewed as caused by ὄρεξις: Aristotle made sweeping claims that suggested this. Now he explicitly recognizes that there is an important class of movements which cannot be so explained. Of the reflex motions, he says here (as in *De Anima* III 9) that the animal's own thought or φαντασία of the object does enter into the explanation of what happens; but there is lacking any resolve or ὄρεξις to perform the action, pursue the object. (Here the *De Anima* puts it better, indicating that it is the ὄρεξις that is lacking; the *De Motu* unclearly speaks of a command of the intellect). So the animal's own φαντασία, or view of the object, is relevant to explaining the leap of the heart; but because its desires are not engaged, what takes place is merely a sudden and partial movement, and no movement from place to place results. In the second group of cases, Aristotle asserts (compatibly with *Physics* VIII) that neither ὄρεξις nor φαντασία is properly in control of any of them. The explanation to be given is simply one that refers to the physiological necessities. The uncertainty of the *Physics* VIII passages as to whether this story holds good for all

On the extensional equivalence of Aristotle's positive and negative accounts

This account of ἑκούσιος movement, Nussbaum explains, unpacks more clearly than the ethical works what is of concern there as well as in the *DeA* and *DeM*:

> to isolate and characterize a group of movements which, unlike various other movements, may be said to be the ones for which the animal itself is the explanation, the ones that are done 'through the creature itself', not through some external force that uses the creature as its instrument (*CE* 147).[51]

But since the ethical works give a primarily negative account of τὸ ἑκούσιον, the question remains whether this positive account of the *DeA* and *DeM* "isolate the same group of actions" and "make the same points about our reasons for drawing the distinctions we draw" (*CE* 148).

Nussbaum argues that in fact the criterion of the *DeM* and *DeA* account of τὸ ἑκούσιον is extensionally equivalent to the criteria of the account in the ethical works. The positive account unpacks what it means in the negative account for the agent to be the ἀρχή or αἴτιον of the action, and like the negative account, excludes from ἑκούσιοι actions those actions performed under force (βία) or through ignorance (δι' ἄγνοιαν). The *DeM*'s positive account of τὸ ἑκούσιον furthermore, shows a connection between what in the ethical works appear to be rather disparate events, acts that occur under force and acts that occur because of ignorance.

Since on the *DeM* view "an action A is ἑκούσιος if and only if it is caused by the animal's own ὄρεξις for A and cognitive states concerning A" (*CE* 148–9), acts that occur under βία, narrowly construed as in the *NE*, are clearly excluded. Likewise, actions performed through ignorance (δι' ἄγνοιαν) would be excluded. For, insofar as these actions are performed in ignorance of particular details, there are legitimate descriptions of the action that do not correspond to

---

animal movements—and the opposing uncertainty of the *De Anima*, where it looked as if desire was involved in the explanation of all movements—are resolved now by saying that there are three relevantly different groups of animal movements. Many movements, including apparently all movements from place to place, require an explanation mentioning both desire and cognition. In other cases, physiology suffices. In the third group, selective cognition, but not ὄρεξις will enter in."

[51]Nussbaum also notes: "This account of the ἑκούσιον seems to be what underlies and explains Aristotle's repeated and entirely consistent ascription of it to other animals and to human children, as well as to human adults: though these less developed creatures lack deliberation, choice, and general principles, they do have in common with human adults that their own view of the world and their own ὀρέξεις, rather than physical necessity, are the causes of their actions" (CE 147–8).

the agent's intentional description at the time of action. Thus, since the agent would not have a desire and cognition to correspond to every legitimate description of the action, under certain descriptions, the agent cannot be said to be the doer of that action. Nussbaum illustrates this point with the case of Oedipus.

When his act is described as killing an old man at a crossroads, it must be ἑκούσιος. "There is the right sort of conceptual connectedness among the contents of desire, belief, and resulting action" (*CE* 149).[52] However, when this action is described as a parricide, the action does not fit the *DeM* criterion for being ἑκούσιος:

> Parricide is not the intentional object of any of Oedipus' orectic or cognitive activities, so far as we know. The *EN* puts this point a little circuitously by saying that the man acted 'out of' ignorance, as if ignorance were the cause of the action. The issue to which this criterion points is more clearly seen in the light of the *De Motu's* way of putting things: the desires and beliefs of the agent are not directed at that action in such a way as to explain it (*CE* 149).

Nussbaum is correct to say that both the *NE* account and the *DeM* account would exclude all acts that occur through ignorance and under βία (as strictly defined in the *NE*) from ἑκούσιοι actions. But her argument is not only that actions which count as ἀκούσιοι in the ethical works do not meet the criteria for being ἑκούσιοι in the *DeM* account. Although she makes a direct statement only about the ignorance case, I take it she holds both acts that occur under βία and acts that occur δι' ἄγνοιαν are also ἀκούσιοι by the *DeM* account. This assertion requires examination. It must be determined whether the *DeM* account will consider these acts ἀκούσιοι (as Nussbaum says) or οὐχ ἑκούσιοι; and whether this distinction in the *DeM* is coextensive with the distinction in the *NE* between ἀκούσιοι actions (those done through ignorance with pain or regret) and οὐχ ἑκούσιοι actions (those done through ignorance without pain or regret).

Let us look more carefully at what Nussbaum says about the ignorance case. She says that Oedipus' action described as a parricide "looks like a paradigmatic case of an action done out of excusable ignorance, and therefore ἀκούσιος" and "described as a parricide, this action is ἀκούσιος by the *DeM*'s criteria as well. There is no ὄρεξις for parricide and no belief concerning parricide that can explain it" (*CE* 149). It will be remembered, however, that by Nussbaum's own account of the *DeM*, motions called ἀκούσιοι include those in which there was some cognitive activity connected with the motion, but no ὄρεξις: examples are the leap of the heart from fear and the sudden erection of the penis. (These were described by Nussbaum as "reflex motions," "sudden and partial movement," but not movement from place to place [*CE* 146]). Motions that are οὐχ ἑκούσιοι by

---

[52]See J.L. Ackrill, "Aristotle on Action," *Essays on Aristotle's Ethics*, ed. A.O. Rorty (Berkeley, 1980) on the individuation of actions in Aristotle.

the *DeM* account involve neither cognitions nor desire for the motion in question, e.g., going to sleep, waking, respiration. Thus, if Oedipus' action is described as a parricide, and "Parricide is not the intentional object of any of Oedipus' orectic or cognitive activities, as far as we know" (*CE* 149), then it seems that this action is more like action called οὐχ ἑκούσιος by the *DeM*, not ἀκούσιος, as Nussbaum says.

Having drawn this conclusion, I should say that I do so not without some hesitation. If one compares by simple gross observation the examples Aristotle gives in the *DeM* for each of the three types of motion with the action of Oedipus, one might reach a different conclusion. The gross similarity between Oedipus' action and ἀκούσιοι or reflex motions seems no greater than its similarity to οὐχ ἑκούσιοι or systemic motions. In fact, the action of Oedipus, on gross observation, is much more like the *DeM*'s ἑκούσιοι motions from place to place. Yet, his act, described as a parricide at least, seems clearly not to be ἑκούσιος by the *DeM* account (as well as by the *NE* account).

It is not that the *DeM* cannot at all explain Oedipus' case as ἑκούσιος motion; it is the particular description of the case it cannot accommodate. Perhaps it is simply not appropriate to ask the *DeM* to explain motions under anything but a neutral description: in this case, Oedipus killed an old man at a crossroad. It is important to know that in the case of Oedipus there was no desire and cognition linked up in such a way so as to have caused a parricide. But on the basis of the *DeM*, when we discover a motion that occurs without desire we also expect it to be a completely different sort of motion than a parricide is. According to the *DeM*, if there is no desire, there may be no motion from place to place at all or the motion is either a reflex or a systemic motion. Under the description "parricide," perhaps, if the *DeM* answers the question at all, it would say there was no motion at all rather than there was ἀκούσιος or οὐχ ἑκούσιος motion. After all, we would say of Oedipus that he did not perform a parricide, and if he did not, no one else did.

The same points can be made about those cases which fall under the *NE*'s strict definition of βία. The *DeM* account would also label these οὐχ ἑκούσιοι rather than ἀκούσιοι since neither the cognitions nor the desires of the person subject to βία account for the action in the appropriate way. Here too it is difficult to compare Aristotle's example of a victim of βία, the man picked up and carried off by a strong wind, to a systemic motion. This victim of βία is better described not as somehow moving but as being moved.

Next, we should consider whether the *DeM*'s reasons for drawing a distinction between ἀκούσιοι and οὐχ ἑκούσιοι motions fits with the reasons for the *NE*'s distinction between ἀκούσιοι and οὐχ ἑκούσιοι actions.

Strictly speaking, Nussbaum overstates the matter when she says the act of Oedipus described as a parricide is ἀκούσιος because it is a clear case of "excusable ignorance." It so happens that Oedipus is pained and feels regret for his act, and so his act is correctly labelled ἀκούσιος. But in the *NE*, acts that occur through excusable ignorance may be ἀκούσιοι or οὐχ ἑκούσιοι, depending on whether or not the agent feels pain or regret.

The *DeM* account does not discuss regret as the way to distinguish ἀκούσιοι and οὐχ ἑκούσιοι actions. In the *DeM*, it is the role of cognitions and desires in the motions that distinguishes all three types of motions. In effect, the *NE* distinguishes two classes, ἑκούσιοι actions and those done under force or through ignorance. The latter are ἀκούσιοι only if accompanied by pain or regret. Actions which are οὐχ ἑκούσιοι are a sub-class of actions done through ignorance, not as in the *DeM*, a strictly third class of motions or actions.[53]

Nussbaum does attempt to integrate regret into the *DeM* account. She thinks the *DeM*'s positive account makes clearer Aristotle's insistence that ex post facto regret accompany an act that occurs through ignorance in order for the act to count as ἀκούσιος: "regret is really what shows us that the agent's desires were not such as to have caused the action. It shows us that he would not have done the action but for the ignorance; it removes the possibility that he would have done it anyway, even in full awareness of the facts" (*CE* 149).[54] Moreover, it points out that regret or even rejoicing at what happened is not sufficient to establish a causal connection between a person and an action. "It is not enough that there is a match between the desire/belief and that which happens. It is also important that it be this desire and this belief that were really at work causing the action" (*CE* 149).

However, Nussbaum's view of the role of regret significantly alters its importance as described in the *NE*. In her view regret is merely a sign about desires which are the essential factor in determining whether a motion or action is ἑκούσιος or ἀκούσιος and plays no role in distinguishing what is οὐχ ἑκούσιος and what is ἀκούσιος. But in the *NE* pain and regret are essential *per se* for designating an action ἀκούσιος and for distinguishing a difference among actions done through ignorance.

---

[53]Since in the ethical works pain is associated with ἀκούσιοι actions in general, and not only some actions which occur through ignorance, rather than reject this category of the οὐχ ἑκούσιοι, it could be expanded to include as well acts which come about through βία, where the agent feels no pain. I suspect Aristotle does not take this route since for his paradeigmatic case of acting under force, not feeling pain is too rare an occurrence.

[54]In ch. 5 I argue that pain and what it says about the agent's desires is more the reason for calling the agent ἄκων than Nussbaum suggests about regret. The question behind the use of ἑκών group words is not the same question whose answer can pinpoint why the action or motion occurred.

But perhaps in my objections I am overlooking what Nussbaum finds central in the *DeM*: ὄρεξις. Under the opposite pair ἑκούσιος and ἀκούσιος, essentially, what Aristotle collects is motion with desire, ἑκούσιος, and motion without desire, ἀκούσιος. Consider Nussbaum's criticism of the *NE*'s distinction of action done through ignorance with regret, ἀκούσιος, and action done through ignorance without regret, οὐχ ἑκούσιος. The criticism rests on the centrality of ὄρεξις. Of Aristotle's οὐχ ἑκούσιος she writes: "Nor does it seem correct to say, as Aristotle does in the *NE*, that such an action, done from ignorance but without regret, is neither ἀκούσιος nor ἑκούσιος, but some third thing, 'not ἑκούσιος.' For surely it is ἀκούσιος, if the desire for it did not cause it, and ἑκούσιος, if it did" (*CE* 149–50). But this criticism, however much it amplifies what truly is central in Aristotle's account in the *DeM*, ὄρεξις, does not explain or take account of the fact that the *DeM* also has a category of οὐχ ἑκούσιος motion. Motions in this category also are not caused by the creature's ὄρεξις; but this does not render such motions ἀκούσιοι.

Nussbaum would neutralize some of my objections by reading Aristotle's examples of ἀκούσιοι motions in Chapter 11 of the *DeM* as a subset of all those motions that could be mentioned. Aristotle's interest is limited in the chapter and so is the list of examples. The examples he introduces with "οἷον" need not be taken to exclude examples that would be more relevant to the ethical works. Moreover, that the *DeM* has a category of motions that are οὐχ ἑκούσιοι need not be reason to be uncritical of the οὐχ ἑκούσιοι category of the *NE*: in regard to "motions" ἑκούσιος and ἀκούσιος may be polar opposites, but in regard to "actions," contradictories.[55] These points are well taken. But the fact remains that, however more consistent his view might have been without οὐχ ἑκούσιοι actions, Aristotle does talk of actions in the *NE* that are οὐχ ἑκούσιοι; and the role of pain and regret in the *NE* is much more important than the role Nussbaum finds for these factors in the *DeM*.

The account of τὸ ἑκούσιον in *De Motu* does fill out to some extent what Aristotle says in the ethical works about τὸ ἑκούσιον; but it also supplies much that cannot easily be integrated or reconciled with the ethical works. Aristotle appears to have imported to his discussion of animal motion terms that were not used in ordinary discourse in quite the same way. It hardly seems likely that when ἄκων or οὐχ ἑκών appear in literature they are describing movement very much like the heart leaping in fear, a suddenly erected penis, or respiration.

Since Aristotle did not create entirely new terms but borrowed from ordinary usage, it is safe to assume there is some overlap in his use of ἑκών group words among the *De Motu*, the ethical works, and ordinary usage, but the extent

---

[55]Prof. Nussbaum discussed with me some of my objections to her account of the *DeM* and made the preliminary replies I report here.

and nature of this overlap is elusive. For example, it may be true of the agent designated ἑκών that the action in question was caused by his desires and cognitions without it being the case that he is called ἑκών because this fact is true. Likewise, when an agent is designated ἄκων or οὐχ ἑκών, it may be true that under certain descriptions of the act, the act cannot be said to have been caused by his desires or his desires and cognitions. But it need not also be the case that on account of this he is called ἄκων or οὐχ ἑκών. Since Aristotle holds that desire is the essential factor in motion from place to place, however involved the agent's cognitions must also be, I suspect it may simply be the prominence of desire or a closely related matter in the ordinary usage of ἑκών group words that prompted Aristotle to designate this sort of motion as ἑκούσιος. In the ethical works too there is reason to think Aristotle is adapting ordinary usage to meet his interests. Here too Aristotle draws a distinction between ἀκούσιος and οὐχ ἑκούσιος action which is not evidently adhered to in literary texts. Moreover, Aristotle's description of his own methodology notwithstanding, his expressed concern in the NE about the usefulness of his discussion for lawgivers (NE 1109b30–35) makes clear that however descriptive his task may be, his purpose contains a prescriptive component as well. This is not to say Aristotle sought to prescribe the general usage of ἑκών group words, but he did expect his work to be useful to those who must legislate and adjudicate with consistency and objectivity. Both of these characteristics demand a systematization of human experience which may prompt new distinctions, like an οὐχ ἑκούσιος action, to deal with the actions of individuals for legislative and judicial purposes, even though in any particular case the distinction may not correspond precisely with an individual's experience.

Overlap between ordinary usage and the ethical works can also be seen in another feature of τὸ ἀκούσιον, its association with pain and regret. The *De Motu* does not discuss this feature although in the ethical works it is characteristic of any action properly called ἀκούσιος. Although Nussbaum finds a role for regret in the *De Motu* as a sign that the "agent's desires were not such as to have caused the action" (*CE* 149), I think the reason for calling an agent ἄκων is more intimately connected with pain than this role suggests. Feeling pain or regret is not sufficient to render an agent (or his action) ἄκων (or ἀκούσιος) but it is more than a sign of τὸ ἀκούσιον.

Summary

Although the *DeM* account and the *NE* account of τὸ ἑκούσιον and τὸ ἀκούσιον do not overlap as much as Nussbaum has claimed, they do fit together in the following ways. In both accounts, actions which take place under βία as delimited by the *NE* and actions which are done through ignorance of the particulars set out in the *NE* are excluded from actions that count as ἑκούσιοι; and, more positively, both the *NE* and the *DeM* seem to isolate the same group of actions as ἑκούσιοι: those actions in which the ἀρχή is in the agent are those which occur because of the desires and cognitions of the agent. However, with more detail, the following differences emerge.

Actions that are ἀκούσιοι by the *NE* view (cases of strict βία and ignorance of detail accompanied by pain or regret), as well as actions called οὐχ ἑκούσιοι by the *NE* view, if they are to count as motions at all by the *DeM* view, seem more akin to the οὐχ ἑκούσιοι motions of the *DeM* view, because they involve neither the desires nor the cognitions of the victim, and because in the *DeM* view, pain and regret are not relevant features. However, I consider problematic the question of whether or not an analogy to systemic motions is even appropriate for actions that come about by force or ignorance. Fortunately, and especially since there is no detectable distinction between the use of ἄκων and οὐχ ἑκών in the passages collected for study, such passages are accommodated well enough by Aristotle's negative view. His positive view adds further insight into the exclusion of these cases from ἑκούσιοι actions, but these cases are not among those Aristotle does not seem able to accommodate at all.

The ἀκούσιοι motions of the *DeM* have no ready correspondent in the *NE* view. The criteria for ἀκούσιοι motions in the *DeM* would exclude both types of the *NE*'s ἀκούσιοι actions, since the *DeM*'s ἀκούσιοι motions involve the agent's cognitions in the appropriate way but not his desires, whereas ἀκούσιοι actions in the *NE* involve neither the cognitions nor the desires of the victims of βία and ignorance. The *DeM*'s ἀκούσιοι motions, moreover, seem even less analogous to the actions depicted in the passages collected for this study than the *DeM*'s οὐχ ἑκούσιοι motions. Something like a blow immediately offered in return for a blow, or a conditioned response to a stimulus, could be considered analogous to the *DeM*'s reflex motions, but such actions are not represented in the passages. Furthermore, any attempt to render an action in the collected passsages analogous by relying on different descriptions of the action and various combinations of the elements of the action under different descriptions, would be unproductive. One could not avoid layers of tenuous hypotheses in such a construction, since the passages themselves do not address the kind of details on which the requisite distinctions are based.

In the following chapter, the APV will be especially scrutinized to see if it can help with those passages we have seen the ANV cannot readily accommodate, especially the ἑκών victim of strict βία and mixed actions which are ἀκούσιοι.

5. The Occasions for Describing Attitude View

Aristotle may not have adequately accommodated all that needed to be accommodated in his account of τὸ ἑκούσιον and τὸ ἀκούσιον in the ethical works. However, the tidy and clear APV need not be preferred to even a partially adequate account that does at least include important factors. There seems to be more to calling an act ἑκούσιος or ἀκούσιος than that the agent's desire did or did not cause it. In fact, in the passages I am studying there seems to be little if any interest in determining why the act happened, at least not in the way the APV is designed to determine this. The ethical works, on the other hand, contain hints at what seems to be at the core of the use of ἑκών group words in the passages studied here but do not give these hints adequate prominence.

We will see that on the whole, Aristotle's account of τὸ ἑκούσιον and τὸ ἀκούσιον, even with the aid of his positive view, does not satisfactorily accommodate the use of these words. This final chapter will contrast and assess interpretations based primarily on Aristotle's positive view and my own, the Occasions for Describing Attitude View.

Description

In my view of ἑκών group words, it is important that the words are used under the particular circumstances described in some detail in the first three chapters, generally, various sorts of compelling circumstances and related circumstances of error and doing harm or wrong. These circumstances provide the occasion for the use of ἑκών group words. From a descriptive viewpoint, their presence prompts interest in the agent's or victim's overall attitude or desires.[1] But when these circumstances pertain, it cannot be taken for granted that what actually happens to a person or what a person does is a clear or an accurate reflection of that person's desires or overall attitude. It is the role of ἑκών group words to describe the agent's or victim's attitude. That an individual's overall attitude or desires cannot be presumed on the basis of external compelling circumstances must also be taken into account in those cases in which ἑκών

---

[1] If none of these occasions pertain, it may be that whether a person is ἑκών or ἄκων is taken for granted or not problematic or simply of no interest. Whether or not ἑκών group words are appropriate on other occasions is taken up briefly later in this chapter. See pp. 165–66

group words are used to describe a third-party, that is, the individual described as ἑκών or ἄκων is not the one who directly does or suffers the action.[2]

I suggest that an agent or victim called ἑκών (or one whose act is called ἑκούσιος) is one whose desire for the act is such that he counts himself especially committed to it and elevates this desire and his commitment to the act above all other desires, despite the difficulties and compelling nature of the circumstances under which the desire and act occurs, and despite whatever other desires he may have. Given the kind of circumstances under which most ἑκών group words are used, it will not be surprising that agents or victims frequently have many conflicting desires relevant to what they do or suffer. An agent or victim called ἄκων (or one whose act is called ἀκούσιος) is divorced from the act. This is not a denial that the ἄκων caused the act, but a way of expressing a distance between a person and what he does or suffers. For the ἄκων Aristotle's insistence that he could act only if he so desired would be a mere formality (however important this point is for other philosophical considerations). The specific desire required in order for the action to take place, the desire in which Aristotle is especially interested, is not the basis of the designation ἑκών or ἄκων. In effect, ἑκών and ἄκων express the agent's or victim's attitude toward what is happening: if ἑκών, a strong positive attitude or commitment; if ἄκων, a strong negative attitude or divorcement.

Test passages for the Occasions for Describing Attitude View

In the following pages I will discuss a select group of examples that represent four types of passages which Aristotle's views in particular do not readily accommodate. Some passages will be interpreted by each of the four views under consideration: the Functional Opposite View (FOV); the Aristotelian Negative View (ANV) which will sometimes be subdivided into the *NE* version and the *EE* version (ANV/*NE* and ANV/*EE*); the Aristotelian Positive View (APV); and the Occasions for Describing Attitude (ODA) View. For other passages, the discussion will focus on the differences between the APV and the OCV. Less will be said about the FOV, since this view has been discussed thoroughly already. But it will be mentioned, especially where some other view allies with it.

---

[2]Although it is true that a person's actions need not accurately reflect his or her attitude, it is also the case that an agent or victim or someone describing the agent or victim, may not truthfully or accurately describe attitude with ἑκών group words. This issue will be taken up at the end of this chapter.

1. The ἑκών victim of force

Consider again the following two examples. In the first, Helen is described by Electra as taken away by force and destroyed ἑκοῦσα; in the second, it is asked whether Eriphyle was killed ἑκοῦσα:[3]

ἡ μὲν γὰρ ἁρπασθεῖσ' ἑκοῦσ' ἀπώλετο,
σὺ δ' ἄνδρ' ἄριστον Ἑλλάδος διώλεσας,
σκῆψιν προτείνουσ' ὡς ὑπὲρ τέκνου πόσιν
ἔκτεινας· οὐ γάρ ⟨σ'⟩ ὡς ἔγωγ' ἴσασιν εὖ.
(Eur. *El.* 1065–68)

⟨Α⟩ μητέρα κατέκταν τὴν ἐμήν, βραχὺς λόγος.
⟨Φ⟩ ἑκὼν ἑκοῦσαν ἢ ⟨οὐ⟩ θέλουσαν οὐχ ἑκών;
(Eur. *Alcmeon* Fr. 68 *TGF*)

These passages can be understood as meeting Aristotle's stringent criteria for βία. The victims are totally passive, but nonetheless ἑκοῦσαι. The FOV cannot accommodate such passages, and since the βία is construed to meet Aristotle's stipulations, on the basis of the ANV we would expect these victims to be excluded at least from being ἑκοῦσαι. However, we can not go so far as to say these victims meet the criteria for being ἄκουσαι, since they do not show evidence of being pained, a characteristic important to Aristotle's account of τὸ ἀκούσιον in general.

The APV does not accommodate the passages since even though they could be seen as cases where each of the characters designated ἑκοῦσα had desires and cognitions that were in accord with the actions, the actions were not directly caused by their desires and cognitions. Merely having a desire and cognition that is the sort that could account for an action is not enough to be the actual cause of that action. The APV is interested in pinpointing the desires and cognitions that actually cause motions. Furthermore, in the *De Motu*, Aristotle distinguishes and labels as ἑκούσιοι, motions that happen through the creature itself. But when a particular agent is called ἑκών or a particular act is called ἑκούσιος, we are informed not only that there has occurred a motion that is the sort which occurs through the creature itself, but also *which* creature has moved. Thus, as the APV explains why a motion occurred, it picks out simultaneously *who* moved. But once it is granted that the βία involved in these passages is actual and overwhelming, there is no questioning that the victims are not those *who moved* but those *who were moved*.

The ODA View explains that these victims, though not the actual movers, have a very positive attitude toward what is happening. We cannot take for granted or assume we can always predict what a person or character feels merely because circumstances are of a certain sort. A person can be acted on, that is,

---
[3] These passages were discussed in ch. 4 pp. 109–110.

not himself be the cause of the action, and still have a positive attitude toward it, be desirous of it, or feel committed or in accord with it. This view is decidedly unlike the APV, according to which, to be ἑκών it is not enough to have a desire and cognition that is of the sort that could cause a certain action. To be ἑκών one's desires and cognitions must be connected with the action such that they are the actual cause of the action. But for the ODA View, to be ἑκών, overall one strongly desires the action without actually being the cause of it. In fact, the particular usefulness of ἑκών group words is that these words can tell us the attitude of a person even when that attitude is unlike what we would expect of someone in that particular situation. Surely, if anything, this is why in many accounts Helen was so frequently upbraided: contrary to expectation about appropriate behavior, and despite the fact that she could not have prevented what was done, Helen desired or approved the act.

Finally, we need not think that these characters are masochists because they are pictured as being committed to what has been described as force. According to the ODA View, their being in accord with or having a positive attitude toward what is ordinarily repulsive, can be tied up with their values and goals, that for the sake of which the act in question is performed.[4] The ODA View allows many factors to influence and be the basis of the designation ἑκών and ἄκων whether or not these factors are made explicit. In the case of Alcmeon's mother, for example, we see ⟨οὐ⟩ θέλουσαν used as the opposite of ἑκοῦσαν, implying that, at least in some cases, "consent" can be an important concomitant or determinant factor for being ἑκών. Similarly, in Chapter 2, I discussed passages in which the use of ἑκών group words seemed connected with decisions based on evaluations of the circumstances at hand and consequences. There it was determined that one could be ἑκών or ἄκων in such cases. For our purposes here, it should be noted that even though one cannot predict whether an agent will be ἑκών or ἄκων on the basis of such information, at least in some cases, choiceworthiness or consent can be seen as factors influencing or perhaps even determining the attitude of an agent. But the ODA View does not regard these or similar features as either necessary or sufficient to render an action ἑκούσιος or ἀκούσιος. The virtue of the ODA View is that it leaves open what factors in any particular case come together in such a way that

---

[4] In *NE* 5.9 Aristotle discusses this fragment of the *Alcmeon*. He considers whether it is possible to be treated unjustly ἑκών. His conclusion is that this is not possible. The discussion itself is difficult and involves factors that are not an obvious part of the discussion of τὸ ἑκούσιον. But my interest here is in noting that Aristotle's discussion of the passage is based on a particular interpretive description of the action: being treated unjustly. Thus, his conclusion that it is not possible to be treated unjustly does not make nonsense out of what the passage actually says. Moreover, since the speaker is a speaker of Greek, I take it that the question makes sense: somehow it is possible to have been killed ἑκοῦσα. For a further *caveat*, see the discussion of this passage in ch. 4 pp. 109–110.

the action is ἑκούσιος or ἀκούσιος, and what factors may happen to be true of an act or person so described. Thus, even though the ODA View holds a consistent and stable interpretation for ἑκών group words for all the passages collected, that is, irrespective of genre, author, or time period, it has room for understanding a variety of factors to be related to the use of these words, and even for there to be differences in the factors which apply according to genre, author, or time period. But unlike the kind of view discussed in Chapter 2, the ODA View does not reduce the meaning of ἑκών group words to any particular factor or set of factors.[5]

This perspective is very different from that of the FOV which focuses only on the presence or absence of compelling circumstances or ignorance and holds these circumstances to exhaust the significance of ἑκών group words. Likewise, the APV and also the ANV are interested only in a particular isolated motion or action and the desires and cognitions immediately responsible for that motion or action. Thus, matters outside the particular isolated motion or action at hand do not affect the designation ἑκών or ἄκων, even if they sometimes enter into the agent's (and Aristotle's) explanation of the agent's choice. Recall *NE* 3.1 where Aristotle tells us that ordinarily no one would choose to throw his cargo overboard, but for the safety of himself and his crew anyone having any sense would do so. But the overall negative attitude of the agent toward this action does not affect whether the agent is to be called ἑκών or ἄκων. Aristotle says he is ἑκών because he is the actual mover of this particular isolated action. The ODA View, in contrast, has room for Aristotle's observation about the relationship between acting ἄκων and choiceworthiness, and can accommodate cases where lack of choiceworthiness is the basis of the designation ἄκων as well as cases where an agent is ἑκών under the same circumstances.

2. More on mixed actions

In these passages, even where the text gives a neutral description of the action, contrary to what Aristotle's positive view would lead us to expect, that is, that the agent would be ἑκών since the desires and cognitions of the agent caused the action, the agent is ἄκων. To discuss these cases I will focus on passages which can be paired on the basis of their sharing very similar circumstances though they differ in their descriptions of the agent as ἑκών or ἄκων. The discussion will show the inadequacy of the APV and other views to accommodate them, since except for the ODA View, each of the views under discussion leads us to expect the agents of the paired passages to be described by the same ἑκών group word. Since neither force, narrowly construed to meet Aristotle's stipulations, nor ignorance of detail is an issue in these cases, in

---

[5]Cf. pp. 73–74, and 102.

general they fall under Aristotle's class of mixed actions. Although I will focus this discussion on a pair of passages in which the relevant constraining circumstance is threatened βία, the same arguments apply to other pairs of passages in which other compelling circumstances pertain.[6]

Consider the following passages from the *Andromache* and the *Prometheus Bound*. In the first, Hermione is speaking to Andromache; and in the second, Io is telling her story to Prometheus.

---

[6] E.g., the agents in the following paired passages act under the constraint of social practices. In particular, the agents act under oaths, orders, demands or requests, and having been chosen or elected to act:

Soph. *Ph*. 1019–28: oath/ἑκών (Philoctetes)
Aesch. *Ag*. 838–44: oath/οὐχ ἑκών (Odysseus)
Od. 19.370–78: order/οὐκ ἄκουσα (Eurycleia)
Eur. *Bacch*. 434–42/#2: order/οὐχ ἑκών (Pentheus' attendant)
Aesch. *PrB* 271–78: request/οὐκ ἄκουσαι (Chorus)
Soph. *OR* 354–62 demand/ἄκων (Teiresias)
Soph. *Ant*. 268–77/#1: chosen/ἄκων (Messenger)
Eur. *IA* 1362–67: chosen/ἑκών (Achilles)

As I showed in ch. 2, since an agent can act ἑκών or ἄκων under compelling social practices, the FOV cannot accommodate these passages. For the FOV expects all agents acting under such constraints to be ἄκοντες. For a similar reason the ANV and the APV also fail to accommodate these passages. The ANV/*NE* expects all the agents to act ἑκόντες since they do not act under its narrow view of βία or through ignorance. If the ANV/*EE* were to apply, i.e., if it were granted that the practices were of the sort that could force one to act and the acts required were not of the sort that should never be performed, it too would fail to accommodate all these passages. For when the view does apply to a passage it amounts to much the same as the FOV: a criterion for being ἄκων is met and all the agents would be expected to be ἄκοντες. The APV in accord with the ANV/*NE* would also expect all of the agents to be ἑκόντες: they do actually perform the acts. The ODA View, however, can accommodate each passage. Because they act under compelling circumstances, the actions are performed whatever the agents feel deeply; but the agents are not rendered ἄκοντες merely because they are constrained by circumstances to act as they do. Some of the agents, those ἑκόντες, have a positive attitude and are in accord with and committed to the actions they perform. Others, those ἄκοντες, act but have a negative attitude and are uncommitted to their acts. The actions performed ἄκοντες need not be generally of the sort the agents would never perform. Odysseus, e.g., would sometimes choose to go to war. Nor are actions performed ἑκόντες the sort that are intrinsically choiceworthy, for example, washing a stranger's feet. However, we may suppose that, given the particular details of the circumstances, the ἄκων agent would not have performed the action except for the compelling practices. But we cannot suppose that the ἑκών agent would have performed the action on his or her own. For example, Philoctetes might have joined the expedition to Troy even if he had not sworn an oath to Tyndarus, but there is no reason to think Eurycleia would have washed Odysseus' feet without orders to do so.

ὦ βάρβαρον σὺ θρέμμα καὶ σκληρὸν θράσος,
ἐγκαρτερεῖς δὴ θάνατον; ἀλλ' ἐγώ σ' ἕδρας
ἐκ τῆσδ' ἑκοῦσαν ἐξαναστήσω τάχα·
τοιόνδ' ἔχω σου δέλεαρ. ἀλλὰ γὰρ λόγους
κρύψω, τὸ δ' ἔργον αὐτὸ σημανεῖ τάχα.
κάθησ' ἑδραία· καὶ γὰρ εἰ πέριξ σ' ἔχοι
τηκτὸς μόλυβδος, ἐξαναστήσω σ' ἐγὼ
πρὶν ᾧ πέποιθας παῖδ' Ἀχιλλέως μολεῖν.
(Eur. *Andr.* 261–68)

τέλος δ' ἐναργὴς βάξις ἦλθεν Ἰνάχωι
σαφῶς ἐπισκήπτουσα καὶ μυθουμένη
ἔξω δόμων τε καὶ πάτρας ὠθεῖν ἐμὲ
ἄφετον ἀλᾶσθαι γῆς ἐπ' ἐσχάτοις ὅροις·
κεἰ μὴ θέλοι, πυρωπὸν ἐκ Διὸς μολεῖν
κεραυνὸν ὃς πᾶν ἐξαιστώσοι γένος.
τοιοῖσδε πεισθεὶς Λοξίου μαντεύμασιν
ἐξήλασέν με κἀπέκληισε δωμάτων
ἄκουσαν ἄκων· ἀλλ' ἐπηνάγκαζέ νιν
Διὸς χαλινὸς πρὸς βίαν πράσσειν τάδε.
(*PrB* 663–72)

Andromache's situation in the first passage is comparable to Inachus' in the second. Inachus is threatened with the destruction of his progeny if he does not drive out his daughter, Io; Andromache is threatened with the death of her son if she does not leave the shrine where she has taken sanctuary. Andromache is an agent victim of βία no less than Inachus: both act on prudential decisions under the threat of violence. The FOV fails to accommodate these passsages. Relying on it, we would expect both Inachus and Andromache to be ἄκοντες. But this is not the case: Andromache is ἑκοῦσα and Inachus is ἄκων. Again, the fact that an agent acts under compelling circumstances is not what determines whether he is ἑκών or ἄκων.

The ANV/*NE* would lead us to expect both Inachus and Andromache to be ἑκόντες since the βία involved does not meet the *NE*'s stipulations. Their acts are mixed acts which are more like ἑκούσιοι acts in the *NE*. This view then accommodates only the case of Andromache. But even this accommodation is unsatisfying since the passages are so similar that we would expect both to be accommodated if one is.

The ANV/*EE* might seem a better fit. Arguments could be made both for and against these situations as cases in which the agents were forced to act as they did because the threats were beyond human nature to endure. But let us assume for the sake of argument that both cases are at least as serious as the *NE* 5/*EE* 4 cases described earlier and different enough from the blind man's bluff example to qualify under the *EE* as cases where it was not in the person's power (ἐφ' αὑτῷ) to act otherwise. Nevertheless, we would still expect both agents to be ἄκοντες. The *EE*'s broadening of what is not in one's power (ἐφ' αὑτῷ) to include cases where nature is overpowered brings it closer to the FOV and therefore to the same objections and conclusions that were made about the FOV: it is not the presence of overpowering circumstances that renders an agent ἄκων.

The APV also fails to accommodate satisfactorily these passages because it too leads us to expect that both Inachus and Andromache would be ἑκόντες, since each is the efficient cause of the action in question. But let us consider the objection that the descriptions of the acts are relevant and explain why one agent is ἄκων and the other is ἑκοῦσα. In the course of this discussion it must be kept in mind that, as I have already pointed out, the passages collected for study do not show any distinction in their use of οὐχ ἑκών and ἄκων. However, in his positive view, Aristotle does distinguish οὐχ ἑκούσιος and ἀκούσιος motion. What is in question in the following discussion which will alter the descriptions of the actions for the purpose of testing the APV, is Aristotle's οὐχ ἑκούσιος motion which involves neither the desires nor the cognitions of the creature. The actions being investigated are too unlike Aristotle's reflex or ἀκούσιοι motions to even consider a redescription involving the agent's cognitions but not his desires.

As the discussion of Oedipus showed in the last chapter, on the basis of the APV an agent's act properly desribed as ἑκούσιος under one intentional description can be οὐχ ἑκούσιος (Aristotle's technical term) under other descriptions. Unlike the case of Oedipus, these passages show no significant difference in what the agent knows when the intentional description is manipulated. But the intentional description may make a difference nonetheless. Consider for example, Aristotle's pilot who ἑκών threw the cargo overboard. If we redescribe the captain as bringing to financial ruin the owner of the cargo, relying on the APV we could explain why he can now be called οὐχ ἑκών: he had no desire, as far as we know, to do any such thing when he threw the cargo overboard, and although we can imagine he knew or expected his action would bring about this consequence, this cognition played no role in the accomplishment of the action.

The descriptions of the acts of Inachus and Andromache could be manipulated in a similar way to render each agent ἑκών under one description and οὐχ ἑκών (Aristotle's technical term) under others. For example, described as saving his progeny, Inachus would be ἑκών; but described as being cruel to Io, οὐχ ἑκών. Likewise, we could say Andromache οὐχ ἑκοῦσα brings about her own death; but Andromache ἑκοῦσα saves her son's life. These descriptions are prejudiced or interpreted descriptions. They say more than would be said, for example, by an observer who reported in neutral terms, i.e., without including goals or desires, only what he could see happening. They are, in fact, very different from the actual descriptions we find in the texts concerning these characters. The actual descriptions are neutral. Inachus is said to have driven out and shut out Io from their house (ἐξήλασέν με κἀπέκληισε δωμάτων). When Hermione tells Andromache she will make her move (ἀλλ' ἐγώ σ' ἕδρας ἐκ τῆσδ' ἑκοῦσαν ἐξαναστήσω τάχα), we infer, because of the sacredness of the place and because she refers to Andromache's son as "bait" that she is not herself going to get Andromache up and out, but rather she expects that Andromache will herself move from the place. Neither of these descriptions approaches the partiality of the prejudiced or interpreted versions given as examples above. The APV, then, appears to accommodate Andromache: she is pictured as moving from the holy place through herself, and as expected she is called ἑκοῦσα. But despite the fact that Io's being driven out of the house can be traced in the appropriate way to the desires and cognitions of Inachus, he did actually do this, Inachus is οὐχ ἑκών (Aristotle's technical term; Text: ἄκων), not what the APV leads us to expect, ἑκών.

The ODA View, on the contrary, can explain both cases. Andromache is pictured by Hermione as totally committed to what she expects her to do. Her commitment on this view goes well beyond that desire the APV focuses on. Hermione is not saying merely that Andromache will herself walk away from the altar. Internally, Andromache is expected to be at one with her act. External circumstances bring about what she does and there will be severe consequences for her. But nonetheless, she will desire and have a completely positive attitude toward what she does and be unconflicted about it.[7] Moreover, Andromache's desire for that for the sake of which she leaves the sanctuary surely is involved in her being ἑκοῦσα, but according to the ODA View, neither desiring that for the sake of which one performs an act is sufficient to render her ἑκοῦσα, nor the fact that Andromache's movement is explained by her own desires and cognitions. Inachus, on the other hand is ἄκων. He divorces himself from his act, has a very negative attitude toward it despite the fact that he desires that for the sake of which he acts, the safety of his progeny. The word ἄκων registers his repulsion at what he does despite the fact that he prefers driving Io out to not driving her out on the basis of the consequences of each alternative.

It is not because someone actually performs an act that he is ἑκών, though clearly action is, as Aristotle has shown us, intimately connected with desire. Nor, as in the case of Inachus, does acting for the sake of something one prefers render an agent ἑκών. Whether an agent is ἑκών or ἄκων in a situation like that of Inachus is a purely personal matter. It depends on what the agent values and sometimes how he responds to the loss of not substantiating some values even as he does substantiate other values.

---

[7]See below, pp. 159, 160–164, on the aggressor's use of ἑκών. This is one case where the aggressor does not minimize the victim's internal state.

It is not impossible to imagine someone doing ἑκών what Inachus did. But such a person would be very different from Inachus. When presented with circumstances where values conflict and cannot all be substantiated simultaneously, one alternative is to reject the claims of the value that must lose out for prudential or other reasons. This is not the response of Inachus. That he values his progeny is evidenced by his act which insures their future. But he has not so hierarchized his values that what he does not do, treat his daughter in an appropriate way, is minimized and devalued. Inachus does not reject the claim of the value he can not substantiate, and ἄκων tells us how important it still is to him. The ODA View allows the ἑκών group word to express the overall attitude of the agent, however many consequences, desirable or otherwise, are involved. In Inachus' case, e.g., we understand that it was never a desire or aim of Inachus to harm his daughter, although he did act to preserve the remainder of his progeny. What ἄκων tells us is not merely that Inachus did not want to harm his daughter, but that despite the desirable consequences of his act, and the fact that he chose to act as he did, his overall attitude toward his act was negative. There is a distance between the agent and his act despite his preference for this act and its consequential value.

This portrait of Inachus need not be taken to reflect badly on Andromache. For hers is a special case. She too makes a prudential decision. But unlike Inachus, she is thoroughly committed to her act. The obvious difference between the two characters is that whereas Inachus trades his daughter for the survival of his progeny, Andromache is to trade her own life for that of her son. Since Andromache's decision involves only (not merely) her own self-sacrifice, it allows for her total commitment to her act. Inachus divorces himself from his act because of the harm to his daughter. In acting ἑκοῦσα Andromache too displays a deep moral sensitivity, ungrudging and total self-sacrifice. We do not expect her to acknowledge the value she does not substantiate in this case. In fact, we would think it odd if she were to save her son by her act but do so ἄκουσα under this description of the act. To be aloof from one's own act of self-sacrifice would detract from the value of the act as an act of self-sacrifice.[8]

---

[8] If we attend the actual descriptions in the texts, the APV is disappointing because it leads us to expect both actions to be ἑκούσιοι. But what if the very presence of the ἑκών group words warrants importing along with the bland descriptions in the texts more interpreted descriptions which the ἑκών group words simultaneously affirm (ἑκών) or deny (ἄκων)? For example, suppose they warrant our understanding further descriptions which specifically detail the end for the sake of which the agents act. Now Andromache's getting up from the altar ἑκοῦσα is tied to her saving her son's life, and Inachus' driving out Io ἄκων is tied to his saving his progeny. The APV still does not explain these texts satisfactorily since these new descriptions still lead us to expect both actions to be ἑκούσιοι. Tying Andromache's ἑκούσιος action to her larger purpose seems to work, but thinking that under such a description Inachus cannot properly be said to be the efficient cause of his action (since he is ἄκων) does not seem plausible.

More on the Aristotelian Positive View and intentional description

Before moving to the next group of passages, it should be noted that when description is taken into account, there are passages the Aristotelian Positive View does seem to accommodate where the ANV failed.[9] Recall the following three passages which were discussed in Chapter 4. The first, from the Theognidean corpus, involves the failure of a lover to achieve his goal:

καλὸς ἐὼν κακότητι φίλων δειλοῖσιν ὁμιλεῖς
ἀνδράσι, καὶ διὰ τοῦτ' αἰσχρὸν ὄνειδος ἔχεις,
ὦ παῖ· ἐγὼ δ' ἀέκων τῆς σῆς φιλότητος ἁμαρτών
ὠνήμην ἔρδων οἷά τ' ἐλεύθερος ὤν.
(Theog. 1377–80)

The ANV failed to accommodate this use of ἄκων because it involves neither βία nor ignorance of the requisite kinds. But under the description used in the text, failing to win the boy's love, the APV can explain that the speaker is ἄκων (here not to be distinguished from Aristotle's technical οὐχ ἑκών for the purpose of argument) because this is not the intentional description under which he acted. The speaker's desires and cognitions are not the explanation of the action so-described.

In the next passage the speaker admits to having committed an injustice while intoxicated:

νοῦ δ' οἶνος ἐξέστησέ μ'· ὁμολογῶ δέ σε
ἀδικεῖν, τὸ δ' ἀδίκημ' ἐγένετ' οὐχ ἑκούσιον.
(Eur. *Auge* Fr. 265 *TGF*)

A similar strategy might allow the APV to accommodate both texts if we grant that in Inachus' case the ἑκών group word imports in addition to the stated description another description (but not one detailing that for the sake of which he acts) under which Inachus cannot properly be said to be the doer of the action, e.g., "Inachus harms his daughter." This description is not capricious; it specifies the other relevant consequence of his act as described in the text, but it is not that for the sake of which he acted. Allowing the ἑκών group words themselves to import a consequence of the act as described which the ἑκών words affirm or deny may allow the APV to accommodate these passages, but it certainly puts a large burden on the ἑκών group words in doing so. Such a story about the use of ἑκών group words gives no clue about when we are to import further descriptions, and when the ἑκών group words really are to be taken with the given descriptions. The Andromache passage, after all, can be accommodated by the APV without elaborate assumptions. Furthermore, since there may be any number of consequences, even serious ones, produced by any one act, there is no obvious way to sift through them to find which consequences are meant to be affirmed or denied by the ἑκών group word.

[9] For Aristotle's technical distinction between ἄκων and οὐχ ἑκών, see above pp. 117, 122–25.

Since the requisite kinds of neither βία nor ignorance are involved, and recalling that Aristotle rejects ignorance of right and wrong as a kind of ignorance relevant to the designation ἄκων, the ANV fails to accommodate this passage too. The ANV leads us to expect the agent to act ἑκών. But in keeping with the APV, the speaker can be understood to admit that calling the action an injustice (ἀδίκημα) is an accurate description, but also to deny that the intentional description under which he acted when drunk included any desires and cognitions productive of an injustice.

The following passage involving drunkenness was discussed in Chapter 4 as a case which can be accommodated by the ANV:

τί ταῦτ' ἐπαινεῖς; πᾶς γὰρ οἰνωθεὶς ἀνὴρ
ἥσσων μὲν ὀργῆς ἐστι, τοῦ δὲ νοῦ κενός·
φιλεῖ δὲ πολλὴν γλῶσσαν ἐκχέας μάτην
ἄκων ἀκούειν οὓς ἑκὼν εἴπῃ λόγους.
(Soph. *TrGF* 929.1-4)

This passage can also be accommodated by the APV. In fact, although on the whole the passages do not provide examples to fit Aristotle's technical use of ἀκούσιος to describe an action like a reflex motion, an action involving the agent's cognitions but not the agent's desires, the activity involved in this passage, hearing, is a very good example.[10] In this passage, whether or not the agent was drunk when he ἄκων heard from someone the words he himself ἑκών said when drunk, does not matter. According to the APV, since the agent heard, although he had no desire to hear, the agent can be said to hear ἄκων.

This last example from Homer is unusual for its description of Zeus as both ἑκών and ἄκων. Zeus gives Hera what she wants, the destruction of Troy, but warns her that he will not tolerate interference from her when he in turn some day may desire to destroy men whom she holds dear:

ὁππότε κεν καὶ ἐγὼ μεμαὼς πόλιν ἐξαλαπάξαι
τὴν ἐθέλω ὅθι τοι φίλοι ἀνέρες ἐγγεγάασι,

---

[10]Since in the ethical works (e.g., *NE* 3.1 and *EE* 2.8) Aristotle rejects the view that the passions constitute superior force, reconciling that Aristotelian view with the APV for cases in which someone is subject to internal force, βία (ia), would be no easy task. But cases of internal force may be more akin to reflex or systemic motions. See e.g., Theog. 371-72 and Simon. Fr. 541.7-11 *PMG*. To accommodate these cases the APV would claim that the force of *eros* or certain desires, e.g., for profit, work like reflex or systemic motions, that is, actions accomplished without the agent's desire. Whether or not Aristotle would accept some view of compulsive or impulsive behavior or drives that work more like reflex or systemic motions, that would include desires of this sort, is very problematic and cannot be taken up in detail here.

μή τι διατρίβειν τὸν ἐμὸν χόλον, ἀλλά μ' ἐᾶσαι·
καὶ γὰρ ἐγὼ σοὶ δῶκα ἑκὼν ἀέκοντί γε θυμῷ·
(*Il.* 4.40–43)

According to the APV, it could be said that Zeus is ἑκών under the intentional description which fits his act: he actually does give Hera what she wants. Then ἀέκοντί γε θυμῷ (with his *thumos* being ἄκων) can be taken to deny that the correct intentional description includes the feelings and desires of his *thumos* linked in such a way so as to bring about the action. Under a description which includes the features of Zeus' *thumos*, Zeus cannot be said to be the efficient cause of the action.[11]

The ODA View too can accommodate all of these passages. But its interest is in the attitude of the agent, and not in specifying whether or not the agent can be correctly identified as the doer of the action. If the intentional description of an action is at issue, where the APV comments on whether or not a particular description is correct as the intentional description, the ODA View comments on the attitude of the agent under that description.

3. Third-party passages

Another group of passages that are difficult for the APV are those where persons and characters other than those directly involved with the action in question are described by ἑκών group words. In these passages, the weaker explanation that the person is or is not the efficient cause of the action at hand seems particularly out of place, since this is a statement of a fact that is generally not at issue. The ODA View explains these occurrences as summary statements of the attitudes of those described by the ἑκών group words. We see especially in these passages how effective a shorthand the use of ἑκών group words can be. Without going into detail about the feelings, desires, beliefs, values, or aims of a person or character, the words can express his deep feelings and attitudes about what is happening. Consider the following four examples where the APV's explanation seems particularly inappropriate or irrelevant.

---

[11] See further discussion of this passage below, p. 145 and n. 15. The APV would handle the other passage in which the agent acts both ἑκών and οὐχ ἑκών, Eur., *IT* 511-12, in a similar way, by explaining there are two intentional descriptions of Orestes' flight, and he can be said to be the efficient cause of his action only under one. The ODA View would also rely on the circumstances surrounding Orestes' flight, the hounding of the Erinyes and the oracles of Apollo, to explain why he is both ἑκών and οὐχ ἑκών, but with interest in his attitude toward his action.

"Ὣς ἄρα φωνήσασ' ἀπεβήσετο, τὸν δὲ λίπ' αὐτοῦ
χωόμενον κατὰ θυμὸν ἐυζώνοιο γυναικός,
τὴν ῥα βίῃ ἀέκοντος ἀπηύρων' ...
(Il. 1.428–30)

Reading βίῃ with τήν, i.e., Briseis, the poet describes the heralds of Agamemnon taking Briseis away by force while Achilles looks on ἄκων. The FOV accommodates the passage by reference to the overall compelling circumstances to which Achilles is subjected. The ANV is at a loss since there is no evidence that Achilles is subjected to overwhelming force by these two heralds. Even if βίῃ is read with ἀέκοντος it would be difficult to imagine the heralds actually constraining Achilles. The APV with its matter-of-fact explanation seems completely irrelevant: it was not Achilles who led Briseis away. The ODA View explains ἀέκοντος as a description or statement of Achilles' deep feelings which are in total opposition to what is actually happening.

In the next example, the poet is speaking about the wall the Greeks built to defend their ships:

οἱ δ' ἐμάχοντο
Ἀργεῖοι καὶ Τρῶες ὁμιλαδόν· οὐδ' ἄρ' ἔμελλε
τάφρος ἔτι σχήσειν Δαναῶν καὶ τεῖχος ὕπερθεν
εὐρύ, τὸ ποιήσαντο νεῶν ὕπερ, ἀμφὶ δὲ τάφρον
ἤλασαν, οὐδὲ θεοῖσι δόσαν κλειτὰς ἑκατόμβας,
ὄφρα σφιν νῆάς τε θοὰς καὶ ληίδα πολλὴν
ἐντὸς ἔχον ῥύοιτο· θεῶν δ' ἀέκητι τέτυκτο
ἀθανάτων· τὸ καὶ οὔ τι πολὺν χρόνον ἔμπεδον ἦεν.
(Il. 12.2–9)

In saying the wall was built although the gods were ἄκοντες (8–9), the poet is unlikely to be saying that the gods did not build the wall, the information gained from the APV. According to the ODA View, the poet tells us, in a word, the gods were totally opposed to the wall being built.

The APV would understand the following passage in which Gylippus is described as ἄκων, as stating that Gylippus did not himself execute the two Athenian generals.

Νικίαν δὲ καὶ Δημοσθένη ἄκοντος τοῦ Γυλίππου ἀπέσφαξαν. ὁ γὰρ Γύλιππος καλὸν τὸ ἀγώνισμα ἐνόμιζέν οἱ εἶναι ἐπὶ τοῖς ἄλλοις καὶ τοὺς ἀντιστρατήγους κομίσαι Λακεδαιμονίοις.

(Thuc. 7.86.2)

Here too this is not a plausible explanation, since it is most unlikely that Gyllipus would ever have performed the execution himself. But that Gyllipus was totally opposed to what happened, the explanation afforded by the ODA View, is an important point and worth emphasizing.

Finally, in the following passage, Herodotus gives his opinion about the Egyptian version of Helen's whereabouts during the Trojan war.

> Ταῦτα μὲν Αἰγυπτίων οἱ ἱρέες ἔλεγον, ἐγὼ δὲ τῷ λόγῳ τῷ περὶ Ἑλένης λεχθέντι καὶ αὐτὸς προστίθεμαι, τάδε ἐπιλεγόμενος· εἰ ἦν Ἑλένη ἐν Ἰλίῳ, ἀποδοθῆναι ἂν αὐτὴν τοῖσι Ἕλλησι ἤτοι ἑκόντος γε ἢ ἀέκοντος Ἀλεξάνδρου. οὐ γὰρ δὴ οὕτω γε φρενοβλαβὴς ἦν ὁ Πρίαμος οὐδὲ οἱ ἄλλοι ⟨οἱ⟩ προσήκοντες αὐτῷ, ὥστε τοῖσι σφετέροισι σώμασι καὶ τοῖσι τέκνοισι καὶ τῇ πόλι κινδυνεύειν ἐβούλοντο, ὅκως Ἀλέξανδρος Ἑλένῃ συνοικέῃ·
> (Hdt. 2.120.1–2)

Herodotus thinks Priam and his advisers were not so demented that they would have allowed such destruction to their city and so many deaths just so Paris could have Helen. They would have given her back to the Greeks "whether Paris (Alexander) was ἑκών or ἄκων" (ἤτοι ἑκόντος γε ἢ ἀέκοντος Ἀλεξάνδρου). This statement surely does not mean what the APV explains: that Paris may or may not have actually handed her over himself; but rather as the ODA View explains, that his feelings would not have been taken into account at all.

On the other hand, there are some passages for which the APV's rather matter-of-fact explanation may be more informative and relevant than the previous examples suggest. This is particularly the case with some passages where the third party is ἑκών. For example, in the *Homeric Hymn to Aphrodite* (145–54), Anchises summarizes the tale a disguised Aphrodite has just told him. Aphrodite told of how Hermes snatched her up (117: ἀνήρπαξε; 121: ἥρπαξε), led her away (122: ἤγαγεν), and after much travelling, finally set her down and told her she was to be the wife of Anchises and bear him children. Aphrodite tells Anchises that Hermes then returned to the immortals, "But I have come to you (Anchises), and strong necessity is upon me" (αὐτὰρ ἐγώ σ' ἱκόμην, κρατερὴ δέ μοι ἔπλετ' ἀνάγκη). Anchises' summary of this last part of Aphrodite's tale is brief: "You came here when Hermes, the immortal messenger, was ἑκών; and you will be my wife forever":

> ἀθανάτου δὲ ἕκητι διακτόρου ἐνθάδ' ἱκάνεις
> Ἑρμέω, ἐμὴ δ' ἄλοχος κεκλήσεαι ἤματα πάντα·
> (HAphr. 147–48)

At first it seems Aphrodite was the victim of superior force and was not herself the ἀρχή of her motion. The APV would explain correctly that Aphrodite's "coming" was not her own action, since her desires and cognitions are not the explanation of her coming. Hermes' desires and cognitions are the explanation of Aphrodite's coming, and he is correctly called ἑκών. But even if this is true at first, is it still true, according to the APV, once Hermes has left?

The FOV would count the order of Hermes as a form of ἀνάγκη and count Aphrodite as ἄκουσα. Aristotle's negative view would not (unless this act is counted under the ANV/*EE*'s broader view of ἀνάγκη). The APV too would count Aphrodite as ἑκοῦσα when she actually approaches Anchises since she does so on her own: she moves her own limbs through her own desires and cognitions (albeit under order of the god). The important question still to be answered is whether the APV would still count Hermes as the efficient cause of Aphrodite's coming to Anchises even after Hermes departed from the scene.

Because of Aristotle's strict view even about mixed actions, the APV would not count Hermes instead of Aphrodite as the efficient cause of her immediately approaching Anchises, but there is room in the APV for accepting Hermes in addition to Aphrodite as the efficient cause of her coming. After all, it is true that because of Hermes' desires and cognitions Aphrodite came to Anchises.[12] Since the passage does not say Aphrodite is ἄκουσα but only that Hermes is ἑκών, the APV can explain without contradiction that there is a legitimate explanation of the action in question, which connects Hermes' desires and cognitions with the action in such a way that the action would not have happened without them. Hermes' desires and cognitions are not merely in accord with the action; they cause it to happen. The APV in this sort of case then does not give an irrelevant or uninformative piece of information.[13]

For the APV to call someone ἑκών, it is not enough that the individual merely have the sort of desires and cognitions that could account for an act. There must be a causal connection between that individual's desires and cognitions and the action. Thus, in some third-party passages the APV's explanation may supply important information. These are passages in which the third party is not merely interested in the action in question but can also be construed as at least one of its doers, and perhaps a doer that might otherwise be overlooked. But in other third-party passages, a statement that the third party is or is not the one whose desires and cognitions caused the action may be true, but it is also uninformative and unsatisfying as an explanation of what is being said of the third party. Because the ODA View's interest is primarily in the attitudes of persons, it can accommodate passages where the person described by ἑκών group words is only interested in the action and not the direct agent or victim as well as cases where the person so described is the agent or victim. Thus the

---

[12]Cf. the discussion of Aspasius' example in ch. 4, pp. 107–110. But it may make a difference to generalization from his point that in his example the person moved and the person who gave the order are the same person.

[13]Other examples include: *Od.* 6.236–43; 15.318–24; 19.85–88; *HDion.* 1–6; Bacchyl. 1.112–118.

ODA View supplies a likely and satisfying explanation of all third-party passages: the attitude and desires of a third party described as ἄκων are thoroughly opposed to the action or event at hand; the attitude and desires of a third party described as ἑκών are thoroughly committed to it. Not only what an agent feels about events is of interest and important to know, but also even what an interested bystander feels about events can often be of interest and important to know. Although one can imagine situations where it is especially relevant to know whether a third party is also a doer of the action, situations where the question who did action A is in question, on the whole in the passages under study, it is not apparent that the interest is in determining who did action A. But in all of these passages it is plausible that there is an interest in how a third party feels about what is happening. The use of ἑκών words gives a quick assessment of the third party's attitude.

4. Views of strong and weak desire

The ODA View is preferable in the following examples too where the APV's weaker explanation is less likely and unsatisfying.

1. Passages like the following, in which βία is narrowly construed to meet Aristotle's stipulations, and the passive victim is ἄκων, can be accommodated by all four views. In this example, Demeter, disguised as an old woman, tells the daughters of Celeus that she came from Crete, and that pirates led her ἄκουσα by force and necessity:

Δωσὼ ἐμοί γ' ὄνομ' ἐστί· τὸ γὰρ θέτο πότνια μήτηρ·
νῦν αὖτε Κρήτηθεν ἐπ' εὐρέα νῶτα θαλάσσης
ἤλυθον οὐκ ἐθέλουσα, βίῃ δ' ἀέκουσαν ἀνάγκῃ
ἄνδρες ληιστῆρες ἀπήγαγον...
(HDem. 122–125)

The FOV and ANV work similarly in this case since for these views the presence of a criterion, βία, is what renders the character ἄκουσα. The APV would explain that the victim is ἄκουσα because she did not move because of her own desire and cognition. This amounts to much the same story as the ANV tells: she was not the starting-point of the motion. One may suspect, however, that this is a rather odd point to make or at least a redundant one given what we are otherwise told. No one is likely to think that the victim was the starting-point of the motion since she tells of pirates who led her away by force and necessity. In any event, the APV provides a weak reading of the passage, devoid of emotional content or report on the victim's internal state. It simply tells us she was not the efficient cause of the action. The ODA View explains the victim is ἄκουσα because she is totally divorced from what is happening to her and has a completely negative attitude about it. We are informed about what is going on within the victim in contrast to what is overtly happening to her. One might say ἀέκουσαν registers the victim's protest. This is not redundant information, however predictable it is that someone would be ἄκων under such circumstances. The ODA View, no less than the FOV and ANV, finds the victim of overpowering force the paradigm of what it is to be ἄκων. But other descriptors tell of what can be seen; ἄκουσα tells what cannot be seen since it occurs within the victim.

2. It was shown in the last chapter that the APV could accommodate the following passages when the appropriate descriptions of the actions are given. The APV can accommodate them, but only with its weak reading of ἑκών group words. Its readings are matter-of-fact, superfluous or uninformative. Of course, I am not suggesting that these views are inadequate simply because the information they supply is boring. However, I am suggesting that we ought not to be easily satisfied with views that reduce ἑκών group words to information supplied in other ways or treat them as synonymous with such features and thus uninformative. The ODA View, on the other hand, providing insight into the victim's internal state, gives a strong reading, not too strong to be plausible and perhaps more plausible because strong.

Recall the following passage from the Theognidean corpus:

καλὸς ἐὼν κακότητι φίλων δειλοῖσιν ὁμιλεῖς
ἀνδράσι, καὶ διὰ τοῦτ' αἰσχρὸν ὄνειδος ἔχεις,
ὦ παῖ· ἐγὼ δ' ἀέκων τῆς σῆς φιλότητος ἁμαρτὼν
ὠνήμην ἔρδων οἷά τ' ἐλεύθερος ὤν.
(Theog. 1377–80)

The failed lover who is ἄκων does not make so unlikely a comment as "I did not intend to fail." Rather, he expresses how very much he wanted to be successful and how deeply he feels his failure even now that he knows he is better off having failed.

The next example is the fragment from Euripides in which the speaker says that the injustice (ἀδίκημα) he did while drunk came about οὐχ ἑκούσιον:

νοῦ δ' οἶνος ἐξέστησέ μ'· ὁμολογῶ δέ σε
ἀδικεῖν, τὸ δ' ἀδίκημ' ἐγένετ' οὐχ ἑκούσιον.
(Eur. *Auge* Fr. 265 *TGF*)

The speaker in this passage does more than deny the description of what he confesses to have done. By expressing his divorcement from the act, his totally negative attitude about it, we can infer his abhorrence for it, and perhaps we are meant to infer something about his character from this abhorrence: it is such that if not for the drunkenness the act would not have been committed.

Finally, recall the passage from the *Iliad* in which Zeus grants Hera the destruction of Troy:

ὁππότε κεν καὶ ἐγὼ μεμαὼς πόλιν ἐξαλαπάξαι
τὴν ἐθέλω ὅθι τοι φίλοι ἀνέρες ἐγγεγάασι,
μή τι διατρίβειν τὸν ἐμὸν χόλον, ἀλλά μ' ἐᾶσαι·
καὶ γὰρ ἐγὼ σοὶ δῶκα ἑκὼν ἀέκοντί γε θυμῷ·
 (*Il.* 4.40–43)

The APV reading of this passage is much too antiseptic: under description A, I do this; under description B, I do not. Any affective content of Zeus' statement must be inferred. But on the ODA View it is not inferred; it is declared openly through the ἑκών group words. Perhaps we can understand Zeus as epitomizing the conflicted state of one who must act in a situation in which prudential considerations conflict with deep feelings or in which two ends really are of equal value but only one can be substantiated. In the ordinary use of ἑκών group words, individuals are not both ἑκών and ἄκων in such circumstances.[14] It is only one horn of the dilemma which is emphasized overall through the use of ἑκών group words. Recall, for example, the action of Inachus (*PrB* 67–72;) who saves his progeny by driving out Io but does so ἄκων. Thus it is striking that Zeus marks both horns through these words. Here according to the ODA View the indication of strong positive attitude and commitment along with strong negative attitude and divorcement shows the extraordinary nature of Zeus' internal state at this momentous point when he grants Hera the destruction of Troy.[15]

3. Since the FOV has been found to be inadequate, we can reassess the discussion in Chapter 2 of lines 27–30 of Simonides' poem to Scopas.[16] These lines need not be understood to express an exclusive disjunction between acting ἑκών and acting under ἀνάγκη, even though there is a superficial disjunction between them. The poet says, "I praise and love everyone who ἑκών does nothing shameful; not even the gods fight necessity":

---

[14]Cf. *EE* 1223b24–26 and the discussion of the characterization of parts of the soul and the whole soul of the *enkrates* and the *akrates* at *EE* 1224b15–1225a1. Aristotle might explain this passage by reference to more than one part of Zeus' soul.

[15]Cf. the case of Orestes (*IT* 511–12) who flees Argos both ἑκών and οὐχ ἑκών. The ODA View would explain this passage too as marking the extraordinary feelings which must be involved for one hounded by the dread Erinyes. Although, as Platnauer, *IT*, notes, this line is "a good Euripidean σόφισμα," perhaps Euripides meant to mimic the expression of the extraordinary feelings of the king of the gods in Il. 4.40–43 (the exception which proves the rule for the usage of ἑκών group words?).

[16]Cf. ch. 2, p. 61

πάντας δ' ἐπαίνημι καὶ φιλέω
ἑκὼν ὅστις ἔρδῃ
μηδὲν αἰσχρόν· ἀνάγκᾳ
δ' οὐδὲ θεοὶ μάχονται.

(Simon. 542.27–30 *PMG*)

The FOV reading can be replaced by one in which what is under discussion is acting ἑκών when beset by compelling circumstances. The ODA View as well as the APV can function when compelling circumstances are treated as a particular occasion under which ἑκών group words are used. But the APV explains that however difficult and compelling circumstances are, agent A is ἑκών as long as the immediate cause of the action as described can be traced to A's desires and cognitions. Thus, when the APV denies someone is ἑκών in connection with some particular act, it can be denying that this person performed the act at all; or more subtlely, it can deny this person performed the act under the given description.[17]

In lines 27–30, the speaker, having just dismissed the probability of discovering the totally blameless person (24: πανάμωμον ἄνθρωπον), sets up his own model of the good man. This is the person who performs a shameful act (αἰσχρόν), but does not do so ἑκών, and, from the statement that not even the gods fight necessity (ἀνάγκᾳ δ' οὐδὲ θεοὶ μάχονται), we are entitled to infer that the poet has in mind specifically shameful acts performed under compelling circusmtances, the kind not even the gods can fight.

The APV could explain performing ἑκών no shameful act or performing such an act οὐχ ἑκών (that is, relying on Aristotle's distinctions, involving neither the agent's desires nor cognitions), by weakening the connection between the agent's desires and cognitions and the action. Thus, if the agent acted while subject to what Aristotle would count as ἀνάγκη, certain instances of force or ignorance, it could be said that the action did not occur because of the agent's desires and cognitions. However, insofar as the poet is replacing the all too rare blameless man (πανάμωμος ἄνθρωπος) whose status is dependent on circumstances or chance (13–16: χαλεπὸν φάτ' ἐσθλὸν ἔμμεναι. / θεὸς ἂν μόνος τοῦτ' ἔχοι γέρας, ἄνδρα δ' οὐκ / ἔστι μὴ οὐ κακὸν ἔμμεναι, / ὃν ἀμήχανος συμφορὰ καθέλῃ·), it is unlikely that his new model for praise is someone who only accidentally, through ignorance, or constrained by force performs shameful deeds. To decide who is the new model for praise on the basis of whether these circumstances pertain is just as dependant on circumstances or chance and only underlines the poet's point that shameful deeds do occur because of ἀνάγκη. The poet starts from this assumption but seeks

---

[17] Cf. Epicharm. 78.1–2 Kaibel (ch. 2, n. 5), and see the discussion of Soph. *Tyro* 665 *TrGF* in ch. 3 p. 85. Also, cf. Aesch. *Eum.* 550, if Wieseler's conjecture ἑκὼν δ' (ἐκ τῶνδ' codd.) is accepted.

some characteristic apart from circumstances or chance, a limitation for everyone, to distinguish his model individual from others.

The APV does have another way of breaking the link between the agent's desires and cognitions and the action, even if the agent is not forced or ignorant of details about the act he performs.[18] The connection would be broken if the agent did not perform the act because it was shameful (αἰσχρόν); that is, it was not a part of the agent's intentional description of the action that the act is shameful. On this interpretation, the new model person does not pursue what is shameful because it is shameful. This strikes me as somewhat peculiar. Although there may be some who pursue the shameful, amongst other reasons to be sure, because it is shameful, I would think that generally, someone who pursues an action because it is shameful rather than say because of the benefits to be accrued, is some sort of social revolutionary if not merely a pervert.

In contrast, when Simonides declares that sometimes circumstances can be so compelling that a person must do something shameful, the ODA View explains that the new model person is an agent who has a completely negative attitude toward the shameful acts he must sometimes perform.[19] Since the ODA View allows for any number of considerations to underlie the agent's attitude, e.g., general values, aims, or considerations of favorable consequences, this limitation on the person who must perform a shameful act, that he not do so ἑκών, but we can infer, ἄκων, is considerable. It suggests that however enormous the good is to be derived from the act, the agent is internally divorced from his act. His attitude is negative; he is repelled and pained by his act

Compared to the APV's assessment that the model person does not perform the act under the intentional description of the act as shameful, the ODA View provides a much more powerful and in my view, plausible, interpretation of the text.[20]

---

[18] I am assuming that the one thing the agent cannot be ignorant about when he performs the act is the fact that it is αἰσχρόν. Since for Aristotle what counts as αἰσχρόν in a culture is clear to all members, I am not supposing Aristotle would be interested in drawing a distinction here between knowing in general what is αἰσχρόν and knowing a particular act to be αἰσχρόν.

[19] My interpretation rests on treating "does nothing shameful ἑκών" as equivalent to "does not do anything shameful ἑκών" and interchangeable with "does something shameful ἄκων." This is warranted since the passages make no clear distinction between οὐχ ἑκών and ἄκων and throughout ἑκών and ἄκων appear to be contradictories.

[20] Simonides' Scopas poem (542 *PMG*), has aroused much scholarly discussion. (For bibliography see B. Gentili, "Studi su Simonide," *Maia* 16 [1964], 274–306, and M. Dickie, "The Argument and Form of Simonides 542 *PMG*," *HSCP* 82 [1978], 21–33). Besides those who are interested in determining the traditional form of the poem, if any, there are those interested in whether or not the poem says something original. However, "ἑκών" has not been a source of

4. Concerning the tortured slaves of the *Palamedes*, the APV explains that the slaves themselves speak the accusations which the torture prompts.

> δούλοις δὲ πῶς οὐκ ἄπιστον; ἑκόντες ⟨τε⟩ γὰρ ἐπ' ἐλευθερίαι χειμαζόμενοί τε δι' ἀνάγκην κατηγοροῦσιν.
> (Gorg. B.11a.11 DK)

Again, this is too matter-of-fact to be of interest or, if it is taken to be informative, would require some unwarranted elaborate scenario to be read into the text. It would require, for example, that we suppose, without any clue in the text, that a denial is being made that accusations were made by others and attributed to the slaves. The ODA View tells a direct and relevant tale: the slaves are totally committed to their act, not merely that they perform it. The passage itself mentions that for the sake of which they act, their freedom (ἐπ' ἐλευθερίαι). On the ODA View we can suppose this goal is so overriding that there is no conflict about making the accusations and that the slaves have a completely positive attitude about their action; in effect, nothing else counts for the slaves. Given their circumstances, the ODA View hardly seems to provide too strong an explanation.

5. Finally, in a passage from Thucydides, Pericles draws a distinction between the citizens accepting the war ἑκούσιοι or not, but there is no alternative of not at all taking up the war:

> εἰδέναι δὲ χρὴ ὅτι ἀνάγκη πολεμεῖν, ἢν δὲ ἑκούσιοι μᾶλλον δεχώμεθα, ἧσσον ἐγκεισομένους τοὺς ἐναντίους ἕξομεν, ἔκ τε τῶν μεγίστων κινδύνων ὅτι καὶ πόλει καὶ ἰδιώτῃ μέγισται τιμαὶ περιγίγνονται·
> (Thuc. 1.144.3)

Pericles calls on the Athenians to recognize what they must recognize: the war is necessary. He then asserts that the more ἑκούσιοι the Athenians are, the less pressing their enemies will be to them, and that the greatest honors arise from the greatest dangers. This is an exhortation to be more accepting of the war. But the acceptance urged by Pericles verges more on enthusiasm grounded in expectation of victory than acquiescence aimed only at producing action. Producing action is the bare interest of the APV. The ODA View would explain that Pericles exhorts the Athenians to be committed to what they do under ἀνάγκη. The fact that they act under ἀνάγκη does not prevent them from being ἑκούσιοι,

---

controversy or confusion. In his commentary, C.C.W. Taylor thought to give some information of ἑκών which he translates "freely," but simply relies on Aristotle (*Plato: Protagoras*, Translated with Notes by C.C.W. Taylor, Clarendon Plato Series, ed. M.J. Woods [Oxford, 1976], 146ff.).

nor are they ἑκούσιοι if they merely fight. Here too, it is a strong commitment that is exhorted, not a request merely to perform the functions of war.[21]

Challenges for the Occasions for Describing Attitude View

As several of the foregoing examples have shown, there are passages the APV cannot accommodate at all and some where its interpretation is unsatisfying. When passages can be accommodated by the APV or the ODA View, frequently the difference between the two views is that the APV provides a minimal explanation of the desire involved and simply identifies or denies someone is the actual agent, whereas the ODA View claims a strong positive or negative attitude, deep commitment to or divorcement from the act. According to the APV an agent is ἑκών if he merely moves his own body (as opposed to someone else moving it). According to the ODA View an agent could move his own body but act ἄκων. A deeper commitment is needed for the agent to act ἑκών. Similarly, one described as οὐχ ἑκών (Aristotle's technical usage), according to the APV, is simply not the person whose desires and cognitions are directly responsible for an action. But for the ODA View, an individual who is οὐχ ἑκών or ἄκων is one whose desires are totally adverse to what is happening even where there is no question of his involvement as efficient agent. Since the APV gives a weak interpretation of acting ἑκών and the ODA View a strong one, we would expect criticism of the APV to center on its saying too little, and criticism of the ODA View to center on its saying too much. In the remaining pages I will discuss the kinds of passages which could be raised as objections to the ODA View's strong reading of ἑκών group words. It will be seen there is a good case for maintaining that the ODA View can accommodate these passages too without being apologetic.

1. Animal agents

The agents in the next group of passages to be discussed are animals. At first sight the ODA View may seem to be much too strong to satisfactorily accommodate them. For we do not ordinarily suppose animals to share the psychological and ethical awareness that seems to be at the root of the ODA View's strong reading of ἑκών group words. However, it will be seen that the ODA View provides a rich and plausible explanation for these passages.

---

[21]See M. Ostwald, *ANAΓKH in Thucydides*, American Classical Studies, 18 (Atlanta, 1988). *Akousa* I was not able to take advantage of this recently published work for the present study.

In a repeated formulaic line, horses said to race off οὐκ ἀέκοντε (τὼ δ' οὐκ ἀέκοντε πετέσθην), are also whipped:

μάστιξεν δ' ἐλάαν
(Il. 5.366; 8.45-46; 22.400; Od. 3.481-86; 3.492-96; 15.190-92);

μάστιξεν δ' ἵππους
(Il. 5.768-69; 10.530-31; 11.519-20);

ἡνίοχος δ' ἵμασεν καλλίτριχας ἵππους
(Il. 11.280-81); and

καὶ μάστιγα λαβὼν μετὰ χερσὶ φίλῃσι
(HDem. 377-79).

If humans were subjected to a whipping there would be no hesitation to count them as victims of force. But it might be objected that horses are regularly lashed to get them going. Thus, it would be inappropriate to count this initial lashing as an act of violence. However, horse training practices represented by Xenophon recommend positive reinforcement and deplore the use of violence.[22] On this point Xenophon mentions as authority Simon, who in an earlier treatise on horsemanship, compared the performance of a beaten horse to that of a beaten dancer.[23] On the whole, Xenophon recommends training horses to respond to very gentle "signs" (σημεῖα),[24] especially sounds.[25] Only once does Xenophon recommend beating a horse and even in this case, leaping over a ditch, he says the horse once beaten will perform the task in the future at the mere sight of a man approaching from behind.[26]

Even granting that the passages being examined involve teams of horses that draw their drivers in chariots rather than the mounted horses discussed by Xenophon, and that "Homeric" practices need not be as enlightened as the behavior modification tactics of Xenophon and Simon, we can infer from these treatises that whipping a horse even as a "sign" still amounts to an overt act of physical force.

---

[22]Xen. *On Horsemanship* 8.13-14. Xenophon says reward and punishment must be used to train horses since they can not talk, but he emphasizes immediate positive reinforcement.

[23]Xen. *On Horsemanship* 11.5-6: ἃ μὲν γὰρ ὁ ἵππος ἀναγκαζόμενος ποιεῖ, ὥσπερ καὶ Σίμων λέγει, οὔτ' ἐπίσταται οὔτε καλά ἐστιν, οὐδὲν μᾶλλον ἢ εἴ τις ὀρχηστὴν μαστιγοίη καὶ κεντρίζοι· πολὺ γὰρ ἂν πλείω ἀσχημονοίη ἢ καλὰ ποιοίη ὁ τοιαῦτα πάσχων καὶ ἵππος καὶ ἄνθρωπος.

[24]Xen. *On Horsemanship* 9.3 and 11.6.

[25]Xen. *On Horsemanship* 9.10.

[26]Xen. *On Horsemanship* 8.4.

The horses in these passages then are agent victims of actual force, but they are not ἄκοντες. Thus, they do not fit the FOV pattern. But since the force involved does not meet the strict requirements of the ANV, the ANV can accommodate the passages. According to the APV, the sense of the passages would be that the actual movement of the horses can be traced to their own desires and cognitions. This is not an irrelevant point given that their actions occur under circumstances of physical force: they are whipped. The APV, in fact, makes clear the actual cause of motion in a situation where there might be some question about what was the actual cause of motion. The particular sort of βία that is applied in these cases is not the sort that could move a horse without the horse's participation; however, insofar as there was force operating on the horses, the APV makes it clear that the animals moved through their own desires and cognitions.

The ODA View, on the other hand, gives a stronger reading to the desires of the horses. What is at stake is not merely that the horses are the actual source of motion, whatever external prodding there may have been, but that they are fully committed to their acts. Admittedly, such a description of an animal may seem rather out of place. Aristotle who holds that τὸ ἑκούσιον is appropriate to animals and children as well as adult humans,[27] seems to tell a more believable tale: animals (and children), like human adults, do move themselves, and the horses of these passages are examples of such movement. However, the fact that the animals involved are horses, an animal with a unique status in epic poetry, is a mitigating factor through which the ODA View provides an even more plausible explanation for these passages than the APV.

The status of the horse in epic is unlike that of other animals. Redfield points this out in his comparison of dogs and horses and their relationships to humans. He explains the relationship between man and dog, the other domesticated companion of man, as "metonymic and metaphoric":

> The dog stands for an element within us that is permanently uncivilized. As the dog is a predator within culture, so the dog in us is the predator within us. Thus metonym and metaphor are linked; the man who is called a dog is likened, as it were, to a lower part of himself. He is thus reduced to less than himself. When we are lacking in αἰδώς, in full social humanity, we are liable to become dogs; that is to say, uncontrolled predatory nature within us is liable to take charge.[28]

The horse, on the other hand, the peaceful, herbivorous helper of the warrior, does not fight as the dog does for the herdsman or hunter. "The horse can help

---

[27]*NE* 1111a25–26; 1111b8–9.

[28]J. Redfield, *Nature and Culture in the Iliad* (Chicago, 1975), p. 195.

him escape from danger, but the warrior must do his own fighting."[29] Contrasting the dog and the horse Redfield says:

> Both are companions and instruments of man, but they both stand to one another rather as Caliban to Ariel. Dogs in Homer are anonymous, but horses have personal names. Horses, like heroes, can have divine parents; they can be immortal; one horse even speaks. Horses thus form a civil series parallel to man.[30]

We should add that in the *Iliad* Achilles' horses cry (17.434–40); Hector's, at least, drink wine (8.187–89), and are treated as humans in other ways too. Redfield, e.g., notes the reciprocity that underlies the speech of Hector to his horses in Book 8.185–197.[31] This speech which immediately follows Hector's exhortation to the Trojans, suggests an even closer partnership between the warrior and his horse than even Redfield depicts. Horses, unlike dogs, are not expected to injure the enemy, but they do fully participate in the warrior's exploits and are included as victors. In this speech, the "we" of λάβωμεν (191) who are to capture the shield of Nestor, and the "we" of λάβοιμεν (196) who are to capture not only that shield but the corselet of Diomedes, refer to Hector and his horses.

Redfield thinks there is parallelism between horse and man and that it is typically exemplified in the Catalogue of Book 2. In the following passage, concluding his list of the leaders of the Danaans, the poet asks the Muse to tell who was the best of these men and who was the best of their horses:

> οὗτοι ἄρ' ἡγεμόνες Δαναῶν καὶ κοίρανοι ἦσαν·
> τίς τ' ἄρ τῶν ὄχ' ἄριστος ἔην, σύ μοι ἔννεπε, Μοῦσα,
> αὐτῶν ἠδ' ἵππων, οἳ ἅμ' Ἀτρείδῃσιν ἕποντο.
> (*Il.* 2.760–62)

But the relationship seems to go beyond parallelism; horse and hero are inextricably fused. Thus, for example, horses themselves are called "prizewinners", ἀεθλοφόροι,[32] but yet the prizes they win are clearly for their owners, not themselves. Consider, e.g., the following passage from Book 9 of the *Iliad*, in which Agamemnon describes the horses he offers to Achilles. He does not speak about what he was able to accomplish with these splendid horses, but rather speaks of the horses as winning prizes for him:

> δώδεκα δ' ἵππους
> πηγοὺς ἀθλοφόρους, οἳ ἀέθλια ποσσὶν ἄροντο.

---

[29]Redfield, p. 196.

[30]Redfield, p. 195 and 260 n. 68 where he notes that one dog does have a name.

[31]Redfield, p. 195.

[32]For example, *Il.* 22.162.

> οὔ κεν ἀλήιος εἴη ἀνὴρ ᾧ τόσσα γένοιτο,
> οὐδέ κεν ἀκτήμων ἐριτίμοιο χρυσοῖο,
> ὅσσα μοι ἠνείκαντο ἀέθλια μώνυχες ἵπποι.
> (*Il.* 9.123–27)

Also, in the Catalogue, the "best of horses" are not identified without reference to their owners. In fact, having asked the questions, "Who is the best of these leaders?" and "Who are the best of their horses?" in the passage just quoted from Book 2, the poet begins by telling us first about the horses, no less worthy a topic than the best warriors. The horses are identified by reference first to their owners, then by physical description and breeding. We then learn without comparable detail that Ajax was the best man while Achilles was angry. But, by far, Achilles and his horses were really best. Achilles' horses have their own names, but here they are nameless and paired with their owner.[33]

Horse and rider or driver are so fused in their joint activity that we readily accept language in which the horse itself is spoken of as itself pursuing the course. But we must not lose sight of the fact that not the horse but the rider or charioteer desires to go and goes where he desires. This point is made clear in two of the passages under discussion. Consider the following formula:

> μάστιξεν δ' ἵππους, τὼ δ' οὐκ ἀέκοντε πετέσθην
> νῆας ἔπι γλαφυράς· τῇ γὰρ φίλον ἔπλετο θυμῷ.
> (*Il.* 10.530–31; 11.519–20)

Surely the *thumos* which wanted the horses to go to the ship, was that of the driver.[34]

Because horses are special in epic and are fused with their riders or drivers in their joint activities, it is not implausible to apply the stronger reading of the ODA View to these passages. Moreover, two passages remaining to be discussed,[35] in which animals are described by ἑκών group words are also replete with strong analogies to human psychology. Thus, in these passages too the strong desiring posited by the ODA View can be supplied by the animal's fusion with his human counterpart. Furthermore, in both passages the animal acts but does so ἄκων. Thus the APV has difficulty accommodating these passages at all. The APV expects agents who are the actual cause of motion to be ἑκόντες.

---

[33]*Il.* 2.763–770.

[34]The control of the driver and the passivity of the horses is also signalled in some of these passages by other activities surrounding the actual flight. The drivers yoke and unyoke the horses, for example, and some horses are fed ambrosia and wrapped in mist. Contrast the fusion of horse and driver with *Od.* 15.182–84 which is restricted to the horse's psychology.

[35]Pherecyd. 150 Kock is also about an animal, but the fragment is too brief for speculation.

Both passages are similes. Ibycus' poem likens the trembling reluctance of one all too experienced in the nets of Cypris to the prizewinning old horse that goes ἀέκων to yet another contest:

Ἔρος αὖτέ με κυανέοισιν ὑπὸ
βλεφάροις τακέρ' ὄμμασι δερκόμενος
κηλήμασι παντοδαποῖς ἐς ἄπει-
ρα δίκτυα Κύπριδος ἐσβάλλει·
ἦ μὰν τρομέω νιν ἐπερχόμενον,
ὥστε φερέζυγος ἵππος ἀεθλοφόρος ποτὶ γήρᾳ
ἀέκων σὺν ὄχεσφι θοοῖς ἐς ἄμιλλαν ἔβα.
(Ibyc. 287 *PMG*)

The poet achieves great pathos by humanizing the old race horse and using ἀέκων explicitly of the horse although it applies in sense to the human speaker too. The poem works by infusing the horse with a human psychology. In effect, the speaker tells us that as Eros draws him into another relationship, he feels just the way he would feel if he were an old race horse led off to another contest. The speaker will soon go off to another love contest, and we can infer that he will go ἄκων. But it is through our understanding of the human's feelings that we understand how the horse feels even though it is the horse's feelings that are used to illuminate the human's feelings.

The APV has difficulty accommodating this passage since the horse does actually move his own limbs: the horse is not dragged to the starting gate. The speaker too, we can infer, will himself be the cause of many actions in the love contest he anticipates. One could object that there is something in the actual descriptions of these actions that renders the agents οὐχ ἑκόντες (Aristotle's technical usage; ἄκοντες generally) even on the APV. For example, if the poet had written only that the horse "goes" rather than that the horse "goes to a contest," the APV would have difficulty accommodating the passage. But because the "going" is further described as "going to a contest," it could be argued the APV can accommodate the passage. The passage would be interpreted as saying the horse does not desire his action under that description. However, unlike the Oedipus model for this kind of objection, I think it likely, despite my ignorance of horse psychology, that the description "contest" is not problematic in this passage. Most likely we are to accept that the horse knows he is going to a contest and moves his own limbs. In contrast, the ODA View explains that saying the horse acts ἀέκων (οὐχ ἑκών in Aristotle's technical usage) is not to deny the action under the given description but to express the horse's attitude about the action he performs. The horse acts, but divorces himself from his act; internally he recoils from the act he performs. In the same way, the human who compares himself to the horse will participate in the new love Eros brings him, but his action does not correspond to his attitude about the action.

In the last animal passage, ἀέκων appears in a simile which compares Menelaus to a lion:

Ἦος ὁ ταῦθ' ὅρμαινε κατὰ φρένα καὶ κατὰ θυμόν,
τόφρα δ' ἐπὶ Τρώων στίχες ἤλυθον· ἦρχε δ' ἄρ' Ἕκτωρ.
αὐτὰρ ὅ γ' ἐξοπίσω ἀνεχάζετο, λεῖπε δὲ νεκρόν,
ἐντροπαλιζόμενος ὥς τε λὶς ἠϋγένειος,
ὅν ῥα κύνες τε καὶ ἄνδρες ἀπὸ σταθμοῖο δίωνται
ἔγχεσι καὶ φωνῇ· τοῦ δ' ἐν φρεσὶν ἄλκιμον ἦτορ
παχνοῦται, ἀέκων δέ τ' ἔβη ἀπὸ μεσσαύλοιο·
ὣς ἀπὸ Πατρόκλοιο κίε ξανθὸς Μενέλαος.
(*Il.* 17.106–13)

The simile follows on a passage (90–105) that details Menelaus' conflict about staying to fight over the corpse of Patroclus who lies dead for the sake of Menelaus' *time*. In this deliberative passage Menelaus counters his concern about *aidos* and *nemesis* if he abandons Patroclus, with a truism about disaster rolling in on one who fights whom "god honors" (θεὸς τιμᾷ), i.e., Hector. He concludes that even a *daimon* could be faced if he and Ajax were to fight together. This latter scenario is the best possible given the circumstances, not absolutely: κακῶν δέ κε φέρτατον εἴη (105). At this point the Trojans led by Hector appear and Menelaus retreats. The passage quoted above details in a simile the manner of his retreat. The way Menelaus keeps turning around even as he goes (ἐντροπαλιζόμενος) is compared to a lion struck with terror by dogs and men with spears and loud voices putting him to flight. The lion is said to leave ἀέκων.

Here too human psychology pervades the animal's. If it were not for the detailed portrait of Menelaus' ponderings, the import of the simile and what we are to make of ἐντροπαλιζόμενος would be moot. We think we know what goes on psychologically in the lion because we understand Menelaus, not vice versa. All we know of the lion is that it is frightened. The lion could be turning to look back for many reasons given that it is frightened, e.g., to keep track of its pursuers. Because of Menelaus' conflict, however, we understand the lion to be torn between fleeing and fighting.

The lion's act as it is described in the poem, the act he performs ἀέκων, is so bare that the APV cannot take refuge in any objection that the lion does not perform the act under the given description. The lion simply goes from the inner court: ἀέκων δέ τ' ἔβη ἀπὸ μεσσαύλοιο (112). Thus the APV could not accommodate this passage where the agent is the cause of his motion but is nonetheless ἀέκων (οὐχ ἑκών in Aristotle's technical usage). The ODA View explains that because of circumstances both Menelaus and the lion are compelled to act as they do, but both are estranged from their actions. We can understand the behavior described by ἐντροπαλιζόμενος as an external representation of the lion's negative attitude toward his action which is noted by ἀέκων.

In general it is much easier to picture ἑκών group words describing animals on the FOV or the APV than on the ODA View. The first two require only a minimal psychological impulse so that animals, like humans, do in fact act under circumstances that may or may not show signs of compulsion and are themselves the causes of many of their actions. Since the ODA View, on the other hand, explains ἑκών and ἄκων as signalling the attitude of an agent, his commitment or divorcement from his action, it might seem to require more than we can comfortably project into animals. However, in the passages we actually have in which animals are described by ἑκών group words, the animals are drawn into the more complex psychological capacities of humans through special close associations with humans. Thus, at least for the extant passages, any superficial inappropriateness the ODA View might project is mitigated. In fact, the ODA View provides a more suitable explanation for these passages.

2. Acting ἑκών opposed to acting under necessity

Although there is considerable variety among those passages in which acting ἑκών is opposed to acting under some form of ἀνάγκη, the Aristotelian Positive View, rather than the strong ODA View, may seem to provide a more suitable explanation for these passages as a group.[36] In some cases, the interpretation of the ODA View, that the ἑκών agent acts with full commitment and a strongly positive attitude, seems no more or less plausible than that of the APV, which pinpoints whose act is in question or distinguishes someone acting from someone acted on by someone or something else. For example, either view can accommodate the distinction Pindar draws between what is gained by force and violence and the gain which is dearest (φίλτατον), what one takes from the home of one who ἑκών gives it:

τὺ δ' ὁπόταν τις ἀμείλιχον
καρδίᾳ κότον ἐνελάσῃ,

---

[36]In some of the examples to be discussed, some threat of force still pertains even as the agent acts ἑκών in the absence of actual force. Such passages have been discussed as evidence against the FOV, since that view treats the threat of force on a par with actual force: there must not be even a threat of force for the agent to be ἑκών. But for Aristotle, even though the ANV/*EE* makes room for the most severe threats of force as a compelling factor able to render a victim ἄκων, for the most part, "mixed acts" are ἑκούσιοι. Moreover, the ANV and the APV are extensionally equivalent in these cases. Where there is no ignorance of detail and no overwhelming force, according to the ANV, the action is ἑκούσιος. Likewise, for the APV, assuming the description of the action fits the intentional description of the agent and that the agent's desires and cognitions are in fact the efficient cause of the action, the action is ἑκούσιος. The ἑκών is the one who actually performs the action, the doer.

τραχεῖα δυσμενέων
ὑπαντιάξαισα κράτει τιθεῖς
ὕβριν ἐν ἄντλῳ· τὰν οὐδὲ Πορφυρίων μάθεν
παρ' αἶσαν ἐξερεθίζων. κέρδος δὲ φίλτατον,
ἑκόντος εἴ τις ἐκ δόμων φέροι.
βίᾳ δὲ καὶ μεγάλαυχον ἔσφαλεν ἐν χρόνῳ.
(Pind. *Pyth.* 8.8–15)

or the distinction Euripides' Macaria draws between giving her life ἑκοῦσα and giving it because she has been chosen by lot to do so:

οὐκ ἂν θάνοιμι τῇ τύχῃ λαχοῦσ' ἐγώ·
χάρις γὰρ οὐ πρόσεστι· μὴ λέξῃς, γέρον.
ἀλλ', εἰ μὲν ἐνδέχεσθε καὶ βούλεσθέ μοι
χρῆσθαι προθύμως, τὴν ἐμὴν ψυχὴν ἐγὼ
δίδωμ' ἑκοῦσα τοῖσδ', ἀναγκασθεῖσα δ' οὔ.
(Eur. *Heracl.* 547–51)

In some cases, although either view may seem applicable, the description of the agent's demeanor or the appearance of other words which describe the agent's attitude toward the action or internal state, can be argued to tip the balance in favor of the ODA View. Consider, for example, the description of Dionysus when apprehended. In contrast to the attendant who was ashamed and acted οὐχ ἑκών, Dionysus was gentle, did not flee, and when οὐκ ἄκων he held out his hands, he did not turn pale, but smiled and bade the attendant bind him and lead him away:

Πενθεῦ, πάρεσμεν τήνδ' ἄγραν ἠγρευκότες
ἐφ' ἣν ἔπεμψας, οὐδ' ἄκρανθ' ὡρμήσαμεν.
ὁ θὴρ δ' ὅδ' ἡμῖν πρᾷος οὐδ' ὑπέσπασεν
φυγῇ πόδ', ἀλλ' ἔδωκεν οὐκ ἄκων χέρας
οὐδ' ὠχρός, οὐδ' ἤλλαξεν οἰνωπὸν γένυν,
γελῶν δὲ καὶ δεῖν κἀπάγειν ἐφίετο
ἔμενέ τε, τοὐμὸν εὐτρεπὲς ποιούμενος.
κἀγὼ δι' αἰδοῦς εἶπον· Ὦ ξέν' οὐχ ἑκὼν
ἄγω σε, Πενθέως δ' ὅς μ' ἔπεμψ' ἐπιστολαῖς.
(Eur. *Bacch.* 434–42)

Or consider the specific references to the ἑκών agent's attitude given by expressions like κατ' εὔνοιαν φρενῶν (with goodwill of heart) (Aesch. *Supp.* 940–41), describing the state in which the suppliant women must be in order for the suit of their Egyptian cousins to be acceptable, and εὐκαρδίως (stout-hearted) which describes Polyxena's preference for how she will give her life (Eur. *Hec.* 549).[37]

But in a number of cases the APV seems to provide a more plausible accommodation. First, consider the passages concerning the Plataean surrender to the Spartans (Thuc. 3.52.2–3; 58.2–3). From the point of view of the Spartan commander, in the earlier passage, there is a contrast between his taking Plataea by force, βία and the Plataeans surrendering ἑκόντες. Whatever the Plataeans do, they are pressed by compelling circumstances: not only are they under siege, but they have also run out of supplies. Still, on the APV, though the Spartan commander wants the city, he prefers that the city be handed over to him through the desires and cognitions of the Plataeans, i.e., through an ἑκούσιος action rather than through his storming the city. There is no reason to think the Spartan commander is even interested in whether the Plataeans surrender fully committed to their act. All he is interested in is that they actually perform the act. His concern about a possible treaty that would return cities taken by force during the war but not those which surrendered ἑκόντες, shows that the compelling circumstances under which the cities would surrender do not automatically render the cities ἄκοντες or prohibit them from being ἑκόντες. In this the ANV and APV concur with the ODA View. But we can also infer from the concern about a treaty that the mere act of surrender, in the absence of an actual assault by the Spartans, will count as ἑκούσιος. This fits with the ANV and APV explanation.[38] Furthermore, in the passage where the Plataeans plead for their lives (Thuc. 3.58.2–3), we need understand them only to be reminding the Spartans that the city came into their power because of an action of the Plataeans themselves, their ἑκούσιος surrender, rather than because the city was stormed.

In other examples too the agent's own movement is implicitly contrasted with his being moved by someone (or something) else. When Poseidon curses whoever ἑκών leaves the fighting (*Il.* 13.219–34), presumably this person is being contrasted with a soldier killed or severely wounded who is thereby compelled to leave the fighting. The threatening alternative of Poseidon in a comic fragment (Plato Com. 24.1–2 Kock), that either the one addressed abandon the sea ἑκών or suffer the effects of Poseidon's trident, also requires only that the addressee move away on his own. When Darius (Hdt. 3.72.5) describes how he and the other conspirators will enter the palace to dispose of the masquerading

---

[37] These expressions and others like them, as well as other words for desiring, could be studied to see if they can give a more specific portrait of the internal condition of the ἑκών and ἄκων. However, Aristotle's attempts in the *EE* and *MM* to define ἑκούσιος and ἀκούσιος action by a particular kind of desire or cognition suggests there is a limit to the usefulness of such an exercise.

[38] See ch.2 pp. 72–73 for a discussion of a possible technical use of ἑκων group words. Cf. the first-strike passage Thuc. 6.36.3–4, ch. 2 pp. 49–50.

Magus, there seems to be no reason to picture the sentries as enthusiastically joining the plot, but only allowing entry without a fight. We can also understand in this way the accusation of the Syracusans and their allies against Gylippus and the harm or wrong he committed (Thuc. 7.81.1). The Athenians escaped by night because Gylippus simply let them go. In effect, Gylippus' accusors trace the movement of the Athenians to Gylippus' desires and cognitions. They have no interest in the depth of his commitment, only in the source and explanation of the action.

In response to this interpretation, the ODA View would point out that although ἑκών seems to indicate mere motion as opposed to deep commitment in these passages, it does so from the point of view of an aggressor who is interested not in the agent's internal state, but only in what he actually does, or not in an accurate assessment of the agent's attitude but in a description of that attitude helpful to his own case. The aggressor's use of ἑκών is, in effect, a rhetorical exaggeration. Two bases for this usage are apparent. First, ordinarily it is the case that humans, as real agents, do what they desire. Ordinarily, overt behavior which can be observed accurately represents what is internal and cannot be seen, an agent's desires. Moreover, there are times when the "mere" performance of an act can be taken to represent even the deep commitment of an agent to his act. One can speculate that this very fact gives rise to the need for something like ἑκών group words to indicate the internal state of an agent or victim to accommodate just those situations where there is some question of whether there is accord between what is observable and what is internal and not observable. Secondly, the paradigmatic case of being ἄκων is being totally victimized by external force. This paradigm fits the ODA View just as easily as the other views since the repulsiveness of such an event is undoubtedly shared by all humans. Thus, the inversion of such circumstances can be rhetorically exploited to claim action is ἑκούσιος if only because the agent acts.

The discussion of passages from the *Philoctetes* will illustrate this aggressor's use of ἑκών more clearly. But first it should be recognized that the exaggeration inherent in the aggresor's use of ἑκών represented in the passages discussed above or in others, is matched in other cases by the enthusiasm or exaggeration of a partisan or an agent who seeks to paint a portrait to his or her advantage. As an example of the aggressor's use of ἑκών, consider the severe interpretation Cassandra gives of Helen's experience in the course of bitter remarks against Agamemnon. Helen, she says, was ἑκοῦσα and was not seized by force:

ὁ δὲ στρατηγὸς ὁ σοφὸς ἐχθίστων ὕπερ
τὰ φίλτατ' ὤλεσ', ἡδονὰς τὰς οἴκοθεν

τέκνων ἀδελφῶι δοὺς γυναικὸς οὕνεκα,
καὶ ταῦθ' ἑκούσης κοὐ βίαι λεληισμένης.
(Eur. *Tro.* 370–73)

For the partisan use, consider the passage discussed earlier in which the agent admits to doing an injustice to someone, but claims the act was not ἑκούσιος:

νοῦ δ' οἶνος ἐξέστησέ μ'· ὁμολογῶ δέ σε
ἀδικεῖν, τὸ δ' ἀδίκημ' ἐγένετ' οὐχ ἑκούσιον.
(Eur. *Auge* Fr.265 *TGF*)

Whatever views were held about actions performed by someone when drunk, and whatever the truth of the matter is, it is certainly to the speaker's advantage to plead that the act was not ἑκούσιος.

3. *Philoctetes and the aggressor's use of* ἑκών

The *Philoctetes* presents uses of ἑκών that represent the aggressor's version and what the ODA View sees as the fundamental use. Without doubt, at lines 981–88, the opposition between Philoctetes going ἑκών and going by force is to be understood as a contrast between Philoctetes as efficient cause moving his own limbs and Philoctetes being carried away:

Φι. ἀπόδος, ἄφες μοι, παῖ, τὰ τόξα.   Οδ. τοῦτο μέν,
   οὐδ' ἢν θέλῃ, δράσει ποτ'. ἀλλὰ καὶ σὲ δεῖ
   στείχειν ἅμ' αὐτοῖς, ἢ βίᾳ στελοῦσί σε.
Φι. ἔμ', ὦ κακῶν κάκιστε καὶ τόλμης πέρα,
   οἵδ' ἐκ βίας ἄξουσιν;   Οδ. ἢν μὴ ἕρπῃς ἑκών.
Φι. ὦ Λημνία χθὼν καὶ τὸ παγκρατὲς σέλας
   Ἡφαιστότευκτον, ταῦτα δῆτ' ἀνασχετά,
   εἴ μ' οὗτος ἐκ τῶν σῶν ἀπάξεται βίᾳ;
(Soph. *Ph.* 981–88)

Odysseus, the aggressor, like the Spartan commander at Plataea (Thuc. 3.52.2–3; 58.2–3), is interested only in overt action. The example reminds us of Aristotle's paradigm of βίαιον and τὸ ἑκούσιον in *NE* 3. The APV then provides an explanation of acting ἑκών which requires only a minimum of desire: enough to walk. This is all Odysseus wants of Philoctetes. The play, however, is itself a lesson in the inadequacy and even perversion of such an understanding of acting ἑκών.

The prophecy of Helenus to the Greeks is central to the play's plot and to our understanding of Philoctetes' return to Troy and what it is for him to go ἑκών. Recovering the prophecy by examining the several references to it throughout the play, however, is not a task that can be successfully completed by merely piecing together the references. The prophecy is never quoted verbatim. References to it could contain at least some of Helenus' words, or could be interpretations, partial or full, of those words. For example, despite all the references to persuasion, it may be that all Helenus said was that Troy cannot be taken without the bow of Heracles. The potency of the bow is such, as Odysseus himself says, that Philoctetes who has it cannot be forced to do anything, least of all surrender the bow (102ff.). Thus, all minds are turned to interpreting or referring to the only possible way of securing Philoctetes' return: persuasion. Or, since Odysseus is well aware of Philoctetes' hatred of him and the Atreidae, and predicts Philoctetes would not come by persuasion (102ff.) because of this hatred, perhaps the emphasis on persuasion that begins with the Trader's recounting of the prophecy is only part of the ruse: a way to divert Philoctetes' attention from the δόλος (deceit) being worked on him by Odysseus and his pupil Neoptolemus.[39]

What we can assume with confidence is that there was a prophecy that something and/or someone the Greeks did not have was needed in order for them to take Troy; and that Philoctetes and/or his bow were mentioned as the someone or something needed. But the closest we can get to the original statement of Helenus is what the play unfolds as fulfilling the prophecy. The actual fulfillment also bridges any gap there might be between the words of the prophecy and its true meaning. One would not be surprised to find ambiguity in the wording of a prophecy or oracle. On this assumption, the procession of references to the prophecy can be understood to organically disclose the prophecy until its final meaning is revealed by the appearance of Heracles and Philoctetes' response. We see then a progression from bare remarks about the bow being needed to take Troy (68–9, 113ff., 196ff.), to remarks about the need for Philoctetes to return and mention of persuading him to do so (592ff., 612ff., 839ff.), to the first mention of a cure for Philoctetes made by Neoptolomus after his break with Odysseus (919), to the fuller speech of Neoptolemus about what is in store for Philoctetes and Troy (1314ff.), to the definitive version in the speech of Heracles and Philoctetes' response (1409ff.).

When Philoctetes replies to Heracles: "οὐκ ἀπίθησω τοῖς σοῖς μύθοις" (1447), obedience and persuasion are fused.[40] Philoctetes does not simply walk on his own with the Greeks, he goes persuaded and committed. In a word, he goes ἑκών, but Philoctetes does not use this word himself. Instead, the speech

---

[39]Not only is the Trader's speech untrustworthy as a true recounting of the actual prophecy since it is on the whole a lie, but also by keeping persuasion in the forefront, it serves to protect the deceit it is perpetrating from detection. In the end, however, its version of the prophecy is ironically vindicated. See A.F. Garvie, "Deceit, Violence, and Persuasion in the 'Philoctetes,'" *Studi clasici in Onore di Quintaro Cataudella* (University of Catania, 1972) and R. Scodel, *Sophocles* (Boston, 1984).

[40]Cf. the state of Philoctetes when Odysseus tells him he must obey (994).

of Neoptolemus, before Heracles' appearance, is as full of details about Philoctetes as Heracles' speech and as full of true understanding, and it is here that Neoptolemus mentions the need for Philoctetes to return to Troy ἑκών (1332). Neoptolemus explains that Philoctetes will be cured by the Asclepiadae only when he comes ἑκών to Troy, and then with his bow and alongside Neoptolemus he will conquer Troy:

> καὶ παῦλαν ἴσθι τῆσδε μή ποτ' ἂν τυχεῖν
> νόσου βαρείας, ἕως ἂν αὐτὸς ἥλιος
> ταύτῃ μὲν αἴρῃ, τῇδε δ' αὖ δύνῃ πάλιν,
> πρὶν ἂν τὰ Τροίας πεδί' ἑκὼν αὐτὸς μόλῃς,
> καὶ τοῖν παρ' ἡμῖν ἐντυχὼν Ἀσκληπίδαιν
> νόσου μαλαχθῇς τῆσδε, καὶ τὰ πέργαμα
> ξὺν τοῖσδε τόξοις ξύν τ' ἐμοὶ πέρσας φανῇς.
> (Soph. *Ph.* 1329–35)

Neoptolemus, however, despite the good faith he has by now shown to Philoctetes by returning his bow and his exhortation to Philoctetes to listen to someone who speaks with goodwill (εὐνοίᾳ:1322), fails to persuade Philoctetes. Philoctetes' speech in reply (1348ff.) and the dialogue with Neoptolemus which follows shows he is conflicted about returning and reluctant to trust Neoptolemus. He mistrusts the Atreidae and is opposed to doing anything that might help them. When Philoctetes says he will never return ἑκών, (οὐδέποθ' ἑκόντα γ' ὥστε τὴν Τροίαν ἰδεῖν [1392]), Neoptolemus gives up his attempt to persuade Philoctetes:

> τί δῆτ' ἂν ἡμεῖς δρῶμεν, εἰ σέ γ' ἐν λόγοις
> πείθειν δυνησόμεσθα μηδὲν ὧν λέγω;
> (Soph. *Ph.* 1393–4)

But finally, after Heracles has spoken, when Philoctetes replies οὐκ ἀπίθησω τοῖς σοῖς μύθοις (1447), we can confidently infer that now Philoctetes, persuaded by Heracles, fulfills the version of the prophecy Neoptolemus delivered: Philoctetes will go to Troy ἑκών.

Philoctetes is now not simply persuaded but committed. Had Philoctetes responded to Neoptolemus' sincere attempts at persuasion, he would have gone persuaded, but he need not have been thereby ἑκών. For he would still have had doubts about the Atreidae (1390) and been reluctant to perform a service he saw primarily as a help to his enemies (1354ff., 1384ff.). As we have seen, a prudential act is not necessarily ἑκούσιος. The persuasion effected by Heracles is complete and unconflicted, and because of this Philoctetes goes ἑκών. The three methods of getting Philoctetes to Troy–deceit, force, and persuasion–were tried in turn until only persuasion was left. When Neoptolemus told the truth, deceit was abandoned. When he gave back the bow, force was abandoned and only persuasion left. But persuasion does not succeed until Heracles persuades.

Heracles' version of the prophecy is much the same as that of Neoptolemus. But the god provides what Neoptolemus could not: "he unites the direct word of the gods with the fullest possible reminder of Philoctetes essential nature, symbolized by the bow he gave him."[41] Now Philoctetes is persuaded and ἑκών. His attitude toward his return could only have been effected by the god, and as it is the attitude with which he actually returns to Troy, it must be what was foretold in the prophecy.[42]

Odysseus' earlier use of ἑκών was a perversion of the intent of the prophecy. Philoctetes could no more have gone under those conditions and fulfilled the prophecy than he could have when he told Neoptolemus that he would never return ἑκών. Philoctetes' attitude is comparable to what Pelasgus would find acceptable for the suppliants, they must have goodwill in their hearts:

> ταύτας δ' ἑκούσας μὲν κατ' εὔνοιαν φρενῶν
> ἄγοις ἄν, εἴπερ εὐσεβὴς πίθοι λόγος.
> . . . . .
> μήποτ' ἐκδοῦναι βίαι
> στόλον γυναικῶν...
> (Aesch. *Supp.* 938–49)

The persuasion Pelasgus describes is not the mere acceptance of the prudential course, but an unconflicted, positive (κατ' εὔνοιαν φρενῶν) response. Such a response is reflected in Philoctetes' farewell to Lemnos. He looks forward to the great destiny to which the judgment of friends and the all-conquering daimon send him:[43]

> ...χαῖρ', ὦ Λήμνου πέδον ἀμφίαλον,
> καί μ' εὐπλοίᾳ πέμψον ἀμέμπτως,
> ἔνθ' ἡ μεγάλη Μοῖρα κομίζει,
> γνώμη τε φίλων χὠ πανδαμάτωρ
> δαίμων, ὃς ταῦτ' ἐπέκρανεν
> (Soph. *Ph.* 1464–68).

---

[41] Scodel, *Sophocles*, 100. Cf. A.F. Garvie, "Deceit," 213–226. For deceit, force, and persuasion and the "heroic will" in the Philoctetes, see B.M.W. Knox, *The Heroic Temper: Studies in Sophoclean Tragedy* (Berkeley, 1964), 119ff. C. Whitman has another defense for the necessity of the god's appearance: "The hero's free will implied the hero's resistance; when Neoptolemus yielded, that will was complete, and ready to choose" (*Sophocles: a Study of Heroic Humanism* [Cambridge, 1951], 187–88).

[42] See Knox, *Heroic Temper*, 137, for the relationship between what must be and the prophecy.

[43] Kamerbeek, *Phil. Com.*, ad loc, suggests the friends are Neoptolemus and Heracles, and the daimon, Zeus.

Odysseus' use of ἑκών at lines 981-88, an aggressor's pale shadow of what the prophecy intends, taunts and teases not only Philoctetes but the audience which would surely reject the mere movement of Philoctetes as ἑκούσιος or as satisfying their loyal expectations for him. Odysseus is not totally void of understanding what it is to act ἑκών, but his understanding is limited to his solitary commitment to success. His disregard for the inadequacy of what he demands of Philoctetes may be a symptom of his own superficiality and disinterest in the outcome the audience and the gods want for Philoctetes, but in his own regard he shows his understanding, however ironically. When Odysseus appears as Neoptolemus considers returning the bow to Philoctetes, at first Philoctetes threatens to kill himself rather than go with Odysseus, but then Odysseus, supposing the bow is under his control, seems to give in to Philoctetes. Odysseus says of himself that he is whatever kind of person is needed (οὐ γὰρ τοιούτων δεῖ, τοιοῦτός εἰμ' ἐγώ· [1049]), and even boasts of how just he can be if that is the contest (1050-51). Then with more deceit in mind or simply in anger or confidence of winning anyway, he says it is his nature to win in all things except toward Philoctetes, and ἑκών he will get out of his way:[44]

νικᾶν γε μέντοι πανταχοῦ χρῄζων ἔφυν,
πλὴν ἐς σέ· νῦν δὲ σοί γ' ἑκὼν ἐκστήσομαι.
(Soph. *Ph.* 1052-53)

Odysseus does not merely signal by ἑκών that he is moving himself out of Philoctetes' path, but that he is now completely giving up his attempts to bring Philoctetes to Troy. But this statement of his committment to leave Philoctetes, whether it is an exaggeration to Odysseus' advantage as part of another ruse, perhaps Philoctetes will give in as he is confronted with a second abandonment, or a sincere statement tied to Odysseus' confidence in his own ability to take Troy even without Philoctetes, is juxtaposed with a strong statement of his commitment to winning, and should be interpreted in conjunction with that statement. Odysseus' most positive attitude and deep commitment is to winning, but it is under the compelling circumstances in which he finds himself that he declares he will yield ἑκών to Philoctetes, as though this one time he is just as committed to losing. Indeed, Odysseus seems to adapt to the needs of the situation quite well as he still aims to win even as, in effect, he denies this to Philoctetes by shifting his strong commitment and positive attitude toward giving in to Philoctetes' wishes, an apparent defeat. By interpreting ἑκών as strong commitment we see more clearly the irony embedded in Odysseus' movement to accepting defeat from declaring his nature is to win.

---

[44]On this controversial point, see Scodel, *Sophocles*, 143 n. 8, where she argues "a deception in which the audience is uninformed would not be normal technique."

Concluding remarks

1. A final comparison of the ODA View with the APV

On the whole, even Aristotle's positive view does not provide a satisfactory explanation of ἑκών group words as we find them used. Not only are there passages where this weak reading is unsatisfactory, but there are passages which Aristotle's account cannot accommodate at all. The ODA View, however, recognizing that ἑκών group words are used on the particular occasions set out in this study, provides a strong reading of these words that reflects the agent's or victim's positive or negative attitude, his commitment to or divorcement from what he does or suffers. In effect, the ODA View expands the role of the affective characteristic Aristotle too acknowledges as fundamental to τὸ ἀκούσιον in general, that is, pain. I have argued that the ODA View reading is not too strong for those passages in which we actually find ἑκών group words used. However, it is too strong to accommodate all actions and not only those circumscribed by the particular occasions determined in this study.

A fundamental difference between the ODA View and Aristotle's account, then, is that Aristotle's account is broader. He treats τὸ ἑκούσιον as the class of motions for which a creature itself is the explanation. Thus, Aristotle includes in his account types of action which are not represented in the passages studied here. In particular, his account includes even the actions of animals and children and sudden actions.

Aristotle argues against the view that anything done through *thumos* (διὰ θυμόν) or appetite (διὰ ἐπιθυμίαν) is ἀκούσιον by pointing out that this would completely prevent an animal or child from ever acting ἑκουσίως.[45] He treats this conclusion as clearly unacceptable. Given the appropriate circumstances, the ODA View too can accommodate ἑκών group words being used to describe an animal or child. Passages in which animals are described by ἑκών group words, for example, were discussed in the last chapter where the ODA View was found to accommodate them readily. But this view would not accommodate every action of an animal, child, or adult. What is perhaps more problematic for the ODA View then, is Aristotle's statement that action that is sudden (ἐξαίφνης) is ἑκούσιος. This point comes up when Aristotle distinguishes τὸ ἑκούσιον from choice (προαίρεσις).[46]

Some of the actions in the passages collected and discussed above may be better classified with τὰ ἐξαίφνης than with actions κατὰ προαίρεσιν. But even actions, which are performed without a full or elaborate choice process, can be accommodated by the strong interpretation of the ODA View. Despite their immediacy, attention is drawn to them as actions performed on the special

---

[45]*NE* 1111a24–26.
[46]*NE* 1111b4ff.

occasions that have been found to prompt the use of ἑκών group words. Consider, for example, the dismounting of the Oceanids from their chariots at the request of Prometheus (Aesch. *PrB* 277–78). However, because of its emphasis on affect, the ODA View is ill-suited to explain sudden actions which in themselves have minimal affective or cognitive foundations and to which special attention is not drawn by the occasions in which they occur. The ODA View is not suited to accommodate the many unremarkable motions and actions creatures perform throughout the day, such as walking about or eating or the sort of casual arm waving motions one might see in the course of a lively conversation. Aristotle, on the other hand, can accommodate these actions readily. However, if my assessment is accurate, the extant passages which have been discussed present particular circumstances that do provide a special affective and cognitive background even for the ordinary actions among them. Thus, since Aristotle's account includes actions which do not occur in the extant passages, actions to which special attention is not called, it is weakened as an account of the actual usage of ἑκών group words. Since the number of these passages is substantial and represents a wide range of genres, I do not hesitate to assume that the extant passages fairly represent usage. Overall, the ODA View better accommodates the actual usage of ἑκών group words, though it is not adequate to cover the larger range of actions Aristotle includes. That this is so is not a reason automatically to dismiss or devalue the ODA View. Rather, it is reason to explore further Aristotle's accounts of τὸ ἑκούσιον and τὸ ἀκούσιον for his specific interests, in order to account for the discrepancies.

2. Is the ODA View too strong?

Even if the ODA View does give a more plausible explanation in most cases than the other views I have considered, no doubt there are many cases, not only among passages in which acting ἑκών is opposed to acting under necessity, but also where acting ἄκων is conjoined with acting under necessity, cases of doing harm or wrong, and third-party passages, in which one might well hesitate to believe that the agent really has the strong attitude toward his action posited by the ODA View. However, I suspect that dissatisfaction with this explanation is due not to the view itself, but to doubt that what is said about a particular agent in a particular context on that view is actually true. In such cases, it is not that the ODA View provides an unacceptable meaning for ἑκών group words, but rather that in a particular case, it seems manifestly false or at least very dubious that the agent described as ἑκών really is completely committed to the action or that the agent described as ἄκων has a strongly negative attitude toward the action. In evaluating the meaning of ἑκών group words care must be taken, therefore, to distinguish between the claim that the words mean such and such and the claim that the words are truthfully or accurately applied in a particular case. Thus, in those passages in which the ἑκών group words are applied by a partisan (including the agent who seeks to paint a portrait to his or her own advantage) or an aggressor, the designation of an agent or victim as ἑκών or ἄκων may simply be inaccurate, but this is not evidence against the ODA View's explanation of the meaning of the words. Furthermore, it should be emphasized that this allowance for the rhetorical usage of ἑκών group words, unlike the attempts to account for exceptions discussed at the end of Chapter 2, maintains the integrity of these words and does not resort to a list of diverse senses in order to account for exceptions to some core explanation that proves inadequate to accommodate the variety of passages in which the words occur. But even in cases in which the interpreter is hard pressed to avoid the view that the circumstances of an action, force or necessity for example, which are so regularly associated with acting ἄκων, are the important meaning to be gleaned from a passage, and even if there seems to be a virtual interchangeability of ἑκών group words and these circumstances, a metonymic relationship whereby one stands in for the other, I would maintain that ἑκών group words still represent the attitude of an agent or victim and ought not simply be reduced to the circumstances which occasion their use. I acknowledge this is a very strong conclusion to reach, and that even I might be hard pressed to deny in a particular case that such a reduction of attitude to circumstances or particular psychological features is inappropriate. Even so, as a general rule, I think this kind of reduction should not be taken for granted as a common occurrence but treated as a possibility to be considered only with great care.

But even granting that ἑκών group words are used under the particular circumstances described in this study and should not be simply reduced to these circumstances, why opt for a strong positive or negative attitude rather than some kind of range from weak to strong? (Perhaps a single range from ἀκούσιος to ἑκούσιος, from the weakest negative attitude to the strongest postive attitude, or a range within what counts as ἀκούσιος and within what counts as ἑκούσιος.) One could, of course, formulate another interpretative view along these lines and determine how well it accommodates the actual occurrences of ἑκών group words. However, for the following reasons, at this point I am not attracted to such a position. I would hesitate to depart from what appears to be the paradigm of who counts as ἄκων, the victim of hands-on physical force. The words ἑκών and ἄκων appear to be used as overall descriptions and to be fundamentally contradictories, and it would be difficult to develop a range position that would not interfere with that strong opposition based on the paradigmatic case. With two apparent exceptions which I think can be accommodated, individuals (or their actions) are not described as simultaneously ἑκών and ἄκων (or ἑκούσιος and ἀκούσιος).[47] But one might expect even more examples than we actually have of someone being both ἑκών and ἄκων if there

---

[47] See discussions of Zeus in *Il.* 4.40–42 and Orestes in Eur. *IT* 511–12.

were some sort of range.⁴⁸ Moreover, a simple rhetorical explanation, the aggressor's and partisan's use of ἑκών group words, can accommodate those cases in which a weaker attitude seems more realistic.

3. A word on translation

It will not have been lost on the reader that, however helpful or insightful this study may be, it has offered no specific suggestions for translating these words. The statements I have made about their meanings are certainly too cumbersome to be used as translations. In fact, I will offer no specific suggestions, except to say that no one word will be appropriate in all cases even if the old standbys "willingly" and "unwillingly" turn out to be useful frequently, and that the translator must use her own judgment about how important it is in any particular case to make especially clear that the words describe the attitude of the agent or victim acting or acted on under particular circumstances. But special care should be taken to avoid translations which simply reduce ἑκών group words to the circumstances that occcasion their use, for example, a translation of ἄκων as "by force" or "in ignorance," or which reduce the overall description of the agent or victim's attitude to some internal factor which may be predicated in a particular case, for example, a translation of ἑκών as "deliberately" or "intentionally."⁴⁹

4. Making room for an ethical view

Finally, for the present I would even stubbornly maintain what may seem to some too strong a view, because the role for ἑκών group words set out by the ODA View makes room for an important ethical view that could easily be overlooked if the attention drawn to an agent's or victim's attitude by these words is minimized. Briefly, this is a view that is neither essentially consequentialistic, that is, one that evaluates actions solely on the basis of their results, nor one that would reject out of hand an action aimed at desirable and good results that can be achieved only by ordinarily unacceptable means. It is a view that, for example, in cases where there is an exchange of some evil for some good or for the avoidance of greater evil, exchanges one might expect take place under circumstances of ἀνάγκη, allows that the agent's attitude makes a difference for our assessment of his character.⁵⁰ The agent who feels no pain in

---

⁴⁸Cf. Aristotle's attempts in the *EE* and *MM* to discover a necessary and sufficient condition for designating an action ἑκούσιος or ἀκούσιος.

⁴⁹See discussion at the end of ch. 2 pp. 73–74.

⁵⁰In his discussion of τὸ ἑκούσιον and τὸ ἀκούσιον, Aristotle too has an interest in our evaluations of those who perform such actions. However, as I understand Aristotle, attitude is not the focus of his interpretation. My suspicion is that Aristotle has reduced τὸ ἑκούσιον and τὸ ἀκούσιον to something more man-

such a situation is much different from the agent who acts but does so with pain and regret.[51] It may have been Simonides' personal effort to turn this ethical perspective into a new model for the good man.[52] But in fact, the study of ἑκών group words has shown that the ancient Greeks were interested at critical moments to stress a personal and internal feature of agents and victims, a feature which is independent of success or failure and cannot be determined solely on the basis of observable overt behavior.

---

ageable for the use of those who must make laws and judgments about these personal, internal, and unobservable matters.

[51]In speaking of pain or regret, I do not mean "guilt" insofar as "guilt" implies the choice itself was somehow mistaken.

[52]See discussions of Simon. Fr. 542 *PMG*.

Index Locorum

This index has two sections. The first section contains all of the occurrences of ἑκών group words collected for this study and lists their assigned categories: (i) = ἀνάγκη (i), βία; (ii) = ἀνάγκη (ii), compelling social practices; (iii) = ἀνάγκη (iii), unavoidable prevailing circumstances; S = supernatural influence; 3p = third party; H/W = harm or wrong; GS = general statement; E = error; and Un = undetermined. A line or section number followed by a slash (/) and a number signifies there is more than one occurrence of an ἑκών group word in that line or section. The larger passages discussed in the text are found in parentheses next to the citation of the line or section number in which the ἑκών group word occurs. If the larger passage contains more than one line or section with ἑκών group words, it is located next to the last line or section contained within it. The second section lists other ancient sources which were discussed in the text.

AESCHYLUS
Agamemnon (*Ag.*)
  38 (i)
  180 (i)
    p. 8 n. 3
  803 (H/W)
    p. 46 n. 16
  841 (ii) (838-44)
    pp. 24, 59, 132 n. 6
  943 (ii)
    p. 57
  953 (i)
  1071 (i) (1069-71)
    pp. 23, 42, 41 n. 10, 72, 78
  1613 (H/W) (1607-16)
    p. 86
Eumenides
  234 (iii)
  550 Wieseler (iii)
    p. 146 n. 17
Prometheus Bound (*PrB*)
  19 /1 (i), /2 (ii) (12-20)
    pp. 8, 27, 38, 43 n. 13, 53
    cont.

(*PrB cont.*)
  218 /1 (iiiS), /2 (ii)
  266 (E) (257-70)
    p. 84
  277 (ii) (277-78)
    pp. 57, 132 n. 6, 166
  671 /1 (i), /2 (i) (663-72)
    pp. 8, 17 n. 20, 19, 19 n. 22, 23, 39, 77, 133-36
  771 (3p)
    pp. 77, 88
  854 (i)
Seven Against Thebes
  1033 (i)
Suppliants (*Supp.*)
  39 (i)
  227 /1 (i), /2 (3p)
  940 (i) (938-49)
    pp. 8, 44-45, 157, 163
Theoroi TrGF
  78c.38 (H/W) (37-38)
    p. 87

ANTIPHON
Oration (Or.)
  1.27 (GS)
    p. 90 n. 21
  5.92 (GS)
    p. 90 n. 21
Tetralogy (Tetral.)
  2.2.6 (GS)
    p. 90 n. 21
  3.1.6 (GS)
    p. 90 n. 21

ARISTOPHANES
Birds
  28 (ii)
  936 (ii)
Clouds (Cl.)
  527 (H/W)
  868 (ii) (860–69)
    p. 57 n. 23
  1194 (ii) (1189–95)
    p. 59
Frogs
  701 (iii)
  1523 (ii)
Knights (Kn.)
  1045 (ii)
  1123 (E) (1119–30)
    p. 83
  1250 (iiiS) (1248–52)
    p. 64
  1269 (H/W)
Lysistrata (Lys.)
  223–24 (ii)
  225–26 (i) (223–28)
    pp. 7 n. 1, 39 n. 7
Plutus
  781 (iiiS)
Wasps
  992 (E)
  1002 (E) (990–92, 999–1002)
    pp. 2 n. 2, 80, 114, 117
  1422 (ii) (1421–25)
    pp. 59, 77 *cont.*

(ARISTOPHANES *cont.*)
PCG 602.1 (H/W) (1–2)
  p. 86

BACCHYLIDES (Bacchyl.)
  1.116 (3p) (112–18)
    p. 142 n. 13
  4.9 (ii)
  17.44 (i) (23, 28, 39–46)
    pp. 7 n. 1, 38

DEMOCRITOS Diels–Kranz
  B.240 (iii, GS)

DRACON
  IG I^3.104.17 (H/W) (16–18)
    p. 86

EPICHARMUS Kaibel
  37 /1 (Un), /2 (ii)
    p. 57 n. 22
  78.2 (GS) (1–2)
    pp. 15 n. 17, 37 n. 5, 85 n. 14, 90 n. 20, 146 n. 17
  100 (H/W)

EURIPIDES
Alcestis
  389 (iii)
Alcmeon (Alcm.) TGF
  68.2 /1 (H/W), /2 (i), /3 (H/W) (1–2)
    pp. 52, 109, 129
Andromache (Andr.)
  36 (i)
  38 (i) (32–40)
    p. 39
  263 (i) (261–68)
    pp. 133–136
  357 (H/W)
  680 (iiiS)
  981 (iiiS) (977–84)
    p. 63 n. 29
Antiope Page
  73 (iiiS)

Archelaus TGF
  245.2 (iii)
Auge TGF
  265.2 (H/W) (1–2)
    pp. 113, 137, 144, 160
Bacchae (Bacch.)
  437 (i)
  441 (ii) (434–42)
    pp. 50, 56–57, 132 n. 6, 157
Cresphontes (Cres.) Harder
  66.21 (iii) (20–22)
    pp. 32, 60
Cyclops (Cyc.)
  258 (i) /1 (i), /2 (i) (253–60)
    pp. 8, 45 n. 15
Dictys TGF
  339.4 (iiiS) (1–6)
    pp. 14 n. 15, 31–32, 60
Electra (El.)
  670 (ii) (669–70)
    p. 57 n. 22
  1065 (i) (1065–68)
    pp. 46 n. 16, 52, 109, 129
Erechtheus (Erech.) TGF
  360.44 (iiiS)
Hecuba (Hec.)
  400 (i)
  548 (i) (542–52)
    pp. 51, 72, 158
Helen (Hel.)
  396 (i) (391–96)
    pp. 9, 45 n. 15
  1640 (3p)
Heraclidae (Heracl.)
  400 (i)
  413 /1 (i, iii), /2 (H/W) (403-14)
    pp. 22 n. 26, 39 n. 7
  531 /1 (iiiS), /2 (iiiS) (528–34)
    p. 65
  551 (ii) (547–51)
    pp. 26, 53, 157
  885 (i) (883–87)
    pp. 17, 17 n. 20, 21, 45 n. 15
  cont.

(Heracl. cont.)
  986 (iiiS) (986–90)
    p. 63
  1364 (iiiS)
Hippolytus (Hipp.)
  319 /1 (iii), /2 (iii)
  324 (E)
  358 (ia, iiiS) (358–61)
    p. 40 n. 8
  693 (iii) (688–94)
    p. 79 n. 2
  1305 (iii)
    p. 79 n. 2
  1433 (iiiS, E) (1431–36)
    pp. 79 n. 1, 115
Hypsipyle (Hyps.) Bond
  60.35 (E) (34–36)
    p. 81
Ion
  [375] (i)
  378 (i)
  380 (i) (369–80)
    pp. 13, 21 n. 25
  642 (iii) (642–45)
    p. 63 n. 29
  746 /1 (iii), /2 (iii) (745–46)
    p. 67
  941 (i)
  1500 (iii)
Iphigenia in Aulis (IA)
  360 (i) (356–69)
    pp. 9, 46
  1149 (i) (1148–52)
    p. 39
  1361 (3p)
  1364 (ii)
  1365 (i) (1361–67)
    pp. 48, 55–56, 132 n. 6
  1456 (iiiS)
  1555 (iiiS) (1552–56)
    p. 65
Iphigenia in Tauris (IT)
  512 /1 (i, iiiS), /2 (i, iiiS) (511–12) *cont.*

(IT 512 cont.)
    pp. 66 n. 31, 68 n. 35, 139 n. 11, 145 n. 15, 167 n. 47
  948 (ii) (947–50)
    p. 58
Krates Page
  10 (iiiS)
Medea
  751 (ii)
Orestes
  381 (ii)
  613 /1 (ii), /2 (ii)
Phoenissae (Phoen.)
  72 (iii)
  433 (ii), 434 (ii) (427–34)
    pp. 25, 53, 53 n. 20
  476 (ii)
  519 (i)
  630 /1 (iii), /2 (i)
Suppliants (Supp.)
  151 (iiiS) (147–51)
    p. 65
  393 (ii)
  857 (ii) (857–59)
    p. 57 n. 22
Trojan Women (Tro.)
  373 (i) (370–73)
    pp. 8, 45–46, 46 n. 16, 52 n. 19
  710 (ii)
  960 (i) (959–60)
    pp. 8, 9, 39
  1011 (i) (1010–22)
    pp. 9, 39
  1037 (iiiS)
    p. 46 n. 16

GORGIAS (Gorg.) Diels–Kranz
  B.11a.11 (i)
    pp. 16 n. 19, 23, 43, 72, 109, 148
  B.11a.14 (i)

HERODOTUS (Hdt.)
  1.35.3 (E)
  1.45.2 (iiiS) *cont.*

(HERODOTUS *cont.*)
  1.89.3 (ii)
    pp. 9, 20, 21, 29, 45 n. 15, 54
  2.65.5 (H/W)
  2.108.2 (iii)
  2.120.1 /1 (3p), /2 (3p) (120.1–2)
    p. 141
  2.131.1 (i)
  2.139.3 (iiiS) (139.2–3)
    pp. 64, 65
  2.162.2 (iii) (162.1–2)
    p. 67
  2.179.1 (H/W)
  3.72.5 (i)
    p. 27 n. 38, 51, 158
  3.75.1 (ii)
  3.88.1 (3p)
  4.43.7 (E)
    p. 83
  4.120.4 /1 (i), /2 (i)
    p. 48
  4.164.3 (iiiS)
  4.164.4 /2 (E), /3 (E)
  5.30.4 (3p)
  5.37.2 (i)
  7.104.3 (i)
    pp. 22 n. 26, 45 n. 15
  7.139.3 (i) (139.3–4)
    p. 39 n. 7
  7.164.1 (i)
  7.222 /1 (i), /2 (i)
  8.10.2 (i)
    p. 49
  8.30.2 (H/W) (8.30)
    p. 22 n. 27
  8.80.1 /1 (iii), /2 (iii)
  8.116.1 (H/W)
  9.7a.2 (iii)
  9.17.1 (i)
    pp. 22, 38
  9.53.2 (ii, H/W)
  9.111.1 (ii)

Index Locorum

HESIOD
Theogony (Th.)
  232 (H/W) (231–32)
    p. 33 n. 52
  529 (3p)
  [730] (3p)
Works and Days
  4 (3p)
  282 (H/W)

HOMER
Iliad (Il.)
  1.301 (i)
  1.327 (ii) (326–28)
    p. 56
  1.348 (i) (345–48)
    pp. 10, 38
  1.430 (i) (428–30)
    pp. 8, 10, 12, 21 n. 25, 40, 77, 140
  2.667 (3p)
  3.66 (iiiS)
  4.43 /1 (iii), /2 (iii) (30–49)
    pp. 68, 139, 145, 145 n. 15, 167 n. 47
  5.164 (i) (163–164)
    p. 48
  5.366 (i)
    p. 150
  5.768 (i) (768–69)
    p. 150
  6.458 (i) (450–61)
    p. 22 n. 26
  6.523 (H/W)
  7.197 /1 (H/W), /2 (i) (191–98)
    pp. 8, 38
  8.45 (i) (45–46)
    p. 150
  8.81 (iii)
  8.487 (iii)
  10.372 (E) (369–75)
    p. 82
  10.530 (i) (530–31)
    pp. 150, 153 *cont.*

(Iliad cont.)
  11.281 (i) (280–81)
    p. 150
  11.519 (i) (519–20)
    pp. 150, 153
  11.557 (iii) (556–57)
    p. 70
  11.716 (ii) (714–17)
    p. 57 n. 22
  12.8 (3p) (2–9)
    pp. 89, 140
  13.234 (i) (219–34)
    pp. 49, 78, 158
  13.367 (i)
  14.105 (ii) (103–8)
    p. 57 n. 22
  15.186 (i) (178–88)
    pp. 7, 39 n. 7, 153 n. 34
  15.720 (3p)
  16.204 (ii)
  16.264 (iii) (257–65)
    p. 66
  16.369 (i)
  17.112 (iii) (106–13)
    p. 155
  17.666 (ii)
  18.240 (ii) (239–42)
    p. 56
  19.273 (i) (270–75)
    p. 10 n. 7
  21.59 (iii)
  22.400 (i)
    p. 150
  23.434 (iii) (433–37)
    p. 68
  23.585 (H/W)
Odyssey (Od.)
  1.79 (3p)
  1.199 (i) (198–99)
    p. 48
  1.403 (i) (397–404)
    p. 39 n. 7
  2.130 (ii)
    .133 (H/W) *cont.*

(Odyssey cont.)
3.28 (3p)
3.213 (i)
.214 (i) (205–17)
  pp. 7 n. 1, 42–43
3.484 (i) (481–86)
  p. 150
3.494 (i) (492–96)
  p. 150
4.372 (H/W)
.377 (iiiS)
4.463 (i)
4.504 (3p)
4.646 (i)
.647 (i)
.649 (i) (645–56)
  pp. 39 n. 7, 46 n. 17
4.665 (3p)
5.100 (ii) (99–101)
  p. 56
5.177 (3p)
6.240 (3p) (236–43)
  p. 142 n. 13
6.287 (3p)
7.315 (i)
9.405 (i) (403–12)
  pp. 8, 39 n. 7
10.266 (ii)
10.489 (iii)
12.290 (3p)
13.277 (iii)
15.19 (3p)
15.190 (i) (190–92)
  p. 150
15.200 (ii)
15.319 (3p) (318–24)
  p. 142 n. 13
16.94 (i), 95 (i) (91–98)
  p. 42 n. 12
17.43 (3p)
18.135 (iiiS) (125–42)
  p. 63 n. 29
19.86 (3p) (85–88)
  p. 142 n. 13 *cont.*

(Odyssey cont.)
19.133 (iiiS) (124–33)
  p. 58
19.374 (ii) (370–78)
  pp. 57, 132 n. 6
20.42 (3p)
20.343 (ii) (339–343)
  pp. 27, 53
21.348 (i) (344–53)
  pp. 7 n. 1, 39 n. 7
22.351 (i) (330–31, 344–53)
  pp. 16 n. 19, 22, 45 n. 15
24.444 (3p)

HOMERIC HYMNS
Homeric Hymn to Aphrodite (HAphr.)
  147 (3p) (147–48)
    p. 141
Homeric Hymn to Apollo
  471 (iiiS)
Homeric Hymn to Demeter (HDem.)
  19 (i)
  30 (i)
  72 (i) (66–73)
    pp. 17, 17 n. 20, 21, 38, 77
  124 (i) (122–25)
    pp. 17, 17 n. 20, 21, 38, 77, 108, 143
  344 (i)
  379 (i) (377–79)
    p. 150
  413 (i) (407–13)
    pp. 17 n. 20, 19, 21, 38, 77
  432 (i)
Homeric Hymn to Dionysus (HDion.)
  5 (3p) (1–6)
    p. 142 n. 13

IBYCUS (Ibyc.) *PMG*
  287.7 (i) (1–7)
    p. 154

ION West
  27.8 (ii)

Index Locorum

PERIANDER Diels-Kranz
  10.3.ζ (H/W)

PINDAR (Pind.)
Nemean
  4.21 (ii)
  6.57 (ii) (55–61)
    p. 57
  8.10 (ii)
Olympian
  10.29 /1 (i), /2 (H/W)
  13.96 (ii) (93–97)
    pp. 57–58
Pythian
  4.165 (ii)
  5.43 (ii)
  8.14 (i) (8–15)
    pp. 7 n. 1, 45, 157
  8.67 (ii)
Fragmenta
  43 (ii)
  169.52 (ii)
  266 (iii)

PHERECYDES (Pherec.) Kock
  145.1 (ii)
  150 (Un)
    p. 153 n. 35

PHOCYLIDES Gentili-Prato
  13 (GS)
    p. 90 n. 20

PLATO COMICUS (Plato Com.) Kock
  24.1 (i) (1–2)
    pp. 27 n. 38, 51, 158

SAPPHO *PLF*
  94.5 (iii)

SIMONIDES (Simon.) *PMG*
  541.8 (ia) (7–11)
    pp. 7 n. 1, 14, 40, 113 n. 32, 138 n. 10 *cont.*

(SIMONIDES *cont.*)
  542.28 (iii)
    pp. 31, 31 n. 46, 33, 61, 85 n. 14, 145–147, 147 n. 20, 169 n. 52

SOPHOCLES
Ajax (Aj.)
  455 (iiiS) (447–56)
    pp. 63–64, 63 n. 29
Antigone (Ant.)
  276 /1 (ii), /2 (H/W) (268–77)
    pp. 55, 132 n. 6
  1340 (H/W)
Oedipus at Colonus (OC)
  [172] (ii)
  177 (i)
  240 (iiiS) (239–40)
    p. 2 n. 2
  522 (iiiS)
  775 (iii)
  827 (i)
    p. 77
  935 (i) (932-36)
    pp. 39 n. 7, 77
  964 (iiiS, E)
  977 (iiiS, E)
  985 (H/W)
  987 /1 (iiiS, E), /2 (H/W) (960–99)
    pp. 2 n. 2, 63, 79 n. 1, 115
  1634 (H/W)
Oedipus Rex (OR)
  358 (ii) (354–62)
    pp. 56–57, 132 n. 6
  591 (iii) (590–91)
    p. 70
  1213 (iii)
  1230 /1 (H/W), /2 (H/W) (1229–30)
    pp. 2 n. 2, 77
Philoctetes (Ph.)
  301 (iii) *cont.*

(*Philoctetes cont.*)
305 (iii) (305–6)
  p. 77
436 (iii)
617 (i)
618 (i) (617–18)
  p. 77
771 /1 (ii), /2 (ii) (769–73)
  p. 57 n. 22
985 (i) (981–88)
  pp. 44, 46, 50, 72, 77, 108, 160, 164
1027 (ii) (1019–28)
  pp. 23–25, 59, 132 n. 6
1053 (iii) (1047–62)
  pp. 68, 164
1179 (ii) (1177–80)
  p. 57
1318 (iiiS) (1314–24)
  pp. 30, 33, 61, 162
1332 (i) (1329–35)
  pp. 77, 162
1341 (H/W)
1392 (i) (1392–4)
  p. 162
Trachiniae (Tr.)
198 /1 (i), /2 (H/W) (192–99)
  p. 86
466 (iii) (465–67)
  p. 67
727 (iiiS, GS) (727–28)
  pp. 80, 90
935 (iiiS, E) (932–935)
  pp. 80, 114, 117
1123 (iiiS, E) (1122–1123)
  pp. 80, 114, 117
1263 (H/W)
Tyro TrGF
665 (E)
  pp. 85, 146 n. 17
TrGF 746 (GS)
  pp. 89–90
TrGF 929.4 /1 (iii), /2 (H/W) (1–4)
  pp. 113, 138

THEOGNIS (Theog.)
371 (ia) (371–72)
  pp. 8 n. 3, 13, 40, 138 n. 10
467 (i)
471 (ii) (467–72)
  pp. 22 n. 26, 28, 38
1343 (ia) (1341–44)
  pp. 7 n. 1, 14, 60 n. 26
1379 (E) (1377–80)
  pp. 80 n. 3, 117, 137, 144

THUCYDIDES (Thuc.)
1.32.4 (i)
  pp. 2 n. 2, 22 n. 26, 46 n. 17
1.52.2 (i)
1.96.1 (i)
1.138.4 (iii)
1.144.3 (iii)
  pp. 29, 62, 148
2.8.1 (iii)
  p. 68
2.89.4 (ii)
2.89.8 (iii)
2.90.1 (iii)
.90.3 (iii)
  pp. 70, 70 n. 38
3.11.4 (i)
3.31.1 (i)
3.33.1 (iii)
3.37.2 (i)
3.39.7 (i)
  pp. 22 n. 26, 45 n. 15
3.40.1 /1 (E, H/W), /2 (GS) (40.1–2)
  pp. 2 n. 2, 89
3.47.3 (iii)
3.47.5 (iii)
3.52.2 /1 (i), /2 (i) (52.2–3)
  pp. 47, 50, 72, 72 n. 39, 158, 160
3.58.3 (ii) (58.2–3)
  pp. 29, 29 n. 41, 47, 50, 53 n. 20, 72, 72 n. 39, 158, 160
cont.

Index Locorum

(THUCYDIDES *cont.*)
3.63.2 /1 (ii), /2 (i)
  pp. 29 n. 41, 46 n. 17, 53, 53 n. 20
3.64.3 (i)
  .64.5 (i)
  .65.1 (i) (64.2–65.1)
  pp. 37 n. 6, 38, 46 n. 17
3.65.2 (i)
3.67.5 (i) (67.4–5)
  p. 53 n. 20
3.82.2 (iii)
  pp. 32, 46 n. 18, 60
3.95.1 (3p)
4.19.4 (i)
  pp. 22, 46 n. 18
4.30 (E)
  pp. 80 n. 3, 114, 117
4.73.2 (iii)
  p. 69
4.78.4 /1 (3p), /2 (3p)
4.83.6 (3p)
4.87.2 (i)
  pp. 18, 38
4.92.2 (i)
4.98.1 (i)
  .98.4 (i)
  .98.6 (i) (98.1–6)
  pp. 17 n. 20, 18, 21, 23, 37 n. 6, 38
5.7.2 (ii)
5.98 (iii)
  p. 70
5.111.3 (iii)
  p. 69
6.8.4 (ii)
6.14 (H/W)
6.25.2 (ii)
6.34.6 (ii)
6.36.4 (i) (36.3–4)
  pp. 49–50, 72 n. 39 *cont.*

(THUCYDIDES *cont.*)
6.44.1 (ii)
  pp. 28, 53
6.69.1 (iii)
6.76.3 (ii)
6.87.4 (i)
  pp. 22 n. 26, 38
6.92.5 (i)
  p. 45 n. 15
7.8.3 (iii)
  p. 69
7.57.2 (i, ii)
  .57.9 (i, ii)
  .57.10 (i, ii) (57.1–10)
  pp. 22, 28–29, 44, 44 n. 14, 46 n. 18, 54
7.81.1 (H/W)
  .81.3 (i) (1–3)
  pp. 22 n. 26, 86–87, 159
7.86.2 (3p)
  p. 140
8.3.1 (i)
  p. 22 n. 26
8.27.3 (i)
  pp. 20, 46 n. 18
8.68.1 (i)
8.73.4 (iii)

UNKNOWN
PMG
  924.14 (ii)
TrGF
  75a /1 (GS), /2 (GS)
  p. 90 n. 20
  80.2 (GS) (1–4)
  pp. 15 n. 17, 37 n. 5, 90 n. 20
  132 (Un)
  [656.10] (Un)
  700.11 (iii)

Other Ancient Sources

ARISTOTLE
De Anima
  3.9
    p. 119 n. 50
De Motu (DeM)
  6
    p. 118
  700b17
    p. 118 n. 45–46
  703b3–11
    pp. 96 n. 4, 119
  11
    pp. 118 n. 44, 124
Eudemian Ethics (EE)
  1188b8–14
    p. 105 n. 20
  1222b15ff.
    p. 98
  1223a4–9
    p. 98 n. 9
  1223a29ff.
    p. 111
  1223b24–26
    p. 145 n. 14
  1224a10–30ff.
    pp. 97, 111 n. 30
  1224b7–14
    pp. 97 n. 6, 106 n. 21
  1224b12
    p. 98 n. 7
  1224b13–15
    p. 106
  1224b15–1225a1
    p. 145 n. 14
  1225a2–27
    pp. 103–104, 103 n. 17
  1247a31–33
    p. 115 n. 40
  2
    pp. 96 n. 3, 99, 105 *cont.*

(*Eudemian Ethics cont.*)
  2.6
    p. 98
  2.7–8
    pp. 102, 108 n. 24
  2.8
    pp. 33 n. 50, 41 n. 9, 138 n. 10
  2.9
    p. 111 n. 28
  4
    p. 133
  8.7–16
    p. 106
Magna Moralia (MM)
  1.14
    p. 41 n. 9
  1.15
    p. 105
  1195a27–b4
    p. 116 n. 42
Metaphysica (Meta.)
  1023a17–22ff.
    p. 97
Nicomachean Ethics (NE)
  1109b30–35
    pp. 112 n. 31, 125
  1109b35–1110a1
    p. 96
  1110a1–3
    pp. 97, 101, 101 n. 13
  1110a3–4
    p. 96
  1110a4–11
    pp. 99, 105
  1110a12–15
    pp. 100–101
  1110a15–19
    pp. 98, 99, 100, 101 n. 13, 116 n. 42 *cont.*

(*Nicomachean Ethics cont.*)
1110a19ff.
  p. 104 n. 18 *cont.*
1110a23–26
  pp. 101, 104
1110a26–29
  p. 104
1110b1–5
  pp. 97 n. 5, 100, 101 n. 13
1110b6–7
  p. 100
1110b11–13
  p. 111 n. 30
1110b15–17
  p. 97 n. 5
1110b18–30
  pp. 111, 113 n. 34, 116 n. 42
1110b24–1111a2
  p. 112
1111a3–7
  pp. 113, 114 n. 37
1111a15–19
  p. 114 n. 37
1111a19–21
  pp. 111 n. 29, 113
1111a23–24
  p. 96
1111a24–26
  pp. 151 n. 27, 165 n. 45
1111b3
  p. 112
1111b4ff.
  p. 165 n. 46
1111b8–9
  p. 151 n. 27
1113b30ff.
  p. 112
1135a23ff.
  pp. 113 n. 33, 114 n. 37
1135a25
  p. 115
1135a26–28
  pp. 97, 98, 106 n. 21 *cont.*

(*Nicomachean Ethics cont.*)
1135a31–b2
  pp. 96 n. 4, 98 n. 8
1135b4–8
  p. 105
1135b11–19
  pp. 115, 116 n. 42
1145b1ff.
  p. 94 n. 2
3
  pp. 96, 98–99, 102, 104–105
3.1
  pp. 33 n. 50, 101, 111–112 n. 30, 112, 131, 138 n. 10
3.1.20-27
  p. 41 n. 9
3.2
  p. 96 n. 4
3.5
  pp. 67 n. 32, 96 n. 4, 116 n. 42
5
  pp. 96, 102, 115, 133
5.8
  pp. 114 n. 37, 115, 133
5.9
  p. 130 n. 4
Physics (Ph.)
  192b8–19
    p. 97
  197a18–20
    p. 115
  8
    p. 119 n. 50
Poetics
  1452a4ff.
    p. 116 n. 42
  1453a7ff.
    p. 115 n. 41
Posterior Analytics (PA)
  94b37–95a3
    p. 98

Rhetoric
  1374bff.
    p. 115 n. 39
  1376b–77a
    p. 23 n. 30

CICERO
De Officiis
  3.26
    p. 24 n. 31

EURIPIDES
Iphigenia in Aulis (IA)
  53–71
    p. 24 n. 31

GORGIAS (Gorg.) Diels–Kranz
  B.11.8–12
    p. 36 n. 3

HERODOTUS (Hdt.)
  3.72.2–3
    p. 51

HOMER
Iliad (Il.)
  1.298–9
    p. 10
  1.324–5
    p. 10
  2.760–62
    p. 152
  2.763–70
    p. 153 n. 33
  8.185–197
    p. 152
  9.123–27
    p. 152–53
  17.434–40
    p. 152
  19.428–30
    p. 10–11 n. 7
  22.162
    p. 152 n. 32 *cont.*

(*Iliad cont.*)
  22.353
    p. 16 n. 19
Odyssey (Od.)
  1.154
    p. 16 n. 19
  15.182–84
    p. 153 n. 34

PHILEMON Kock
  31.4–5
    p. 31

PROCLUS
Chrestomathia
  103.25–28
    p. 24 n. 31

PSEUDO-APOLLODORUS (Ps.-Apoll.)
  3.6.2
    p. 104 n. 19
  3.7.5
    p. 104 n. 19
  3.10.9
    p. 24 n. 31

SOPHOCLES
Antigone (Ant.)
  79
    p. 11
  223ff.
    p. 26 n. 37
  229–30
    p. 26 n. 37
  272–75
    p. 26 n. 37
  663
    p. 12
  781ff.
    p. 14 n. 15
  907
    p. 11, 11 n. 8

Odysseus Mainomenos Radt
  462–69
    p. 24 n. 31
Philoctetes
  68–69
    p. 161
  102 ff.
    p. 161
  113 ff.
    p. 161
  196 ff.
    p. 161
  592 ff.
    p. 161
  612 ff.
    p. 161
  839ff.
    p. 161
  919
    p. 161
  994
    p. 161 n. 40
  1348 ff.
    p. 162
  1354 ff.
    p. 162
  1384–90
    p. 162 *cont.*

(*Philoctetes cont.*)
  1409ff.
    p. 161
  1447 ff,
    pp. 161–62
  1464-68
    p. 163
Trachiniae (*Tr.*)
  497–50
    pp. 9, 14 n. 15, 79 n. 1

THUCYDIDES (Thuc.)
  1.43.3
    p. 77
  3.27.1
    pp. 30, 62
  3.47.3
    pp. 30, 62
  4.84
    p. 18
  6.36.3–4
    pp. 49, 70 n. 37, 158 n. 38
  7.139.3–4
    p. 22

XENOPHON
On Horsemanship
  8.4–11.6
    p. 150 n. 22–26

General Index

Ackrill
 p. 121 n. 52
Adkins
 pp. 16 n. 19, 41–42 n. 10, 78
αἰτία (see motion)
αἴτιος
 pp. 98, 98 n. 9, 116 n. 42
akrasia
 p. 41 n. 9
akrates
 pp. 93 n. 1, 97 n. 6, 98 n. 7, 106, 106 n. 21, 111, 145 n. 14
Allen, J.T., and Italie
 pp. 5–6 n. 6
Allen, T.W., Halliday, and Sikes
 pp. 19 n. 22, 77
alliance
 pp. 28–29, 53–54, 53 n. 20, 60
ἁμαρτάνειν
 pp. 79 n. 1, 80, 82–85, 82 n. 10, 87, 117; ἁμάρτημα 114 n. 37, 115, 115 n. 41, 116 n. 42; ἁμαρτία 79 n. 2, 90
Andrewes, Gomme, and Dover (also see *Com. Thuc.*)
 pp. 20, 28 n. 39
anger
 pp. 76, 90
appetite
 pp. 112, 118, 165
ἀρχή (see motion)
Aspasius
 pp. 103 n. 15, 107–10, 107 n. 23, 110 n. 26, 142 n. 12
ἀτύχημα (see chance)

Austin
 p. 3 n. 3
Badham
 pp. 5–6 n. 6
beauty
 pp. 67, 67 n. 32, 111
beliefs
 pp. 121, 139
Benveniste
 p. 58 n. 24
Beta
 p. 110 n. 27
Bond
 pp. 81 n. 8, 82 n. 9–10
Bremer
 p. 82 n. 11
Brodaeus
 p. 12 n. 12
Campbell
 p. 90
Carrière
 pp. 14, 14 n. 14
Casaubon
 pp. 23 n. 29, 41 n. 10
cause (see motion)
chance (τύχη)
 pp. 30, 32, 32 n. 49, 60–61, 63 n. 29, 66 n. 31, 69, 115, 146–47; mischance (ἀτύχημα) 80 n. 3, 114 n. 37, 115–16, 115 n. 41, 116 n. 42–43
Chantraine
 pp. 2 n. 2, 5 n. 6
choice
 pp. 22, 68, 100–3, 120, 165

choiceworthy (αἱρετός)
    pp. 100–2, 100 n. 11, 101 n. 13, 130–31, 132 n. 6
Classen and Steup
    p. 77
cognition
    pp. 101, 119, 119–20 n. 48, 121–23, 125–26, 129–31, 134–35, 137–38, 141–43, 146, 149, 151, 156 n. 36, 158–59, 158 n. 37; cognitive 118, 118 n. 45, 120–21, 166
Collard
    pp. 5–6 n. 6
command (see orders)
Com. Thuc.
    pp. 20 n. 24, 22 n. 28, 28 n. 39–40, 29 n. 42
consent
    p. 130
contributes nothing (μηδὲν συμβάλλεται)
    pp. 97–98, 100 n. 13, 101, 101 n. 13–14, 106–7, 106 n. 21, 107 n. 22, 108 n. 24, 110
curse
    pp. 65, 79 n. 2
deceit
    pp. 24, 80, 80 n. 4, 161–62, 161 n. 39, 163 n. 41, 164, 164 n. 44
decision
    pp. 68–71, 73–75, 77, 130, 133, 136, 145
demand
    pp. 27–28, 51, 53, 55–58, 132 n. 6
Denniston and Page
    p. 41 n. 10
description of action
    pp. 120–22, 125-26, 130 n. 4, 131, 134–39, 136–37 n. 8, 139 n. 11, 144–47, 154–55, 156 n. 36, 159, 168
desire
    pp. 1, 14, 41 n. 9, 75, 101, 104, 105 n. 20, 106, *cont.*

(desire *cont.*) 108, 111–12, 119, 119–20 n. 48, 121–31, 134–35, 137–39, 138 n. 10, 141–43, 146–47, 149, 151, 153–54, 156 n. 36, 158–60, 158 n. 37
Dickie
    pp. 32 n. 47, 147 n. 20
Diels and Kranz
    pp. 5–6 n. 6
Dihle
    p. 1 n. 1
disease
    pp. 14 n. 15, 30, 36, 60–61, 63
Dodds
    p. 63 n. 30
Donlan
    p. 32 n. 47
Dover (see Andrewes, Gomme, and Dover, and also *Com. Thuc.*)
    p. 28
dreams
    p. 64
drunk
    pp. 112–13, 113 n. 34, 137–38, 144, 160
Dunbar and Marzullo
    pp. 5–6 n. 6
election
    pp. 55–56, 60, 132 n. 6
Ellendt and Genthe
    pp. 5–6 n. 6
enkrates
    pp. 93 n. 1, 97 n. 6, 98 n. 7, 106, 106 n. 21, 111, 145 n. 14
ἐπ' αὐτῷ (see power)
Erbse (see Snell and Erbse)
eros (ἔρως)
    pp. 14, 14 n. 15, 36, 41, 79 n. 1, 80 n. 3–4, 104, 138 n. 10, 154
error
    pp. 73 n. 40, 77, 79–88, 79 n. 1, 91, 93, 109 n. 25, 114–17, 114 n. 38, 127

General Index

Eustathius
    p. 11 n. 8
ἐφ' αὐτῷ (see power)
ἐφ' ἡμῖν (see power)
fate
    p. 16 n. 19
Fatouros
    p. 5 n. 6
fear
    pp. 18, 51, 69–71, 121, 124
Fitzgerald
    p. 2 n. 2
forgetting
    p. 83
forgiveness
    pp. 89, 112, 112 n. 31
Fraenkel
    p. 78
Frazer
    p. 55 n. 21
Frisk
    pp. 2 n. 2, 5 n. 6
Gagarin
    p. 86 n. 15
Garvie
    pp. 161 n. 39, 163 n. 41
Gauthier and Jolif
    pp. 2 n. 2, 96 n. 4, 113 n. 33, 114 n. 36
Genthe (see Ellendt and Genthe)
Gentili
    pp. 133, 147 n. 20
Gerth (see Kühner and Gerth)
gods
    pp. 13, 13 n. 13, 14 n. 15, 29–33, 42, 50, 60–61, 63–64, 63 n. 29–30, 65, 79 n. 1, 88–89, 88 n. 17, 140, 146, 164
Gomme, Andrewes, and Dover (also see *Com. Thuc.*)
    p. 20 n. 24
goodwill
    pp. 157, 162–63
Gottschalk
    pp. 16 n. 19, 41–42 n. 10

Greek law
    p. 76
Grene
    pp. 88, 89 n. 18
Griffith
    pp. 9 n. 4, 77, 85 n. 13
Halliday (see Allen, Halliday, and Sikes)
Harder
    p. 32 n. 49
Harrison
    p. 33 n. 51
Hesychius
    p. 2 n. 2
Hofinger
    p. 5 n. 6
homicide law
    pp. 1, 76, 86, 86 n. 15,
hospitality (ξενία, *xenia*)
    pp. 16 n. 19, 55, 58, 60, 74
How and Wells
    p. 29 n. 43
ignorance (ἄγνοια)
    pp. 73 n. 40, 77, 79–80, 81 n. 7, 82, 85, 89, 89 n. 19, 91, 93 n. 1, 96, 96 n. 4, 99, 100–3, 109 n. 25, 111–17, 111 n. 28–29, 113 n. 34, 114 n. 35 and 37, 116 n. 42–43, 120–21, 123–25, 123 n. 53, 126, 131, 137–38, 146, 147 n. 18, 154, 156 n. 36
indexes
    pp. 5–6 n. 6
intentionality
    p. 1
internal force
    pp. 13–14, 36 n. 3, 40–41, 40 n. 8, 60 n. 26, 112–13, 138 n. 10
Italie and Radt (see also Allen and Italie)
    pp. 5–6 n. 6
Jackson
    p. 116 n. 42

Jacobi
  pp. 5–6 n. 6
Jebb
  pp. 2 n. 2, 11, 11 n. 9, 24 n. 32, 77
Joachim
  p. 116 n. 43
Jolif (see Gauthier and Jolif)
  p. 116 n. 42
Kaibel
  pp. 5–6 n. 6
Kamerbeek
  pp. 11, 11 n. 9, 24–25, 24 n. 32, 77, 90, 144 n. , 163 n. 43
Kannicht and Snell
  pp. 5–6 n. 6
Kenny
  pp. 96 n. 3, 98 n. 8, 100 n. 11, 101 n. 14, 106, 107 n. 22
κλοπή
  pp. 23–25
Knox
  pp. 144 n. , 163 n. 41–42,
Kranz (see Diels and Kranz)
Kühner and Gerth
  p. 7 n. 1
lawgivers
  pp. 103 n. 16, 125
laws (νόμοι, *nomoi*)
  pp. 16 n. 19, 55, 58, 60
Leaf
  pp. 11 n. 8, 77
legal usage
  pp. 72, 90–91 n. 21
Liddell and Scott
  p. 11 n. 8
liturgy
  p. 28
Lobeck
  p. 90
Lobel and Page
  p. 5 n. 6
lottery (or lot)
  pp. 26–27, 26 n. 37, 53, 55, 60 157

love (also see eros)
  pp. 79 n. 1, 80 n. 3, 117, 137, 154; lover 117, 137, 144
λυπηρόν (see pain)
MacDowell
  pp. 23 n. 30, 28 n. 39, 33 n. 51
madness
  pp. 24–25, 63–64, 66 n. 31, 113–14, 113 n. 34
Maidment
  p. 2 n. 2
Marzullo (see Dunbar and Marzullo, and Prendergast and Marzullo)
Maschke
  pp. 1 n. 1, 2 n. 2, 73 n. 41, 75–76
Matthaei
  pp. 24, 24 n. 33
meaning list approach
  (see sense list approach)
μηδὲν συμβάλλεται (see contributes nothing)
Michael of Ephesus
  p. 96 n. 4
Minton
  p. 5 n. 6
miscalculation
  pp. 80, 80 n. 3, 82, 84–85
miss the mark
  pp. 82, 84–85, 87, 117
mixed actions
  pp. 99–106, 126, 131–32, 156 n. 36; mixed cases 108
motion
  ch. 4–5 *passim*; αἰτία pp. 98, 101 n. 13, 116 n. 42, 120; animal 97, 103 n. 16, 118–20, 119–20 n. 50, 151; ἀρχή 96–98, 98 n. 9, 100–101, 101 n. 13, 103, 106 n. 21, 107–108, 110, 120, 126, 141; cause of 22, 120 n. 51, 123–25, 129–31, 142, 151, 153, 155; cause of action 121, 127–28; *cont.*

(motion cont.)
  doer 121, 136 n. 8, 139, 142–43, 156 n. 36; efficient cause 134, 136 n. 8, 139, 139 n. 11, 142–43, 149, 156 n. 36, 160; move limbs 108–109, 142, 154, 160; move body 100–101, 149; move body parts 98–102, 101 n. 13, 106–107, 109; move oneself 151, 164; ὁρμή 97–98, 97 n. 6, 103, 106 n. 21; reflex 119, 119 n. 20, 121–22, 126, 134, 138, 138 n. 10; systemic 119, 122, 126, 138 n. 10; source of 98, 100, 101 n. 13, 107, 151, 158–59; starting-point 96–98, 100–101, 106–108, 110, 116 n. 42, 143; walk 110, 135, 161
nature (φύσις)
  pp. 96 n. 4, 97–98, 104, 119, 134
Neuhausen
  p. 1 n. 1
nomos (νόμος) (see law)
νόσος (see disease)
nous (νοῦς)
  pp. 118, 118 n. 45
Nussbaum
  pp. 94 n. 2, 118–26 *passim*
ξενία (*xenia*, see hospitality
oath
  pp. 24–26, 25 n. 35, 33, 33 n. 51–52, 53–55, 53 n. 20, 59–60, 59 n. 25, 132 n. 6
O'Brien
  pp. 1 n. 1, 2 n. 2, 77
old age
  pp. 67
oracles
  pp. 26, 42 n. 11, 64–65, 66 n. 31, 72, 79 n. 1, 104 n. 19, 139 n. 11, 161
orders
  pp. 16 n. 19, 23, 27–29, 36 n. 3, 53, 55–58, 57 n. 22, *cont.*

(orders cont.)
  60, 74, 76, 132 n. 6, 142, 142 n. 12; command p.52
ὄρεξις (*orexis*)
  pp. 118, 119–20 n. 50, 120–22, 120 n. 51, 124
Ostwald
  pp. 114 n. 35, 149 n. 21
Pacuvius
  pp. 24 n. 31, 25 n. 34
Page (also see Denniston and Page, and Lobel and Page)
  pp. 5 n. 6, 23 n. 29
pain (also see regret)
  pp. 81 n. 7, 104, 111–13, 115, 116 n. 42, 117, 121, 123–26, 123 n. 53–54, 147, 165, 168, 169 n. 51
paralogos (παραλόγως)
  pp. 114 n. 38, 115, 116 n. 42, 117
passion
  pp. 13, 14 n. 15, 30, 32 n. 47, 36 n. 3, 41, 61, 76, 104, 138 n. 10
pity
  pp. 112, 112 n. 31
Platnauer
  pp. 66 n. 31, 145 n. 15
pleasure
  pp. 104–105; pleasant 111
Powell
  pp. 5–6 n. 6
power, in one's (ἐπ' αὐτῷ, ἐφ' αὐτῷ, ἐφ' ἡμῖν)
  pp. 67 n. 32, 96 n. 4, 98–99, 98 n. 8–9, 103–104, 106, 108, 117, 134
Prendergast and Marzullo
  pp. 5 n. 6
profit
  pp. 14, 41, 44 n. 14, 45, 54, 138 n. 10
prophecy
  pp. 64, 160–64, 161 n. 39
Radt (see Italie and Radt)

General Index

Rassow
    p. 96 n. 4
Redfield
    pp. 151, 151 n. 28, 152 n. 29–31
reflex motions (see motion)
regret (also see pain)
    pp. 81 n. 7, 111–13, 115, 116 n. 42, 117, 121, 123–26, 123 n. 54, 168, 169 n. 51
remorse
    p. 111 n. 30
repentance
    p. 111 n. 30
requests
    pp. 27, 55–57, 132 n. 6,
rhetorical usage
    pp. 4, 72–74, 73 n. 40, 159, 167–68; emphasis 19 n. 21
Richardson
    pp. 19 n. 22, 77
Robortello
    pp. 23 n. 29, 41 n. 10
Rogers
    pp. 2 n. 2, 77
Romagnoli
    p. 14
Rose
    p. 110 n. 27
Rüter
    p. 15
Schreckenberg
    pp. 16 n. 19, 41–42 n. 10, 78
Scodel
    pp. 142 n. , 143 n. , 161 n. 39, 163 n. 41, 164 n. 44
Scott (see Liddell and Scott)
sense list approach
    pp. 3–4, 4 n. 5, 5, 73–75, 81 n. 6, 89 n. 19, 102–103, 106, 108, 167
Sikes (see Allen, Halliday, and Sikes)
Slater
    pp. 5–6 n. 6
Smyth
    p. 32 n. 48
Snell and Erbse (also see Kannicht and Snell)
    p.15 n. 16
Socratic paradox
    pp. 2 n. 2, 77, 88 n. 16
Sorabji
    pp. 30 n. 44, 33 n. 50
Spengel
    p. 96 n. 4
Stanford
    p. 42 n. 11
starting-point (see motion)
Stephanus
    p. 12 n. 12
Steup (see Classen and Steup)
Stewart
    pp. 96 n. 4, 116 n. 42
stout-hearted
    pp. 157–58
systemic motion (see motion)
Taylor
    pp. 133 n. , 147–48 n. 20
technical usage
    pp. 4, 37 n. 6, 67 n. 32, 72–73, 72–73 n. 39, 76, 109 n. 25, 135, 137 n. 9, 154, 158 n. 38
thumos (θυμός)
    pp. 104, 112, 118, 139, 153, 165
tithe
    pp. 9, 20–21, 29, 54, 60
translation
    pp. 2, 2 n. 2, 3–5, 11, 73, 74 n. 42, 75, 77, 147–48 n. 20, 168
τύχη (see chance)
Vernant
    pp. 1 n. 1, 78
von Essen
    pp. 5–6 n. 6
Vos
    p. 16 n. 19
Warner
    p. 2 n. 2

Wecklein
    p. 77
Weiss
    p. 2 n. 2
Wells (see How and Wells)
West
    pp. 5–6 n. 6
Whitman
    p. 163 n. 41
Wieseler
    p. 146 n. 17

will
    pp. 1, 1 n. 1, 76–77, 143 n. , 163 n. 41
Winnington–Ingram
    p. 63 n. 30
wishes
    pp. 103, 106, 108, 110
Wooley
    p. 16 n. 19
xenia (see hospitality)